Meuejarei

# HR Vision
# Managing a Quality Workforce

# HR Vision

# Managing a Quality Workforce

Stephen Connock

INSTITUTE OF PERSONNEL MANAGEMENT

© Institute of Personnel Management 1991

All rights reserved. No part of this publication may be reproduced, stored in an information storage and retrieval system, or transmitted in any form by any means, electronic, mechanical, photocopying, recording or otherwise, without the written permission of the Institute of Personnel Management, IPM House, Camp Road, Wimbledon, London SW19 4UX

Typeset by The Comp-Room, Aylesbury
and printed in Great Britain by Short Run Press Ltd, Exeter

**British Library Cataloguing in Publication Data**

Connock, Stephen
   HR vision : strategies for a quality workforce.
   I. Title
   658.3
   ISBN 0-85292 466-6 Casebound edn.
   ISBN 0-85292 482-8 Paperback edn.

The views expressed in this book are the author's own and do not necessarily reflect those of the Institute

# Contents

| | | |
|---|---|---|
| *Acknowledgements* | | ix |
| Chapter 1 | Introduction | 1 |
| 2 | HR vision and changing business strategies | 8 |
| 3 | Developing the HR vision | 24 |
| 4 | The manpower context | 37 |
| 5 | Resourcing strategies | 59 |
| 6 | Reward strategies | 89 |
| 7 | Development strategies | 111 |
| 8 | Creating the right environment | 144 |
| 9 | Conclusions: implementing HR strategies | 165 |
| Index | | 174 |

# List of Tables

| | | |
|---|---|---|
| 1 | Share of production and exports of manufactures, by country group | 10 |
| 2 | Tactics used by excellent marketeers | 20 |
| 3 | The influence of organisation culture | 29 |
| 4 | The population of sixteen-to-nineteen-year-olds | 39 |
| 5 | Attitudes of final-year undergraduates to information in a recruitment brochure | 72 |
| 6 | Practices affecting retention of women, other than child care and career breaks | 83 |
| 7 | Factors young people consider when applying to employers | 84 |
| 8 | Example of course content in the cadetship scheme run by Pearl Assurance and Peterborough Regional College | 86 |
| 9 | The changing emphasis on which factors to reward | 96 |
| 10 | The changing structural parameters of pay systems | 96 |
| 11 | The effects of performance-related pay in local authorities | 103 |

# List of illustrations

| | | |
|---|---|---|
| 1 | The development of personnel management and human resourcing | 5 |
| 2 | The context in which competitive strategy is formulated | 9 |
| 3 | SWOT analysis | 25 |
| 4 | Unemployment in the UK | 38 |
| 5 | Estimates of the size of the labour force | 40 |
| 6 | Change in the output of school leavers | 41 |
| 7 | Actual and estimated graduate output | 42 |
| 8 | Quantitative and qualitative changes in occupational structure | 43 |
| 9 | Tabulating staff distribution by location, grade and function | 48 |
| 10 | Tabulation of staff distribution, including grade and sex | 49 |
| 11 | Tabulating staff distribution by location, function, sex and age | 50 |
| 12 | Tabulating recruitment by grade, sex and function | 51 |
| 13 | Tabulating promotion by grade, sex and function | 52 |
| 14 | Tabulating resignations by grade, sex and length of service | 54 |
| 15 | Corporate recruitment advertising | 64 |
| 16 | Advertising aimed at recruiting women staff | 66 |
| 17 | Poster advertising aimed at London commuters | 69 |
| 18 | Analysis of recruiting effectiveness | 75 |
| 19 | Salary structure with defined maxima and minima | 98 |
| 20 | The old and new pattern of increments at NatWest | 101 |
| 21 | Typical matrix of performance-related salary increases | 102 |
| 22 | A model of the competence dimensions of a manager | 117 |
| 23 | Core competence in customer service | 123 |
| 24 | Examples of competence assessment | 128–9 |
| 25 | Performance management at Birmingham and Midshires | 131 |
| 26 | Stages in career development | 135 |
| 27 | The sales and production pattern at a manufacturer of consumer durables | 147 |

28  Annual hours worked at a manufacturer of consumer durables   148
29  Part-time working   153

# Acknowledgements

The publications team at the IPM (Chris Handley, Judith Tabern, Anne Cordwent and Matthew Reisz) have been extremely helpful during the writing of this book. I hope their faith has been rewarded! Others also deserve my thanks. Friends and colleagues at Pearl Assurance, including in particular David Davies and Ian Worner, have been the source of much advice and encouragement. So have George Blair, Christine Porter, David Rees and George Spencer. They cannot be blamed for any gaps or shortcomings in the text – that responsibility rests with me alone. I am also very grateful to Anne Watson, who made light work of typing my messy manuscript. Writing a book as well as being General Manager (Human Resources) for Pearl Assurance inevitably means that limited leisure time becomes writing time. My wife Margaret and children Adrian and Mark have put up with this for longer than was reasonable. Without their support and patience the book would not have been published.

Stephen Connock<br>1991

CHAPTER 1

# Introduction

Writing in 1988, John Humble bemoaned the fact that Human Resources Managers do not have the power and influence to do their job as effectively as they could. Logically, he said, this was nonsense. 'The human resource is as important as money, markets and physical products. The average Personnel Manager is just as well trained, productive and committed as his or her average peers. Unfortunately, reality does not match logic.'[1] As one of his six steps to improve the situation he suggested a definition of the basic mission of the Human Resources (HR) function. Why does it exist? What is it trying to achieve? This book will follow this approach in concentrating on the identification of a Human Resources 'vision'. This vision is vital to the development of human resources strategies which derive from and support it. HR strategies in turn lead to annual plans and budgets, together with performance indicators and processes of measurement.

The identification of a separate HR vision is a natural evolution of HR management (HRM). The 1970s concentration on industrial relations has faded in all except the most highly unionised organisations. Instead, the development of HRM has been seen as providing a more effective link between business strategies and HR. In 1986 Hendry and Pettigrew interpreted 'strategic HRM' as establishing 'A coherent approach to the design and management of personnel systems based on an employment policy and manpower strategy, and often underpinned by a "philosophy" '.[2] Despite this reference to 'philosophy', few writers have concentrated on HR vision as such. Most have continued to emphasise HR activities, such as management development and training. Derek Torrington, for example, stated in 1991:

> HRM is no revolution but a further dimension to a multi-faceted role. It will probably embellish personnel expertise and authority in two ways, by finally making training important and by helping managers grant more dignity to working people by concentrating more on getting the contract right and less on supervision and motivation.[3]

This book will point to a key role for the HR Manager in defining HR vision and developing associated HR strategies. Nor are these only 'third-order' strategies.[4] HR vision, including a philosophy of how to treat people in the organisation and the importance of people to the organisation, can be a fundamental component of 'first-order' business strategies. In this the HR contribution to the creation and maintenance of a quality workforce and therefore to overall organisational effectiveness is central.

## WHAT IS HR VISION?

In his 1990 book *Practical Management Development* Gordon McBeath identified the importance of vision as:

> fundamental to good leadership in that it provides the 'grand design' as a framework for all shorter term strategies, decision and behaviour. It influences not only the broad direction of the organisation but also its culture, and provides the concept which conveys to followers an excitement and 'dimension of vision'.[5]

An HR vision will have some of the following characteristics:

- It will be cohesive, providing a common thread through business mission and subsequent HR strategies.
- It will be specific enough to provide direction yet general enough to remain relevant despite fluctuations in conditions in the short term.
- It will be inspiring, aiming at 'excellence' as defined by the organisation.
- It will describe core values strongly held by the organisation.
- It will provide a yardstick by which to judge the future performance of the organisation.

As Tom Peters has said;

> Visions are aesthetic and moral – as well as strategically sound. Visions come from within – as well as from outside. They are personal – and group-centred. Developing a vision and values is a messy, artistic process. Living it consciously is a passionate one beyond any doubt.[6]

Developing an HR vision is relevant to small and large organisations in both private and public sectors. It can stand as a separate concept, or be embraced wholly or in part within the organisation's mission. In addition, vision is closely related to leadership. A clear vision of the future and an ability to translate that vision into practical strategies are key components of leadership, and this applies to human resources as well as management generally. A further link is with 'culture', an overworked concept in the early 1990s, but one best summarised by the phrase 'the way we do things here'. Changing culture – the values, beliefs and related behaviours of people in the organisation – will also be linked with clarity of vision.

Chapter 2 describes the changing business context in which the HR vision is developed. It does this by first considering the importance of the strategic planning process and second by discussing changing organisation strategies.

*Introduction*

This includes reviewing marketing, customer services and manufacturing strategies. HR vision can be developed only from a thorough understanding of both the planning process and the way a business is evolving to achieve its objectives. Next, in chapter 3, the components of HR vision will be considered. Inevitably, each organisation must develop its own vision separately. However, there are pointers from the literature which can be examined. The characteristics of the HR vision described above will be developed at greater length in chapter 3.

## HR STRATEGIES

Having examined the planning process, changing business strategies, and the components of HR vision, the next phase in managing a quality workforce is the development of HR strategies for achieving that vision. These HR strategies are developed within the context of available manpower resources. Chapter 4 analyses this manpower context, taking into account external and internal labour market trends. Demographic trends were potentially, until the impact of the recession in 1990/91, a major constraint on organisational growth. Short-term changes in the level of unemployment have softened the impact of these demographic changes. However, the underlying trends remain clear, and the HR vision and strategies must unfold in the context of the long-term trends rather than be deflected by short-term changes. Long-term, there are, too, major implications for the workforce arising from rapid developments in technology. These and other indications for labour productivity will also be considered in chapter 4.

The range of appropriate HR strategies arising from developing the HR vision in the context of internal and external manpower trends is wide. In this book the focus is on the following strategies:

- *Resourcing strategies* (chapter 5). Recruiting quality staff to meet the business needs of the future. The importance of market research, of targeting recruitment on specific areas and skills, of improving recruitment professionalism generally. Many ideas from marketing and sales are adopted in this review of improving recruitment effectiveness. Equal opportunities are also likely to be at the forefront of the HR vision, and this chapter considers strategies for improving the flow of 'women returners' to the organisation. A further resourcing issue discussed here is school leavers.
- *Reward strategies* (chapter 6). This area is likely to be central to achieving the HR vision. There are key needs of flexibility, adaptability and innovation in the HR vision of the future. Reward structures must support such flexibility. This chapter considers approaches to job evaluation, to performance-related pay, to market-related salaries, to bonus schemes, and to conditions of employment, to maximise flexibility and reward achievement.

- *Development strategies* (chapter 7). The HR vision is also likely to have major implications for training and development strategies. This chapter considers the likely core competences emerging from the HR vision, and explores training and development strategies to achieve these future competences. This chapter also considers potential assessment, performance management and career management. Performance management provides a necessary and vital link between the overall vision and individual objectives and priorities.
- *Creating the right environment* (chapter 8). Again, the theme of flexibility and greater responsiveness to changing customer requirements has implications for patterns of working time. Options such as the 'annual hours' approach and increased use of part-time working are considered in this chapter. In addition, the growing importance of the right working environment is explored.

Finally in chapter 9, implementation issues are considered, including the vital role of communication in achieving understanding of the vision. How the HR Manager judges the effectiveness of HR strategies is also reviewed. Despite the continuing importance of industrial relations, that subject is not covered here. The interested reader is referred to Chris Brewster and Stephen Connock's book *Industrial Relations: Cost-effective Strategies* (Hutchinson, London, 1985).

## THE ROLE OF THE HR MANAGER

The term 'HR Manager' is used throughout this book. It is a general label for those 'Personnel Directors', 'Personnel Managers', Department Managers (Personnel)', functional specialists such as Management Development Manager, and line managers who have responsibility for HR vision and strategies. Personnel officers and students will, too, find much of this book of relevance. However, it is essentially aimed at those HR specialists who have some authority or 'freedom to act' to determine and implement HR strategies. Of course, this will be in conjunction with line managers. As John Purcell has said:

> If corporate philosophies are important it must be the personnel department's function to cultivate and disseminate them, or at least those which relate to the management of people. Guideline policies and long-term action plans which need to be adopted by divisional boards then follow, matched with multi-media corporate communication efforts which articulate those statements of vision.[7]

Why 'HR Manager' and not 'Personnel Manager'? There has been much debate on the change from 'Personnel' to 'Human Resources', some commentators seeing merely a change of name but not of substance, others a marked shift from an industrial relations to a strategic development and training emphasis.[8] John Bramham in his book *Human Resource Planning*[9]

# Introduction

shows the emergence of HR as in Fig. 1. Undoubtedly, 'personnel managers' can still perform all the requirements of HR management. As the term HR suggests a greater emphasis on development, on planning, on formulating managerial values, on vision, on the 'architect' model rather than the 'clerk of works' model[10] it is preferred in this book.

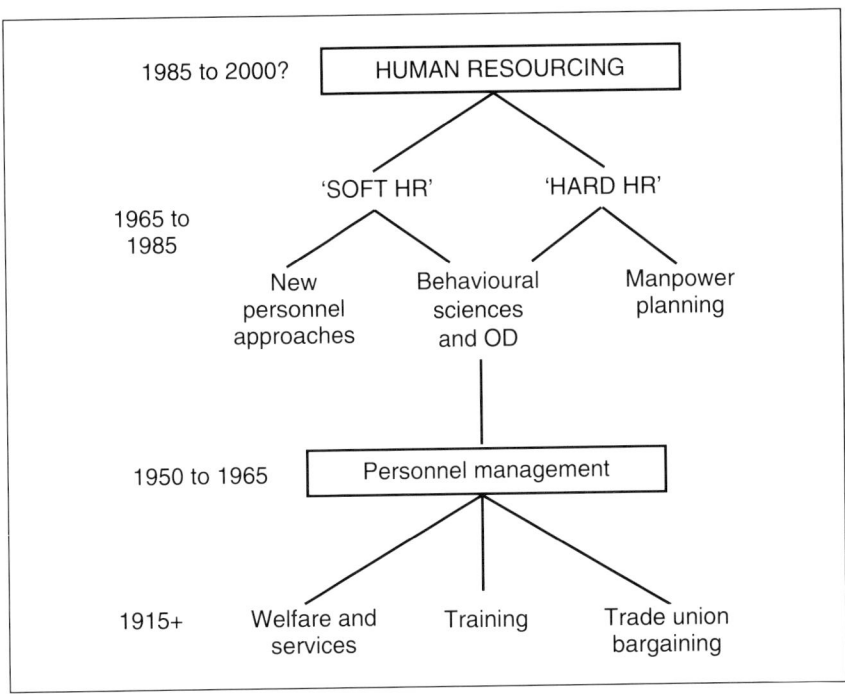

**Fig. 1. The development of personnel management and human resourcing.**

From J. Bramham, *Human Resource Planning*, IPM, London, 1989, p. 6

'HR Managers' collectively continue to be confronted by tensions and ambiguities in their role. These were very well analysed by Karen Legge in her book *Power, Innovation and Problem Solving in Personnel Management* (McGraw-Hill, London, 1978). Since 1978 the renewed confidence of line managers to handle industrial relations in particular, and HR in general, has if anything added to the role uncertainties. Business unit devolution has also been further developed in the 1980s, creating additional tensions between the corporate HR function and the HR function within the operating units. If the HR Manager is feeling beleaguered in this highly political context, there is to compensate increasing recognition that people are fundamental to organisational effectiveness. Internal cost pressures, and external competitive forces, lie partly behind this renewed focus on the need for a productive, trained, flexible and innovative workforce. In short, a *quality* workforce. The HR Manager who focuses on HR vision and HR strategies to create and maintain a quality workforce to support business objectives will demonstrate an 'added value' for the HR function. This will temper, if not remove, some of the tensions and ambiguities surrounding the role.

## A FOCUS ON QUALITY

Alongside HR vision and strategies lies this concept of a quality workforce. Quality in this context has several dimensions for employers, including:

- A customer service orientation.
- Taking personal responsibility for quality output.
- Well trained and developed staff to meet quality requirements.
- Employee involvement in all aspects of quality.
- Maintaining quality standards.
- Communication and recognition programmes which reinforce quality.
- Searching for continuous improvement.
- Knowledge of and identification with quality from staff at all levels.

Customer care initiatives can raise the profile of quality, as can 'Quality Improvement' programmes. This book, through its focus on vision and strategies, keeps stressing quality as a high priority throughout.

## SOLUTIONS, NOT PROBLEMS

Finally, the book is 'solution-centred'. Some textbooks say they will be this, then devote most of the analysis to a restatement of the problem. The authors, one feels, mean well but have not 'been there'. HR Managers can quickly detect whether a proposal is indeed rooted in experience, and 'adds value' to their thinking, or whether the writer is only touching on the true issues.

Solutions can be expensive, and careful analysis is required. We need, too, to keep our feet on the ground. As organisations contract, concentrate or collaborate, or expand, acquire, divest, decentralise, new issues, new strategies, across the spectrum of HR management will be required. Few have been unaffected by the sometimes painful process of strategic reappraisal which has characterised most organisations in the 1980s and early 1990s. Developing an HR vision and HR strategies is a fundamental component of the response to competitive and quality pressures, aimed at ensuring organisational success in the future.

# REFERENCES

1  JOHN HUMBLE, 'How to improve the personnel service', *Personnel Management*, February 1988, p. 30.

2  C. HENDRY AND A. PETTIGREW, 'The practice of strategic human resource management', *Personnel Review*, Vol. 15, No. 3, 1986, p. 21.

3  DEREK TORRINGTON, 'Human resource management and the personnel function' in JOHN STOREY (ed.), *New Perspectives on Human Resource Management*, Routledge, London, 1991, p. 68.

4  JOHN PURCELL, 'The impact of corporate strategy on human resource management', in JOHN STOREY, (ed.), *New Perspectives on Human Resource Management, op. cit.*, p. 72.

5  GORDON MCBEATH, *Practical Management Development: Strategies for Management Resourcing and Development in the 1990s*, Blackwell, Oxford, 1990, p. 125.

6  TOM PETERS, *Thriving on Chaos: Handbook for a Management Revolution*, Macmillan, London, 1989, p. 401.

7  JOHN PURCELL, 'Is anybody listening to the corporate personnel department?', *Personnel Management*, September 1985, p. 30.

8  For further information see LAURENCE HARDY, KEVIN BARHAM, SARA PANTER and AMELIE WINHARD, 'Beyond the personnel function: the strategic management of human resources', *Journal of European Industrial Training*, Vol. 13, No. 1, 1989, pp. 13–18; M. ARMSTRONG, 'Human resource management: a case of the emperor's new clothes?', *Personnel Management*, August, 1987; D. GUEST, 'Human resource management: a new opportunity for psychologists or another passing fad?', *Occupational Psychologist*, No. 2, 1988.

9  J. BRAMHAM, *Human Resource Planning*. IPM, London, 1989.

10 SHAUN TYSON and ALAN FELL, *Evaluating the Personnel Function*, Hutchinson, London, 1986, p. 46.

CHAPTER 2

# HR vision and changing business strategies

Strategic planning processes have increased in importance in organisations in recent years. As competitive pressures increase, and as clarity of business strategy becomes vital to give shape and direction to the process of managing complex change, so planning itself becomes a key priority. There are external and internal factors impacting upon business strategies. Michael Porter in his book *Competitive Strategy* (1980)[1] showed this diagrammatically as in Fig. 2. HR Managers need to be closely involved in the evolution of competitive business strategies to ensure that the HR strategies totally support the business direction of the organisation. To do otherwise is to run the risk of HR becoming marginalised, and of other functions developing a role in strategic HR management.

This closeness of fit is typically shown in the following way:

Corporate mission → Development of HR vision → Identification of HR strategies → Implementation

However, this may underplay the formative impact of developing the HR vision on the corporate mission itself. Business strategies are developed in a more complex, interactive way than the above scheme shows. There are many interrelated components, including developments in information technology, organisation, finance and marketing which will impact upon, shape and themselves be shaped by changing business strategies.

This interactive link between business strategy and HR strategy is hardly surprising. Yet HR managers have not always risen pro-actively to the potential of their role in strategic planning. Some academic writers, too, have categorised HR strategies as 'third-order', behind 'first-order' strategies like 'long-term direction of the firm'[2]. More worrying, perhaps, is the often low credibility of the HR function in the organisation, and the limited business skills of many HR practitioners. This may mean they are not invited to a place at the strategic planning top table, even though there is a space with a label marked 'HR'.

In asserting a major role in linking HR management with developments of corporate mission, the HR Manager must be aware of developments in business strategies. Steeped in this understanding, the HR Manager can then better develop the HR vision. The production of the master strategy, the 'visionary projection of the central and overriding concepts on which the organisation is based',[3] will follow.

*Changing business strategies*

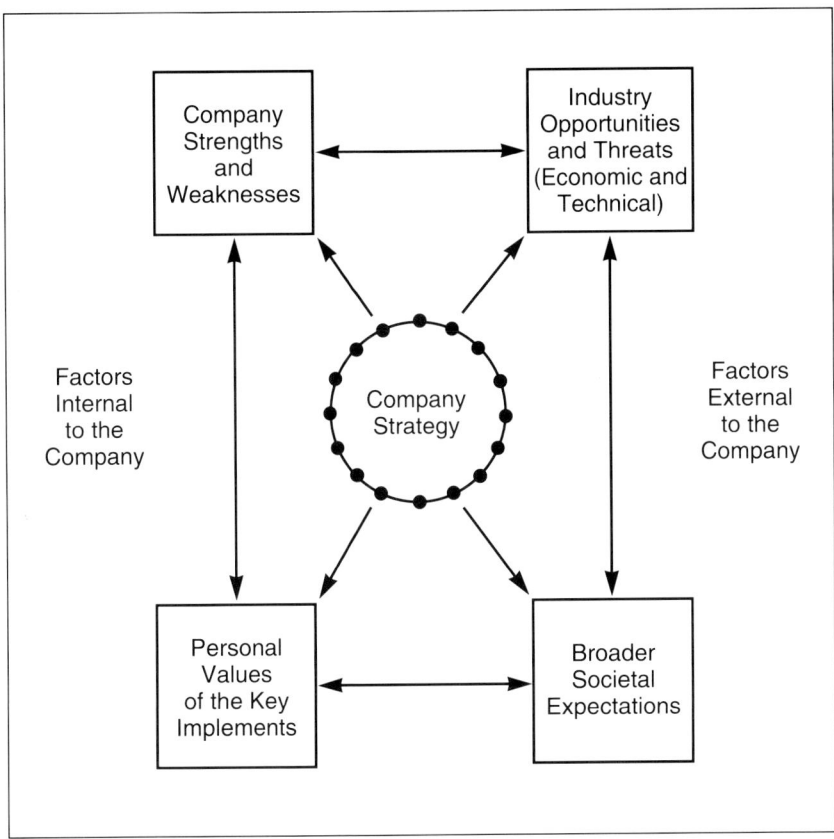

**Fig. 2. The context in which competitive strategy is formulated.**
From Michael Porter, *Competitive Strategy*, Collier-Macmillan, London, 1980, p. xviii

## DEVELOPMENTS IN BUSINESS STRATEGIES

HR Managers operate in a context of rapidly changing business strategies. The changes themselves are complex; no generalised pattern can be easily identified. This chapter explores the main pressures on organisations within which business strategies are being developed. These pressures will be discussed under the following headings: (1) competitive pressures, (2) technological change. Next there will be a brief analysis of how organisations are responding strategically to the pressures, including identifying strategic businesses, changing marketing strategies and adopting a customer service orientation. The components of HR vision and HR strategies can then be explored in chapter 3 in the context of those changing business strategies.

## Competitive pressures

Increasing competitive pressures on organisations have arisen from many directions, including:

- New sources of competition worldwide, including developing countries.
- Government policy changes, including deregulation/'liberalisation' and privatisation.
- Cost pressures, including material and labour costs.

Each of these components will be examined in turn.

### Worldwide competition

The composition of world trade has changed, away from agricultural products towards industrial products and minerals, and trade has spread regionally throughout the world. Developing countries in particular have become more important. Exports from developing countries have continued to grow even during the slowdown in economic growth since 1973. Table 1, for example, shows the shares of production and exports of manufactured goods by country group for 1965, 1973 and 1985. The growth in the share of exports of developing countries from 7·3 per cent in 1965 to 17·4 per cent in 1985 provides tangible evidence of the increasing competition in world markets from this source, especially as the range of manufactured products has itself become more sophisticated. The competitive advantage of developing countries has reflected the availability of raw materials or cheaper labour. As a result the leading position in, for example, shipbuilding, textiles and the steel industry of Western industrial countries has been lost.

**Table 1. Shares of production and exports of manufacturers by country group**

| Type of economy | Share in production | | | Share in exports | | |
|---|---|---|---|---|---|---|
| | 1965 | 1973 | 1985 | 1965 | 1975 | 1985 |
| Industrial market economies | 85.4 | 83.9 | 81.6 | 92.5 | 90.0 | 82.3 |
| Developing countries | 14.5 | 16.0 | 18.1 | 7.3 | 9.9 | 17.4 |
| Low-income | 7.5 | 7.0 | 6.9 | 2.3 | 1.8 | 2.1 |
| Middle-income | 7.0 | 9.0 | 11.2 | 5.0 | 8.1 | 15.3 |
| High-income oil exporters | 0.1 | 0.1 | 0.3 | 0.2 | 0.1 | 0.3 |
| Total | 100.0 | 100.0 | 100.0 | 100.0 | 100.0 | 100.0 |

Source: World Development Report, World Bank, Oxford University Press, Oxford, 1987, p. 47.

*Japan.* Newly industrialised countries in South East Asia have been growing particularly rapidly in recent years. In addition, the well known position in world trade of Japan requires discussion because of its impact on competitive

## Changing business strategies

pressures worldwide. Japan's share of world production doubled in the period 1965 to 1984. This success is remarkable, given that the country has few vital raw materials and is geographically distant from the key export markets of the USA and Europe. How has it been achieved?

> by single-minded co-operation between government, banks and industry; by setting priorities based on a national consensus; by carefully selecting particular branches of industry as spearhead sectors for export; by giving preferential treatment to these selected products; by exploiting the experience curve and sophisticated quality methods to boost their price/performance ratios and quality image and – last but not least – thanks to the tremendous drive and loyalty of the Japanese workers.[4]

In addition, the Japanese have been engaged in direct investment worldwide. In the period 1951 to 1984, US$61,276 million were invested by Japan around the world, with 29 per cent of this investment going into North America, and 4 per cent to the UK.[5] Of interest in the context of business strategies is the evidence that the Japanese operate more effectively in the UK than their domestic counterparts[6]. This is associated with better use of factory space, technically superior production methods, less material wastage and lower inventories, more efficient work organisation and clearly defined lines of responsibility, more rigorous quality control and testing procedures, and better labour utilisation and motivation.

*Multinational corporations.* The activities of multinational companies generally are a key issue in understanding the nature and extent of competitive pressures in the late 1980s and early 1990s. Manufacturing multinationals have been attracted to foreign investment for the following main reasons:

- To overcome tariff and/or quota restrictions.
- To satisfy customer demands for local services or supply.
- To make cost-effective use of local raw materials.
- To increase competitiveness by establishing production where labour costs are comparatively low.

There are also important economies of scale to be gained by multinational corporations operating on a global scale, for example in research and development, purchasing, manufacturing and distribution. Companies like Coca-Cola and McDonald's have been very successful in applying franchising and distribution concepts on a global scale.

Overseas multinational companies are identifying strategic markets like the UK, and in order to penetrate these markets they are introducing or building a presence in the region. This presence often involves the development, production and distribution of the full product range – gaining the advantages of vertical integration – and enables the detailed monitoring of the competition from a local base.

Related to the extension of the activities of multinational corporations has been the rapid development of collaborative ventures between large businesses. There is both a cost and a marketing dimension to such collaborative ventures. Research and development costs, for example, can be very high – in some companies research and development expenditure can amount to between 5 per cent and 10 per cent of sales revenue. Collaboration can spread the costs, and risks, of research and development.

## Deregulation, liberalisation and privatisation

This chapter has been concerned to focus attention on the developing nature of worldwide competition, on the impact of both Japan and the newly industrialising countries and on the growth of multinational corporations. HR Managers must understand the implications of these global developments on their business. Such pressures affect industries like consumer electronics, shipbuilding, steel, chemicals and electrical components. They do not, however, affect large parts of the British economy, such as local authorities or transport, and only to a limited (but increasing) extent is the financial services sector affected.

These sectors face other competitive pressures, often associated with the processes of deregulation/liberalisation and privatisation. These processes are closely related in their underlying philosophy, and reflect changes in political thinking and in priorities. Essentially they seek to improve efficiency by increasing competition, and have been closely associated in the UK with the Conservative government since 1979. Both processes have separate characteristics, and each will be examined individually.

*Deregulation/liberalisation* has been defined as 'the sweeping away of restrictions on consumer choice and the introduction, or extension, of competition on the supply side of the market'.[7] For example, the Telecommunications Act, 1981, eased the previously restrictive conditions governing the attachment of customers' equipment to the public network. The Act was soon followed by Mercury receiving in 1982 a twenty-five-year licence to operate a digital network allowing public access. It was assumed that the threat of competition would encourage the main supplier (in this case British Telecom) to become more cost and performance-conscious.

Deregulation of financial services has also had a profound effect on the traditionally tight restrictions on the range of business financial institutions may undertake. The clearly defined boundaries between, for example, banking, insurance and securities trading has been significantly reduced, creating substantial competitive pressures between banks, building societies and insurance companies. A similar policy thrust can be identified underlying the 'Big Bang' – deregulation of the stock exchange on 27 October 1986 – with boundaries between jobbing and broking eliminated, and membership requirements relaxed.

Other sectors where government buying is involved have also seen significant effects of liberalisation. In defence, for example, the 'cost-plus' approach to contracting has been replaced by competitive tendering. In the health service, as in the case of BT, purchasers have said they will be buying equipment from wherever the best value for money is to be found, and not necessarily from traditional suppliers. The creation of an 'internal market' in the health service from April 1991 is a further example of building competition within sections of the economy.

*Privatisation.* The Labour governments of the 1970s had formed British Aerospace, British Shipbuilders and the British National Oil Corporation (BNOC). The political philosophy changed radically, however, in 1979. Sales of public-sector housing were an early manifestation of the policy change. In addition, many local authorities began contracting services out to private business. As early as 1984 over fifty local authorities had privatised at least one service in this way. The privatisation programme itself commenced in October 1979, with £276 million raised by the sale of shares in British Petroleum, and this was followed by British Aerospace (1981–85), Cable & Wireless (1981–85), Amersham International (1982), Britoil (1982–85), Jaguar (1984), British Gas (1986), the British Airports Authority (1986), electricity supply (1989), and so on.

What is the rationale behind this policy? George Yarrow has identified the following elements:

- Improving efficiency by increasing competition and allowing firms to borrow from the capital market.
- Reducing the public-sector borrowing requirement.
- Easing problems of public-sector pay determination.
- Reducing government involvement in public-sector pay determination.
- Widening the ownership of economic assets.
- Encouraging employee ownership of shares.
- Redistributing income and wealth.[8]

'Privatisation is likely (but not inevitably) to lead managers to place greater emphasis on profit goals,' says Yarrow.[9]

The combined effect of deregulation/liberalisation and privatisation has been substantial. Managers have been stimulated to become more cost and efficiency-oriented by the increased threat of competition, and to define more clearly their strategic mission within which they can maximise their competitive advantage.

## Cost pressures

In the late 1970s, the 1980s and the early 1990s business costs were significantly affected by high inflation levels. In the UK import prices also continued to be affected by the fluctuation in the value of the pound. In the period October 1985 – October 1986, for example, sterling had fallen against the weighted basket of EMS currencies by 22 per cent.[10] Whilst entry to the EMS has stabilised this element, the fluctuations have had a profound impact on the business results of companies dealing with imported products and components, and sharpened substantially their cost-cutting response in the 1980s.

Interest rates, too have remained high and have added a considerable burden to the costs of many organisations. The significance of interest rates on industry costs has been quantified by the CBI. The confederation estimates that each 1 per cent cut in the basic rate reduces industry's costs by about £210 million.[11]

The impact of inflationary pressures on material and fuel costs in the 1980s and early 1990s, continuing high interest costs and the impact of higher import costs have all contributed in different ways to a sustained managerial review of business strategies and business costs. The recession of the early 1990s further hastened this review process. There has been renewed interest in logistics and in 'supply management'. Key performance criteria have been developed in the materials area generally, and in manufacturing industry there has been a continuing sharp focus on reducing stock levels.

For manufacturing industry material costs are a significant aspect of total costs. Employment costs are vital, too, and in other sectors of the economy such as insurance they can account for 90 per cent or more of total business costs. This area has been seen as one in which costs are at least more subject to managerial control than may be the case with, say, the cost of purchasing key commodities from overseas markets. This manpower context is explored in chapter 4.

## Technological change

Alongside the competitive pressures produced by the opening up of world markets, by the processes of deregulation and privatisation and by cost increases, technological changes have had an effect on all organisations. Central to the impact of new technology has been the development of microelectronics, whose influence is ubiquitous and whose power enormous.

For management the advantages of the application of new technology have been well summarised as follows:

> Computerised information systems have enormously reduced the time taken to process information and can provide obvious benefits to customers/users. Manufacturing processes can be more rapid – and the consequent increased volume can reduce unit costs. Productivity can also improve through manning reductions, although this does not always follow from the introduction of new technology. Production and development lead times can be reduced through the use of, for example, computer-aided manufacture (CAM) or computer-aided design (CAD). Modern computer techniques of 'on-line' data processing provide the opportunities for information to be updated by the minute and this means production schedules can be re-planned continuously in the light of changing circumstances. It is this ability which has led to computerised planning and control systems in many manufacturing organisations, with consequent savings on stocks and improvements in lead times and deliveries to customers.[12]

In manufacturing there has been much discussion of the 'factory of the future', centring around the use of robotics, and computer-integrated manufacturing (CIM) technology. Automation has progressed in many industrial sectors, and in specific applications, but new technologies open up the possibilities of system-wide automation, with significant cost savings realisable. The introduction of such 'flexible manufacturing systems' is also related to the need for greater responsiveness to changing customer requirements.

There are enormous issues here for businesses in the future. The widespread introduction of personal computers, integrated into local area networks and communicating with the mainframe, make possible speedy, accurate and flexible responses to operational requirements. In insurance, banking, finance, manufacturing, hotels, air transport and so on the microelectronic impact is still in its infancy.

Organisations in the public and private sector faced by these competitive pressures and technological changes have responded strategically in different ways, with some underlying similiarities of process. In this context, organisations have sought 'a deeper and more determined sense of strategic mission or purpose',[13] with new marketing and customer service strategies and new manufacturing processes. It is to this area that we now turn.

## CHANGING BUSINESS STRATEGIES

Clarity in strategic thinking contributes to giving organisations competitive advantage. Michael Porter has described a set of analytical techniques for developing strategy, and the main elements of his approach are worth noting.

- Analyse the industry in which the firm competes. How might the industry change in the future, taking account of such factors as technological changes, substitute products and competitive policy?
- Examine the sources of competitive advantage. What factors determine a business's cost position, and what differentiates the firm's product/service relative to competitors'?
- Analyse existing and potential competitors who might affect the company. Understand the logic of each competitor's strategy, how it thinks and its likely future moves.
- Assess the company's competitive position. What are its competitive advantages and disadvantages?
- Determine actions. The chosen strategy must be translated into concrete actions.[14]

Organisations have been analysing these and related issues in some depth. Indeed, the process can go too far, producing 'analysis paralysis'. Generally, however, clearer objectives have been identified, covering long-term as well as short-term profitability, dividend growth, market share, sales growth, diversification, employment and social responsibilities. The separate needs of internal and external customers are becoming better understood. The 'competition' is being analysed. There is a better understanding of the organisation's image in the market place, of the possibilities of substitution, and how to gain competitive cost advantages through, say, economies of scale or vertical integration. Company culture has been discussed, and attempts to change managerial value systems have been introduced. Product life cycles and experience curves are regularly monitored, and budgetary systems reviewed for continuing relevance and effectiveness. Present strategies are being scrutinised, against a background of what is changing internally and in the external environment. New strategies are evaluated: are they internally consistent? Do they make good use of the organisation's skills? Do they fit the external environment? Are the time scales appropriate? Do they achieve the organisation's objectives?

In the context of rapidly changing competitive pressures, and with technology evolving equally fast, answering these and other questions has produced considerable changes in business strategies in recent years. One of the main changes has been a marked trend to 'stick to the knitting', to concentrate on that in which the organisation has a particular experience or skill. Diversification, regarded in the 1970s and much of the 1980s as an appropriate strategy, is now seen in many cases to have overstretched resources, both of capital and of staff. This problem is more acute in organisations which have attempted to manage their acquisitions direct. Others, adopting a hands-off, holding-company approach, judging performance against 'bottom line' criteria and allowing considerable local management discretion, have been more successful in managing diversification.

Disinvestment, and concentration on core products or business, can therefore conserve resources and ease resourcing problems. Concentration can, of course, also lead to rapid expansion and growth, albeit within more narrowly defined parameters. Successfully refocusing business goals can in turn lead to resourcing difficulties if market share and profit objectives are fully met. The manpower planning consequences of a growth strategy need to be understood.

There have been numerous examples of the process of strategic analysis leading to changing business portfolios. In 1987 Thorn–EMI sold its consumer electronics division to Thomson of France. Prior to this restructuring, Thorn had sold its 'white-goods' division to Electrolux. At the end of this far-reaching rationalisation programme – forty-one businesses were sold between 1985 and 1987 – Thorn purchased the third leading US consumer electronics rental company. The strategy related to the company pursuing global markets in its remaining core businesses (rental and retail, defence electronics, music and lighting).

Many other examples could be quoted. Lucas Industries disposed of its vehicle lighting operations in the UK in 1987; ICI swapped its polyethylene business for BP's PVC business; Smith's Industries acquired significant US avionics businesses, giving it new capabilities in airborne electronic systems and equipment for navigation and weapon systems. Prudential Assurance sold its estate agency chain in 1990–91 to concentrate on its core business of insurance and related services.

Indeed, the UK merger boom of the mid-1980s can be seen in part as a reflection of the reshaping of companies' strategic portfolios. The year 1986 was a record one in terms of money spent acquiring companies in Britain. In 1985, it has been estimated, some 46 per cent of all ownership changes were divestments, compared with 36 per cent in 1980. The remarkable growth of management buy-outs, from virtually no recorded incidents to over 200 a year since 1983, is also a reflection of parent-company strategic realignment.

The creation of devolved 'strategic business units' has also been noticeable in recent years. The movement towards more decentralised organisation structures built around business centres is generally related to the necessity to sharpen managerial accountability for profit and loss, or service standards, for sharpness can be lost in a functional organisation. It may not always be possible because of size or political factors to introduce integrated business structures, although the experience of many of the so-called 'excellent' companies suggests that this form of organisation is most appropriate. For example, in the case of Motorola, 'It became clear to top management that a centralised highly directive corporate structure would not produce the kind of commitment, effort and innovation needed to succeed.' The company was therefore 'radically decentralised . . . creating many new "presidents" in the process, each with a small entrepreneurial business to run as he saw fit (as long as the actions of each complemented and abetted the thrust of the corporate plan)'.[15] Within the business-centred organisations, more integration of marketing, development and production under 'general managers' is also occurring.

There has, however, been little rigorous analysis of the human resources implications of devolution. Devolution can have some worrying implications, including:

- Duplication of services, leading to increased head count.
- 'Boundary problems', leading to role confusion.
- Line management reluctance to release staff for cross-business unit moves which could impede individual development and be counterproductive organisationally.
- Worsening communications across business units within the same organisation.

All these issues can be effectively managed, and on balance do not detract from the overall advantages of greater accountability and commitment to specific business unit goals.

Also under this heading of changing business strategies are mergers, acquisitions and joint ventures. Joint ventures, for example, as indicated when discussing collaboration on research and development (R&D) expenditure above, can provide an opportunity to share expensive research costs as well as opening access to key markets and an opportunity to develop world products to a global standard. Joint ventures can enable scarce skills to be deployed across separate organisations to the mutual advantage of both. As with mergers and acquisitions, a wider pool of talent can be available to the organisation. In one recent study, manpower levels in 52 per cent of acquired companies in the sample had increased one year after acquisition. The source of recruitment for new senior managers was 38 per cent from the buyer's ranks, showing the impact of the wider pool of talent following an acquisition.[16]

The question of subcontracting is also relevant to revised organisational strategies. In the public sector compulsory competitive tendering and the creation of direct service organisations (DSOs) have focused attention on the subcontracting of certain activities. As one senior politician put it:

> Direct Service Organisations should challenge the overheads allocated to them from central services if they are to successfully compete with private firms. If need be they should be prepared to break away from central services if they can get the same standard of service outside their local authority at a more competitive price . . .
>
> The efficiency of departments including personnel, computing, printing, legal and finance will all reflect in the efficiency of the DSO.[17]

Others would add catering, security, cleaning, internal transport, postal services, photocopying services, and so on, to the list of activities which could be subcontracted.

Subcontracting is driven more by desire for cost savings and by 'focus' than by manpower resourcing difficulties, although the latter are relevant in certain specialist activities such as security, legal and computing work. Companies can place responsibility on the subcontract organisation for providing a full service at an agreed price. All resourcing problems, including providing sickness and holiday cover, are delegated to the contract organisations. These in turn will need to think carefully about their manpower requirements. For the main organisations the key question relates to quality of service. Can quality be guaranteed? There are other items including tradition, image, industrial relations, safety which will need to be weighed in the balance when considering subcontracting.

Organisations therefore have certain strategic options available to them, including concentrating resources on 'core' activities, acquisitions, mergers or joint ventures. Organisations can also structure themselves differently internally, say, by decentralising authority to discrete business units. Some functions can be subcontracted. All these strategic options have human resource implications which need to be evaluated.

## MARKETING AND CUSTOMER SERVICES

Closely related to the consideration of strategic issues within organisations is the renewed focus on marketing and customer services. Cultures which have been technically led or production-oriented are moving rapidly towards this marketing and customer focus. Components of the trend include:

## Changing business strategies

- Putting the customer first, not distribution systems.
- Giving satisfaction over time – not just profits this month.
- Using all the company's resources – not just one department's.
- Innovating – not just sticking to formulas.[18]

Some writers have developed further the tactics used by 'excellent marketeers'. Michael Nevens, for example, contrasts the 'market-focused' approach from those emphasising a technology or engineering-driven approach. This analysis is shown in Table 2. In more recent years emphasis has also been placed on market differentiation, on market positioning (what are the target markets?) and on market segmentation.

One 'six-point plan' for marketing excellence stressed:

- A genuine marketing orientation (not just lip service).
- Responsiveness to change.
- Adopting defensible positions in the market place.
- Flexibility in operating systems and practices.
- Adopting a balanced product portfolio.
- A 'bottom line' bias.[19]

Closely related to this area are the 'total quality' programmes and customer care initiatives which have been a major and successful feature of revised organisational strategies in the 1980s and 1990s.

These programmes reflect the reality of customers having increasingly wide choices, which will further extend following 1992. Customers are becoming more discerning, too, and expect a personalised, effective and – in short – a quality service. The management consultancy A. T. Kearney in a report on *Creating the Environment for Total Quality Management* drew attention in 1991 to the following factors.

- Sixty-eight per cent of the customers who stop doing business with a company do so because of poor service.
- Customers are five times more likely to leave on account of poor service than on account of poor product quality or high cost.
- The average unhappy customer tells nine other people about the experience. Thirteen per cent tell twenty or more people.
- Losing a customer costs as much as five times the annual value of that customer's account.

On the other hand, the report states, 'The average happy customer tells five other people and many of those become customers of the business that was praised'.[20]

## MANUFACTURING TRENDS

Given these strategic realignments, new marketing and customer service responses, and technological changes, manufacturing processes have inevi-

## Table 2. Tactics used by excellent marketeers

| Market-focused | Technology or engineering-driven |
| --- | --- |
| Segments by customer applications and economic benefits received by the customer | Segments by product |
| Knows the factors that influence customer buying decisions; focuses on a package of values that includes product performance price, service, applications | Assumes that price and product performance/technology are the key to most sales |
| Uses market research and systematic collection of sales reports to track market changes and modify strategy | Relies on anecdotes and has difficulty disciplining sales force to provide useful reports |
| Makes and manages marketing investment in the same way as R&D investment | Views marketing as a cost centre with little of the value associated with an investment |
| Communicates with the market on a segment | Communicates with customers as a mass market |
| Talks about customer needs, share, applications and segments | Talks about price performance, volume and book-to-bill ratios |
| Tracks product customer and segment P&Ls and holds junior managers responsible for them | Focuses on volume, product margins and cost allocations among divisions; junior managers not held accountable, owing to 'political' nature of allocations |
| Sees channels as extensions of the sales force or ways to get to users | Thinks of distribution channels as customers |
| Knows the strategy, assumptions, cost structure and objective of major competitors | Knows competitive channels as customers |
| Has annual marketing plan and uses it to manage the function; integrates marketing plan with other functions | Looks at marketing plan only when it is time for the new version; treats marketing as an independent function |
| Management reviews spend as much time on marketing as on R&D and sales | Marketing not reviewed outside budget time |

Source: Michael Nevens, *Electronic Business*, 15 June 1984.

## Changing business strategies

tably had to adapt fundamentally. As a survey in the *Economist* put it, 'The name of the game in manufacturing has become, not simply quality or low cost, but 'flexibility' – the quest to give the customer his or her own personalised design, but with the cheapness and availability of mass-produced items.'[21]

The motivation behind the extension of new technology into manufacturing includes the need to extend the manufacturer's ability to become more responsive to changing customer demands. Product life cycles are shortening; car models, for example, which used to be in production for twelve years or more, are now replaced every six years or less. Television sets in production for three years would now be in production for eighteen months on average. Consumer tastes can change quickly, and customers expect an impressive range of products or services to cater for their particular requirements. The concept of fixed production lines ('dedicated automation') producing standardised products continues to give major economies of scale advantages but cannot respond adequately to changing customer demands.

It is in this context that production processes are being redesigned, with significant advantages in reducing throughput times, reducing stock levels, reducing waiting times through better alignment of operating cycles within the factory, and improving quality. The main elements of these changes include:

- Introduction of computer-integrated manufacturing technology. Although the factories exploiting CIM are still relatively few, the number is growing rapidly.
- CIM enables data on many different aspects – manufacturing, marketing, planning, personnel, finance, supplies – to be processed automatically, instructing the factory's manufacturing process to make changes according to customer requirements or business forecasts.
- This integrated approach to manufacturing also informs flexible manufacturing systems (FMS), which are spreading rapidly. Introducing FMS is seen as a three-to-five-year programme, involving three discernible stages:

1 *Preparation.* Communicating the shift in technology and strategy through the organisation, installing an integrated managerial outlook, redefining job context and retraining.
2 *Optimisation.* Optimisation of existing manual operations, analysing inefficiencies and bottlenecks.
3 *Installation.* Only when manual operations have been optimised.[22]

Robotics will figure prominently in these manufacturing systems, forming 'islands of automation' linked by mechanised supply processes for materials flow.

- 'Just in time' delivery patterns have also featured strongly, with major implications for stock levels and throughput times.
- Computer-aided design: the spread of CAD systems has already had a major impact on development lead times. By linking CAD to the manufacturing process further improvements in lead times can be effected.

Developments in office automation also proceed rapidly, particularly in sectors like insurance which involve processing large quantities of paperwork. Although the advantages of such automation are generally impressive (e.g. the use of word processors), costs can be high and technical problems can cause delay and operational problems.

## SUMMARY

The picture is emerging of astonishing change, in business strategy, in marketing and customer service strategies, and in manufacturing processes. These changes are driven, as this chapter has shown, by competitive pressures on organisations in the public and private sector, and by rapidly evolving technology. In this fast-moving business world the HR Manager contributes through the HR vision and revised HR strategies. As the HR vision concentrates on core values, it is less susceptible to revision as business circumstances change. The vision, too, must adapt to new requirements. The HR strategies and annual plans will need to be fundamentally reviewed to accommodate the developments described in these pages.

## REFERENCES

1 MICHAEL PORTER, *Competitive Strategy: Techniques for Analysing Industries and Competition*, Collier-Macmillan, London, 1980, p. xviii.

2 JOHN PURCELL, 'The impact of corporate strategy on human resource management' in JOHN STOREY (ed.), *New Perspectives on Human Resource Management*, Routledge, London, 1991, p. 72.

3 M. RICHARDS, quoted in GERRY JOHNSON and KEVIN SCHOLES, *Exploring Corporate Strategy*, Prentice Hall, Englewood Cliffs, N.J., 1988, p. 119.

4 Dr W. DEKKER, in a speech delivered at the International Symposium on Japan's long-term future, 26–7 November 1984.

5 JOHN H. DUNNING, *Japanese Participation in British Industry*, Croom Helm, London, 1986, p. 2.

6 *Ibid.*, p. 95.

7 MARGARET SHARP, 'Europe – collaboration in the high-technology sector', *Oxford Review of Economic Policy*, Vol. 3, No. 1, spring 1987, p. 60.

8 GEORGE YARROW, 'Privatisation in theory and practice', *Economic Policy* 2, April 1988, pp. 324–77.

9 *Ibid*, p. 327.

10 *Economic Survey of Europe*, Economic Commission for Europe, Geneva, 1987, p. 33.

11 Goldman Sachs international monetary indicators and CBI estimates, quoted in CBI *Economic Situation Report*, March 1987, p. 25.

12 CHRIS BREWSTER and STEPHEN CONNOCK, *Industrial Relations: Cost-Effective Strategies*, Hutchinson, London, 1985, p. 16.

13 RICHARD S. HARDSCOMBE and PHILIP A. NORMAN, *Strategic Leadership: the Missing Links*, McGraw-Hill, Maidenhead, 1989, p. 4.

14 MICHAEL PORTER, 'Corporate strategy – the state of strategic thinking', *Economist*, Vol. 303, No. 7499, 23 May 1987, p. 22.

15 P. T. BOLWIJN and T. KUMPE, 'Towards the factory of the future', *McKinsey Quarterly*, spring 1986, p. 41.

16 JOHN W. HUNT, STAN LEES, JOHN J. GRUMBER and PHILIP D. VIVIAN, 'Acquisitions – the human factor', *London Business School and Egon Zehnder International*, March 1987, p. 51.

17 WARD GRIFFITH, 'Fees for "house" work – the personnel department as consultancy', *Personnel Management*, January 1989, p. 37.

18 STEPHEN KING, 'Has marketing failed, or was it never really tried?', *Journal of Marketing Management*, I, 1985, pp. 1–19.

19 G. HOOLEY and J. E. LYNCH, *Marketing lessons from UK's high-flying companies*, Institute of Marketing, Maidenhead, 1985, pp. 8–10.

20 A. T. KEARNEY, *Creating the Environment for Total Quality Management*, 1991, p. 4.

21 'Factory of the future', *Economist*, Vol. 303, No. 7500, 30 May 1987, p. 1.

22 BOLWIJN and KUMPE, *op. cit.*, pp. 47–8.

CHAPTER 3

# Developing the HR vision

There are a few HR processes which can be taken 'off the shelf' and applied to the organisation. Certain job evaluation techniques, for example, or team briefing systems can be implemented with minimal adaptation. Other HR developments can only be generated from 'within', reflecting fundamentally the unique circumstances of each organisation. Developing the HR vision is in this category of uniqueness.

The HR Manager considering developing the organisation's HR vision will need to be steeped in the changing business context summarised in chapter 2. From this deep understanding of the mission and strategic goals of the organisation the HR vision can unfold. There will be examples where this mission will be interchangeable with all or part of the HR vision. In cases where the chief executive of the organisation personally drives a clear vision for the business, as well as for HR, the HR Manager's role will be more to develop subsequent HR strategies to implement this vision. Most likely, the HR Manager will work in partnership with senior line managers in articulating the HR vision. This partnership is vital to the effectiveness of the developing vision.

What is the difference between mission and vision? In their book *A Sense of Mission* Campbell *et al.* state:

> A Vision and a Mission can be one and the same. A possible and desirable future state of the organisation can include all the elements of Mission – purpose, strategy, behaviour standards and values. But Vision and Mission are not fully overlapping concepts. Vision refers to a future state, 'a condition that is better . . . than what now exists', whereas Mission more normally refers to the present . . . A Vision is, therefore, more associated with a goal whereas a Mission is more associated with a way of behaving.[1]

How is this vision to be identified? The HR Manager and the review team can adopt processes common to strategic planning to assist in the task. Generally the process of conducting a strategic review of HR embraces a number of distinctive phases:

- Review of current HR strategies.
- Reappraisal of future HR opportunities and threats.

## Developing the HR vision

- Define critical success factors for the future.
- Construct HR architecture.
- Identify and test the emerging HR vision and strategies with key managers.
- Define HR performance indicators, to judge progress over time.

In developing the HR vision the review of current strategies and reappraisal of future opportunities and threats will be the key starting point in redefining or producing the vision for the future of HR in the organisation. The often used SWOT analysis, covering strengths, weaknesses, opportunities and threats, remains a simple, relevant and effective building block (Fig. 3). The SWOT analysis will identify the effect of external developments on the HR vision as well as reviewing internal aspects specific to the organisation.

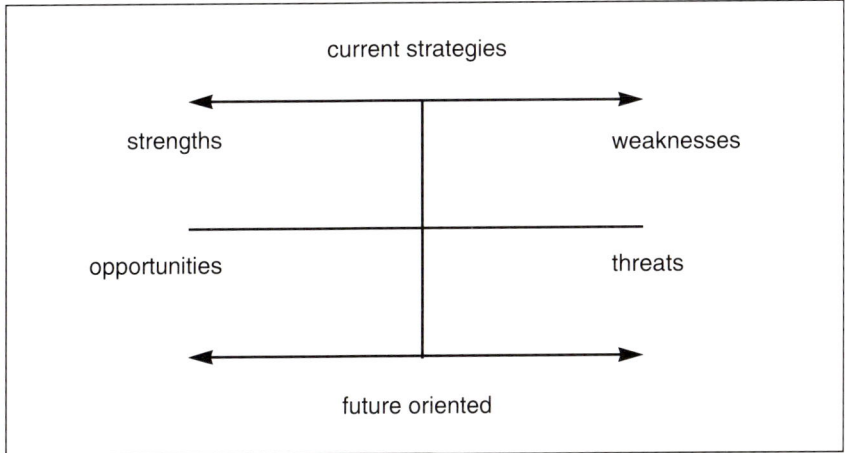

**Fig. 3. SWOT analysis: strengths, weaknesses, opportunities and threats**

In one 1991 study of culture change in the NHS, four key questions were asked at this investigation stage of the review process:

1 Where are we now? What are the problems?
2 Where do we need to be? What will it look like?
3 How can we change? What are the techniques?
4 When should we measure results? How can we do it?[2]

In the 'Where are we now?' question, the views and opinions of more than 1,000 staff from different grades, disciplines and locations throughout the organisation were collected by interviews, questionnaires and group discussions.

SWOT analyses can be conducted for each discipline within HR, since the analysis of industrial relations will be different from the analysis of management development. A SWOT analysis for the organisation generally will be necessary to uncover common threads and underlying core values. Emerging from this analysis will be indicators for the context of the HR vision for the future. Obviously the team charged with the strategic review needs to be honest in its appraisal of today's strengths and weaknesses. Some dearly held initiatives may need to be frankly reappraised and found wanting. This can be a painful but necessary process.

Even more difficult — but equally important — is seeing future trends. Hopefully the changing business strategies will have pointed the way. Issues such as the need for increased flexibility, adaptability, innovation and a customer service orientation may have already emerged clearly. Others will require managers in the review team who have a strategic ability which they can articulate. Scarcity of such strategic ability may be a weakness in the current organisation which will render the development of the HR vision more difficult. In this situation the appointment of an external 'change-agent', or the use of consultants, can provide the needed expertise.

Critical success factors seek to describe the major outcomes sought by the organisation from HR in the future. These outcomes reflect the deep analysis of changing business strategies, and state the HR milestones necessary if the organisation mission is to be successful.

These critical success factors will lead to the construction of the HR architecture. This is a blueprint for the future which describes the HR milestones likely to be necessary to achieve the business strategies. It draws out, as a design would, the key interdependences between the HR milestones.

One American study[3] constructed a series of HR milestones from three different business strategies. The three strategies were: innovation strategy; quality enhancement strategy; cost reduction strategy. The HR practices necessary to support each competitive strategy included:

*Innovation strategy*

- Jobs that require close interaction and co-ordination among groups of individuals.
- Performance appraisals that are more likely to reflect longer-term and group-based achievements.
- Jobs that allow employees to develop skills that can be used in other positions in the firm.
- Compensation systems that allow employees to be shareholders and provide more freedom to choose from a mix of components.
- Broad career paths.

'These practices facilitate cooperative, interdependent behaviour that is oriented toward the long term, and foster exchange of ideas and risk taking.'

*Quality enhancement strategy*

- Explicit job descriptions.

*Developing the HR vision*

- High levels of employee participation in decisions relevant to immediate working conditions and the job itself.
- Mix of individual and group criteria for performance appraisal.
- Egalitarian treatment of employees.
- Some guarantees of employment security.
- Extensive and continuous training and development of employees.

'These practices facilitate quality enhancement by helping to ensure highly reliable behaviour from individuals who can identify with the goals of the organisation and, when necessary, be flexible and adaptable to new job assignments and technological change.'

## Cost reduction strategy

- Fixed job description that allows little room for ambiguity.
- Narrowly defined jobs and career paths that encourage specialisation and efficiency.
- Short-term results-oriented performance appraisals.
- Close monitoring of market pay levels when making compensation decisions.
- Minimal levels of employee training and development.

'These practices maximise efficiency by providing means for management to monitor and control closely the activities of employees.'

We may not agree with each HR practice listed here, and others could be added. It illustrates how the 'HR architecture' can be designed. HR activities and processes are beginning to be clustered around changing business strategies. Some underlying requirements – for example, 'risk taking' and 'adaptability' – can be identified for the HR vision.

In practice, many organisations will be wanting to pursue business strategies which produce innovation, which enhance quality *and* which reduce costs. The signals for the workforce can be confusing and even contradictory if HR processes are designed to meet specific competitive strategies when different strategies exist at the same time in the organisation. In this position, greater clarity of the underlying corporate mission may be required, accompanied by clarity in the underlying HR vision.

## DEFINITION OF THE HR VISION

Chapter 1 defined the characteristics of the HR vision, and they can be restated as follows. The HR vision will be:

- *Cohesive* – providing a common thread linking business mission with subsequent HR strategies.
- *Specific* enough to provide direction, yet *general* enough to accommodate short-term changes.

- *Long-term* in aims and relevance.
- *Simple*.
- Describing the *core values*, *beliefs* and *moral principles* of the organisation.
- Providing a *yardstick* by which to judge future performance.

The HR vision is cohesive in that it supports and complements changing business strategies, from which HR strategies will be developed. This is a complex process. Gerry Johnson and Kevin Scholes in their book *Exploring Corporate Strategy* (1988) stress the complex characteristics of strategic decisions, which demand an integrated approach to managing the organisation.[4] The HR vision provides the overall direction for HR in the organisation, integrating diverse elements by finding the core values and common thread which capture the essence, the philosophy, on which subsequent behaviour is based.

The vision needs to be specific to suggest appropriate behaviour but general enough not to be rendered obsolete by changing business circumstances. 'Long-term' will be for each HR Manager and the review team to decide upon. Setting a twenty-year time frame for the vision to be achieved may not be helpful in that circumstances are likely to change fundamentally in that time frame. Setting a five to ten-year target seems sensible in constructing the HR vision.

The vision needs to be simple because it must be capable of translation into memorable phases and concepts which can be communicated throughout the organisation. Successful philosophies lend themselves to simple explanations.

The identification of 'core value' beliefs and moral princples is fundamental to the development of the HR vision. This component of the vision links the subject very closely with organisation culture. This has been defined in an IPM study of *Changing Culture* as 'the commonly held and relatively stable beliefs, attitudes and values that exist within the organisation'.[5] The characteristic patterns of behaviour in the organisation, the rites, rituals and symbols are consequently seen as manifestation of the underlying culture. The authors of the IPM study go on to state:

> Culture influences what the executive group attends to, how it interprets the information and the responses it makes to changes in the external environment. Culture is a significant contributor to strategic analysis and the development of strategy. Since culture influences what other members of the organisation attend to, how they interpret this information and react, it is a significant determinant of the success of strategic implementation. Culture influences the ability of the organisation both to conceive and to implement a new strategy.[6]

This is shown schematically in Table 3.

Clearly, then, the HR vision will relate closely to organisational culture, particularly through the attempt to articulate, and probably change, underlying values, beliefs and subsequently the behaviour of staff. Culture change prog-

*Developing the HR vision*

**Table 3. The influence of organisation culture**

| Cultural type | Dominant objectives | Strategies | Systems |
|---|---|---|---|
| Defenders | Desire for a secure and stable niche in market | Specialisation; cost-efficient production, marketing emphasises price and service; tendency to vertical integration | Centralised; detailed control; emphasis on cost efficiency; formal planning |
| Prospectors | Location and exploitation of new product and market opportunities | Growth through product and market development; monitors environmental change; multiple technologies | Emphasis on flexibility; decentralised control; use of *ad hoc* measures |
| Analysers | Desire to match new ventures to present shape of business | Steady growth through penetration; exploitation of applied research; followers in the market | Very complicated; co-ordinating roles between functions; intensive planning |

Source: Allan Williams, Paul Dobson and Mike Walters, *Changing Culture: New Organisational Approaches*, London, IPM, 1990, p. 31.

rammes often incorporate elements that would be part of the HR vision as defined in this book. For example, in changing culture at Unisys the following messages were emphasised:

— The customer comes first.
— We work as a team.
— We back the innovator.
— We honour high ethical standards.
— Quality in everything we do.[7]

These would be typical components of an HR vision statement. The likely components are the subject of the next section.

## COMPONENTS OF THE HR VISION

Accepting that each organisation needs to consider its own HR vision, there are in the literature many clues to the direction such a vision may take in the years leading up to the turn of the century. Tom Peters in *Thriving on Chaos* developed the following picture of the successful firm in the 1990s and beyond. It will be:

- Flatter (have fewer layers of organisational structure).
- Populated by more autonomous units.
- Oriented towards differentiation, producing high-value goods and services, creating niche markets.
- Quality-conscious.
- Service-conscious.
- More responsive.
- Much faster at innovation.
- A user of highly trained, flexible people as the principal means of adding value.[8]

Picking up the HR theme more directly, Peters says increasing labour value will mean:

> continuously retraining employees for more complex tasks, automating in ways that cut routine tasks and enhance worker flexibility and creativity, diffusing responsibility for innovation, taking seriously labour's concern for job security and giving workers a stake in improved productivity via profit-linked bonuses and stock plans.[9]

Philip Sadler in *Designing Organisation* (1991) identifies the following main features of companies that have transformed their culture:

- Profound respect for the individual.
- The customer is king.
- Building teams, creating networks, doing things through task forces, project groups and informal co-operation.
- Delegation, decentralisation and autonomy.
- A strong emphasis on innovation.
- Women are treated as persons, judged on their performance and achievements.

Above all, he says, 'there is an all-pervading sense of a dedication to excellence and achievement. Goals are clearly stated. Above-average performance is rewarded and recognised'.[10] Reinforcing the importance of the HR vision, Sadler says that employees are 'turned on' and become committed when:

- The values are clearly articulated and constantly reinforced.
- The values are ones they can identify with and adopt as their own.
- Top management 'lives' the values.[11]

Within the NHS the Grampian Health Board has published 'a vision for the 1990s' which identifies many of the core values likely to be relevant to many organisations:

## Developing the HR vision

Our vision for the 1990s is concerned with the equitable provision of healthcare. We state that we will consciously and visibly build and utilise a strong sense of team identity and commitment to the board's goals.

Our aim is to provide effective healthcare to our community in a professional manner. We believe that our approach to the way in which we work together to achieve this should be that:

- We should be results-oriented and focused on our strategic objectives;
- We should be participative in our approach to management and encourage managers to be innovative and take decisions for themselves.
- We should be people-oriented, recognising the valuable contribution made by individuals;

*As a senior management team we are therefore committed to:*

Collective achievement of the strategy
Responding to opportunities positively and tackling problems as they arise
Taking a corporate view rather than being concerned only with our own unit or department interests
Taking our decisions having sought the views of our colleagues where appropriate
Delivering against our own objectives
Supporting others in delivering against the objectives of the senior management team
Putting forward our views rationally and accepting decisions reached
Recognising the contribution our staff make to the achievement of our objectives
Providing career development opportunities for staff with a view to achieving their, and the organisation's objectives
Regularly reviewing the working arrangements of the senior management team to maximise our effectiveness

As managers we are committed to:

Improving the quality and delivery of care
Ensuring that staff are briefed on the board's objectives and are clear about their own objectives and limits of authority
Utilising to the maximum the skills of our staff
Encouraging staff to take decisions for themselves within the limits of their authority
Concentrating on achievement
Encouraging individuals to find solutions rather than putting forward problems

Fostering the building of teams to promote achievement
Increased participation in 'Resourcing Grampian' (a performance-improvement training programme)
Encouraging a sense of belonging to a hospital or unit/department
Being supportive to staff in their endeavours, allowing them an opportunity of putting forward their views and encouraging their initiative[12]

As indicated earlier, there can be close links between quality improvement programmes and HR management. Rank Xerox in their 'Leadership through quality' programme re-emphasise the key role of the customer in stating that their view of quality is that:

- It refers to conformance to customer requirements, giving the customer no more and no less than he/she requires.
- The customer is defined as anyone who receives a service, either inside or outside the organisation.
- Acceptable performance is measured in terms of satisfying customer requirements, not in terms of percentage of defects.
- The emphasis is on error prevention, not error detection.[13]

Management action/behaviour to support this focus includes:

- Assuring strategic clarity and consistency.
- Providing visibly supportive management practices, commitment and leadership.
- Setting quality objectives and measurement standards.
- Establishing an environment so each person can be responsible for quality.[14]

British Airways, too, developed a 'service-oriented business' which included the following objectives:

1 To provide the highest level of service to all customers, passengers, shoppers, travel agents and freight agents.
2 To preserve high professional and technical standards in order to achieve the highest levels of safety.
3 To provide a uniform image worldwide and to maintain a specific set of standards for each clearly defined market segment.
4 To respond quickly and sensitively to the changing needs of present and potential customers.
5 To maintain and, where an opportunity occurs, expand the present route structure.
6 To manage, operate and market the airline in the most efficient manner.
7 To create a service and people-oriented work environment, assuring all employees of fair pay and working conditions and continuing concern for their careers.[15]

*Developing the HR vision* 33

From these and other examples certain themes consistently emerge as components of the HR vision. These include:
- A strong customer orientation at all levels.
- A focus on innovation.
- The provision of leadership to generate enthusiasm throughout the organisation.
- Employees are trusted; there is 'respect for the individual'.
- Openness in communication.
- An emphasis on teamwork.
- An emphasis on continuous improvement, with every individual having personal accountability for this improvement process.
- Achievements are rewarded within a 'results-oriented' culture.
- Providing opportunities for all staff to influence the shaping of their role (the word 'empowerment' is often used in this context).
- Delegation of authority.
- Providing opportunities for individuals to develop to their full potential.
- A search for total quality – 'right first time'.
- A need for flexibility, adaptability and willingness to change at all levels.

## ORGANISATIONAL IMPLICATIONS

These components of the HR vision have implications for the shaping of HR strategies. Payment systems, appraisal schemes, the working environment and other subjects must support the vision. The emphasis on the individual and 'respect' for the individual requires carefully thinking through. These issues are explored in later chapters. At this stage the main implications for organisations can be considered. There are three:
- A 'flatter' organisation, with fewer middle management positions.
- A devolved organisation, away from functional responsibility.
- A move towards project, or matrix, organisations.

Each will be considered in turn.

### Flatter organisation

Long management hierarchies are a feature of many organisations in both the private and the public sector. This creates many difficulties. Individuals are unsure of their accountability, since overlapping tasks are numerous. Each layer 'second-guesses' the level below, often adding little value to the overall process. Authority levels can become compressed, with the necessity for sometimes unimportant matters to be referred upwards. Certain employees in this context may have little to do, which can be demotivating for other staff. This slack in the organisation is not only demotivating but adds significantly to the cost structure of the business. Individuals lower in the hierarchy can become frustrated by the lack of discretion, leading to higher turnover and lower morale.

If the HR vision emphasises innovation, taking personal responsibility for operational activities, improving quality and responsiveness, then individuals at all levels will need the space hierarchically to impact upon their job. Greater 'freedom to act' will require the definition of performance standards to ensure that this freedom is correctly deployed. Staff will need to be equipped with the necessary level of training to ensure they have the skills and knowledge to undertake their newly empowered responsibilities. Information technology is relevant in this context, enabling, for example, information to be available at all levels of the organisation.

Spans of control are likely to increase. Tom Peters says there could be fifty to seventy-five 'direct reports' for first-line supervision in the future.[16] Flattening the structure has implications for middle and senior managers. Competences for these levels will need to be redefined as their roles become strategic, and more involved in coaching, counselling and overall performance improvement.

These changes have other implications. Fewer positions in the hierarchy means fewer promotion opportunities. This will necessitate a review of growth options for employees in their current role, a theme which will be covered in more detail in chapter 7. In addition the HR Manager may have to manage a surplus of middle managers arising from the process of flattening the organisation. There will be few HR Managers who lack experience of 'down-sizing' operations. Early retirement schemes which enhance the level of pensionable earnings can be the key to successful management of change in this area. The rapid growth of out-placement schemes for middle managers is indicative of the pace of change. Out-placement can provide helpful support to individuals realigning their career.

## Devolution

Decentralisation has already been referred to above in the context of changing business strategies. Devolution here means the shift of responsibilities away from functional specialists and back towards line management. This may be a major component of the HR vision, especially associated with the role of first-line management. Supervisors generally lost authority and credibility in the 1970s. The trend was largely a result of changes in employment law which led companies to centralise decision-making, thus hopefully avoiding costly penalties at industrial tribunals. The growth in trade unionism in that decade was a further factor that led to the supervisor's HR role being reduced. Faced by militant demands from confident union officials, negotiating authority moved to functional specialists and senior line managers. Supervisors did not just lose authority and credibility – they lost their confidence too. It is now being restored as managers become familiar with employment law, as trade

*Developing the HR vision*

union membership declines and as the role of first-line management is re-emphasised in the HR vision.

Devolution of operational authority from functional specialists to line managers means that the functional specialists can concentrate on longer-term issues, on performance standards, on providing advice and guidance on more complex subjects. 'Strategic controls' will need to be defined within which the devolved line authority operates.

## Project organisation

The third main organisational implication is the increased trend towards project organisation. This is linked with the 'self-managed teams' concept already referred to. In manufacturing there has been increased use of 'semi-autonomous' work teams taking responsibility for production as well as routine maintenance and other traditional support activities. Project teams are an excellent method of progressing strategically central priorities within the organisation, as well as of breaking down traditional barriers between jobs and categories of jobs. Managing multi-functional project teams alongside traditional line organisation requires, however, careful management. Clear project accountability and devolved authority are central to effective management.

## MANAGING A QUALITY WORKFORCE

If the HR Manager has conducted the HR strategic review and emerged in conjunction with senior line managers with a definition of critical success factors; with a detailed HR architecture; with a well thought-through HR vision; and with performance indicators to judge progress – then the next stages are to translate this material into practical HR strategies for managing a quality workforce.

Again, it must be stressed that each organisation will need to develop the right HR strategies to fit both the HR vision and the corporate mission and strategic objectives. This book does not attempt to explore HR strategies which relate to specific business strategies. The emphasis here is on the strategies which may relate to the HR vision. HR strategies are chosen which are more likely to have a wider relevance to this vision, and include: resourcing strategies (chapter 5), reward strategies (chapter 6), development strategies (chapter 7) and strategies for creating the right environment (chapter 8). Organisations will find some aspects of more relevance than others, depending on their stage of development. First, however, it is necessary to review the manpower context in which in the 1990s HR vision and the HR strategies will unfold.

## REFERENCES

1 ANDREW CAMPBELL, MARION DEVINE and DAVID YOUNG, *A Sense of Mission*, Economist Books – Hutchinson, London, 1990, pp. 38–9

2 HANCE FULLERTON and COLIN PRICE, 'Culture change in the NHS', *Personnel Management*, March 1991, p. 50.

3 RANDALL S. SCHULER and SUSAN E. JACKSON, 'Linking competitive strategies with human resource management practices', *Academy of Management Executive*, Vol. 1, No. 3, 1987, p. 213.

4 GERRY JOHNSON and KEVIN SCHOLES, *Exploring Corporate Strategy*, Prentice Hall, Englewood Cliffs, N.J., 1988, p. 8.

5 ALLAN WILLIAMS, PAUL DOBSON and MIKE WALTERS, *Changing Culture: New Organisational Approaches*, IPM, London, 1990, p. 11.

6 *Ibid.*, p. 29.

7 *Ibid.*, p. 216.

8 TOM PETERS, *Thriving on chaos: Handbook for a Management Revolution*, Macmillan, London, 1988, p. 27.

9 *Ibid*, p. 22.

10 PHILIP SADLER, *Designing Organisation: the Foundation for Excellence*, Mercury, London, 1991, pp. 142–3.

11 *Ibid.*, p. 112.

12 FULLERTON and PRICE, *op. cit.*, p. 51.

13 WILLIAMS *et al*, *op. cit.*, pp. 2–5.

14 *Ibid.*, p. 206.

15 CAMPBELL *et al.*, *op. cit.*, p. 127.

16 PETERS, *op. cit.*, p. 301.

CHAPTER 4

# The manpower context

HR vision and HR strategies exist in a changing manpower context in the 1990s. The recession in 1990–91 diminished the impact of medium-term demographic changes affecting the supply of labour. Unemployment in 1990–91 steadily increased, as shown in Fig. 4 on page 38. Rapidly rising unemployment and a record level of business failures in 1990–91 led to an understandable movement away from considering underlying demographic changes. The rapidity with which demographic change went out of fashion is remarkable. Training courses on the subject were cancelled and many books placed in the bottom drawer.

The easing of the labour market for IT specialists, accountants and other specialisms was very marked. General categories, such as school leavers, are available because of the reduced level of business demand in the context of recession. Yet quality staff may still be difficult to attract and retain despite growing unemployment. Equally important are the impact of the underlying supply-side demographic trends in the UK. It will be a symptom of short-term thinking at its worst if HR Managers play down the medium-term changes, since the organisation's ability to meet its objectives could be compromised by manpower developments in the mid-1990s. An upturn in the economy is certain – only the timing remains unclear. Despite, therefore, the short-term easing of labour market difficulties and despite 'down-sizing' in many organisations, the medium and long-term external manpower context remains highly relevant and must be reviewed in detail. Three aspects will be considered here: (1) supply-side demographic trends, (2) supply-side education trends, (3) demand-side trends. Following the review of external trends, the necessity to conduct a 'manpower audit' of internal resources will be explored. Finally the chapter concludes with a review of the key issue of the productivity of the organisation's resources.

## THE EXTERNAL LABOUR MARKET

### Supply-side demographic trends

The main supply-side changes in the UK workforce are well known, and before the recession of 1990–91 were one of the most debated aspects of HR management. They will only be summarised here:

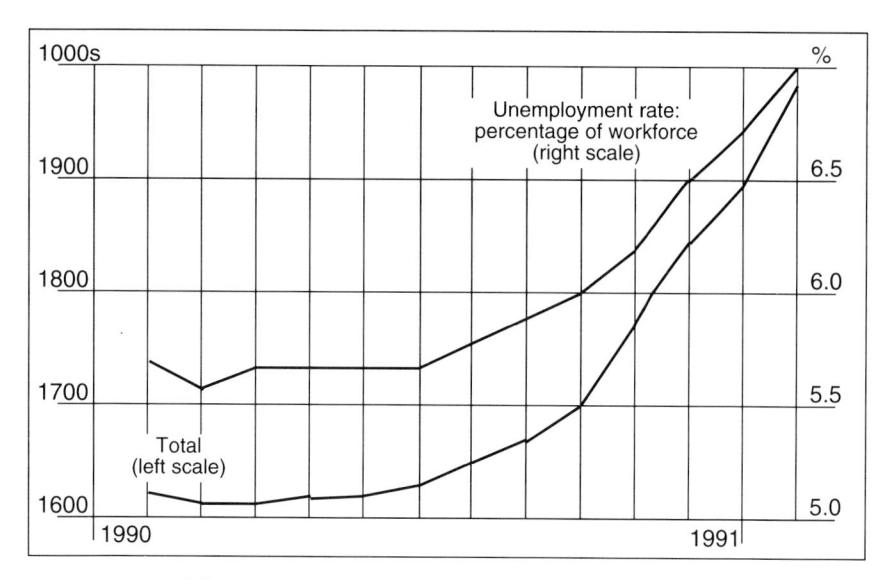

**Fig. 4. Unemployment in the UK, 1990–91.**
From *Management Today*, May 1991, p. 48

- The number of young people entering the labour market has been falling since the mid-1980s. The population of sixteen- to nineteen-year-olds is expected to fall to a minimum of 2·6 million in 1994, over 1 million down on its peak in 1982.[1] The numbers increase slightly in 1995 but by 2001 have still not recovered to the outflow of the late 1980s. There are considerable regional variations in this picture, too. With the percentage reduction in the population of sixteen-to nineteen-year-olds at 24·9 per cent (1987–95), the reduction is 29·7 per cent in Scotland; 18·4 per cent in East Anglia. (See Table 4.)
- Despite this reduction in the number of sixteen-to-nineteen-year-olds, the size of the overall labour force is, notwithstanding rising unemployment in the short term, projected to increase by about 1 million in the year 2000 over 1988.[2] This overall increase contains certain important trends:
- The adult labour force is expected to expand, with about 2·3 million more people aged between twenty-five and fifty-four in the labour force by the turn of the century, compared to 1988. This is shown graphically in Fig. 5.
- There are expected to be significantly more women in the workforce. By the year 2000 almost 45 per cent (12·3 million) of the labour force are likely to be women, compared to 42 per cent (11·4 million) in 1988.
- The workforce is an ageing one, with around a third of the labour force aged forty-five or over by the end of this decade.[3]

Here are the main medium and long-term supply-side changes on which HR Managers need to focus in relation to their vision and HR strategies. Fewer

## Table 4. Population of sixteen-to-nineteen-year-olds ('000)

| Region | 1987 | 1995 | % change |
| --- | --- | --- | --- |
| South East | 1,046 | 809 | −22.7 |
| East Anglia | 124 | 102 | −18.4 |
| South West | 272 | 213 | −21.6 |
| West Midlands | 329 | 240 | −26.9 |
| East Midlands | 246 | 185 | −24.8 |
| Yorkshire and Humberside | 315 | 232 | −26.3 |
| North West | 400 | 286 | −28.5 |
| Northern | 188 | 139 | −26.0 |
| Wales | 172 | 134 | −22.1 |
| Scotland | 339 | 238 | −29.7 |
| Great Britain | 3,431 | 2,578 | −24.9 |

Source: Office of Population Censuses and Surveys.

school leavers, more women returners and a changing age profile of the workforce.

What is behind these changes? As one study put it:

> Between 1946 and 1964 the future of the labour force into the 21st century was being shaped by a nearly 20 year long babies boom. This was slow and irregular at first but gathered momentum in the mid-1950s
> . . .
> School leaver rolls continued to rise through the 1970s, laying the foundations for a buyers' market for young recruits. Aided by the recession at the start of the decade, this culminated with the historically high levels of youth unemployment of the early 1980s.
> This was not the end of the workforce consequences of the babies boom – it was just the start.[4]

To the influx of 'baby boomers' further factors need to be added to explain these supply-side changes. First, a continuing drop in the fertility rate since the 1960s.[5] Second, changing expectations among women, who are increasingly seeking a return to work after having children. Third, improved health generally and a continuing increase in longevity rates.

Later chapters describe the range of strategic options available to HR Managers to handle these supply-side changes in the size and composition of the labour force.

### Supply-side education trends

*School leavers.* The reduction in the stock of sixteen-to nineteen-year-olds in the mid-1990s poses problems for employers, particularly those recruiting

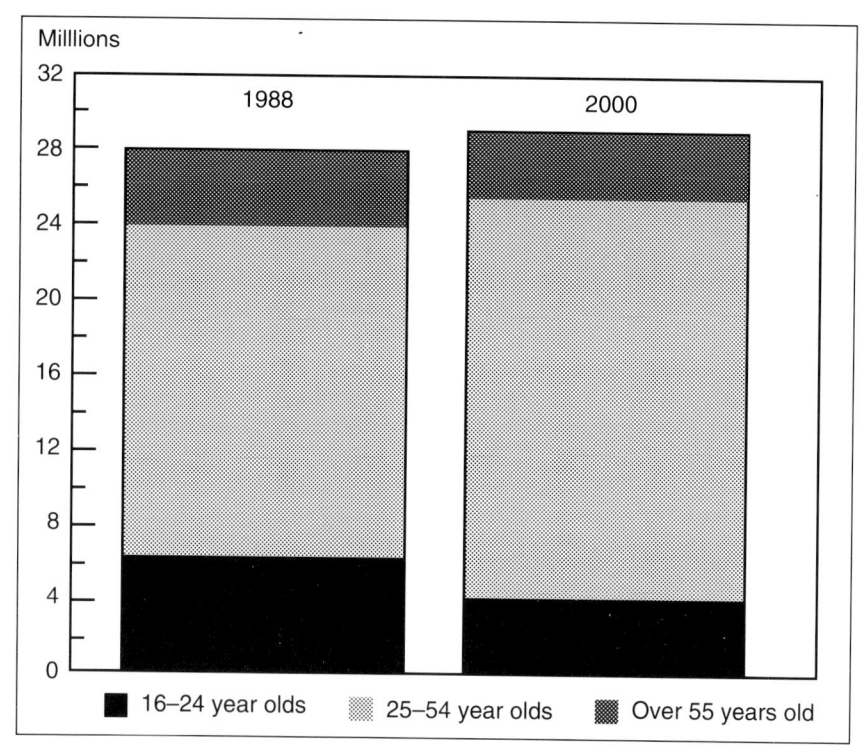

**Fig. 5. Estimates of the size of the labour force, Great Britain, 1988, and projection to 2000.**
By 2000 71 per cent of the labour force will be aged twenty-five to fifty-four; the percentage was 68 in 1988

From Department of Employment figures

clerical staff, who are confronted by a smaller pool of potential recruits. This is not their only problem. The proportion of school leavers going into higher education is also expected to increase. Inevitably the number of young people available for work who achieve better GCSE and A-level qualifications will fall sharply. As an *Employment Gazette* study put it, 'In 1994 there will be some 20,000 fewer better qualified new labour market entrants than in 1987.'[6]

Thus, as qualification levels increase, higher proportions of sixteen-year-olds (from a reduced number anyway) will choose to enter further education on leaving school. Employers will also continue to be concerned at the high number of young people who leave school with no qualifications whatsoever. In 1990 the figure was still running at 40 per cent of the total. This is worrying, especially as the organisation's HR vision may well focus on 'high quality' staff.

As the Institute of Manpower Studies has pointed out, the medium-term problem of declining numbers of school leavers, coupled with an increase in the numbers pursuing further education, can be exaggerated still further by

*The manpower context*  41

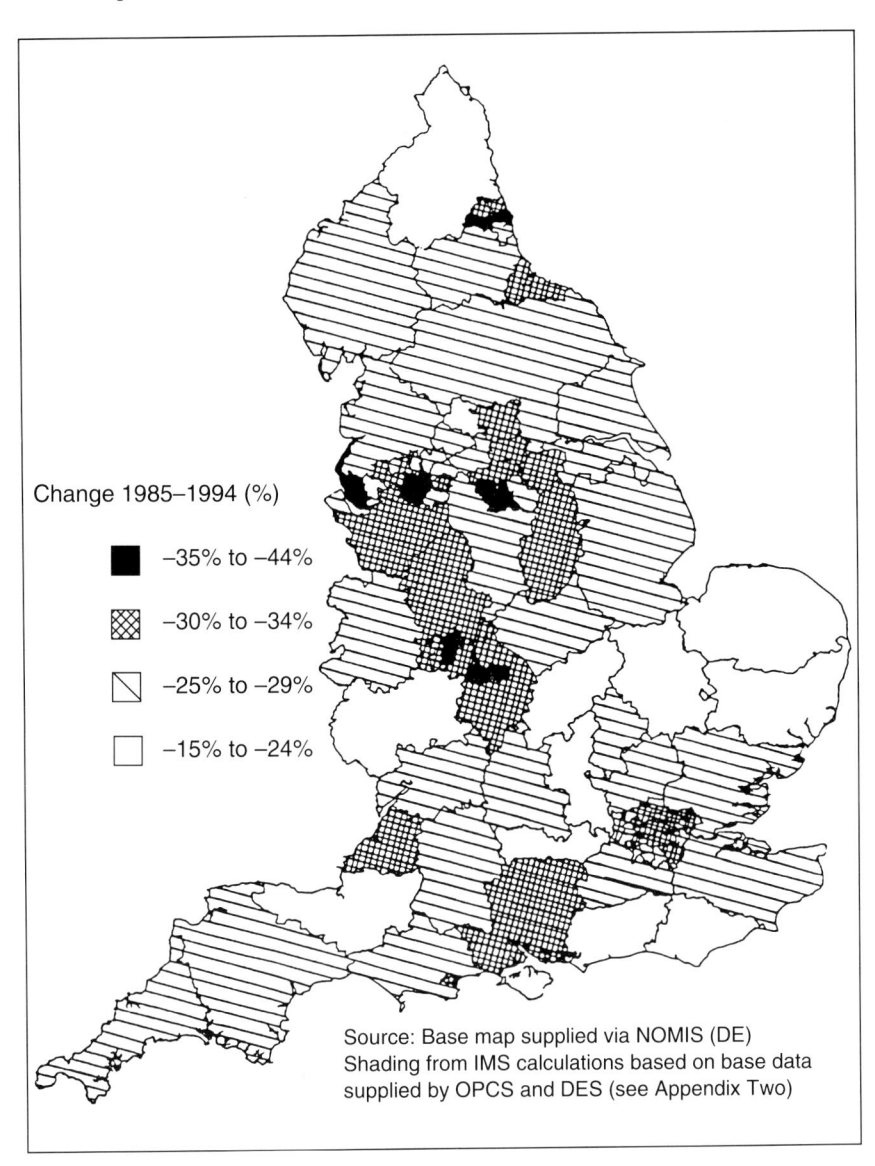

**Change 1985–1994 (%)**

■ −35% to −44%

▩ −30% to −34%

▨ −25% to −29%

☐ −15% to −24%

Source: Base map supplied via NOMIS (DE)
Shading from IMS calculations based on base data
supplied by OPCS and DES (see Appendix Two)

**Fig. 6. Change in the output of school leavers, by English local education authority, 1985–94.**

From Richard Waite and Geoffrey Pike, *School Leaver Decline and Effective Local Solutions*, IMS report No. 178, Brighton, p. 45

local variations. Table 4 has already revealed the decline in the population of sixteen-to-nineteen-year-olds by region. Figure 6 takes this analysis a little further by showing changes specifically in school leaver output by English local education authority, 1985–94.[7] Whilst broad north and south differences are apparent, considerable variation exists between close geographical areas. Not for the first time in this book, it will be obvious that employers need to study the supply-side statistics for their own labour market carefully. An approach to studying the labour market is described below.

*Graduate output.* Still on the subject of supply-side education trends, the position of graduates also needs to be covered. Once again, in the short term there seems little problem: indeed, in 1991 there appear to be more high-quality graduates available than jobs to be filled. The Institute of Manpower Studies has produced helpful research which shows that in 1987 over 200,000 students entered full-time courses of study in higher education. The universities accounted for over 60 per cent of the new first-degree graduates in 1988.[8] The Secretary of State for Education announced in January 1989 that he wanted to see a doubling in the number of students over the next twenty-five years.

Such an increase, together with a projection through to the year 2000, is shown in Fig. 7. From this, the IMS suggested the following compositional changes in the supply of graduates in the 1990s:

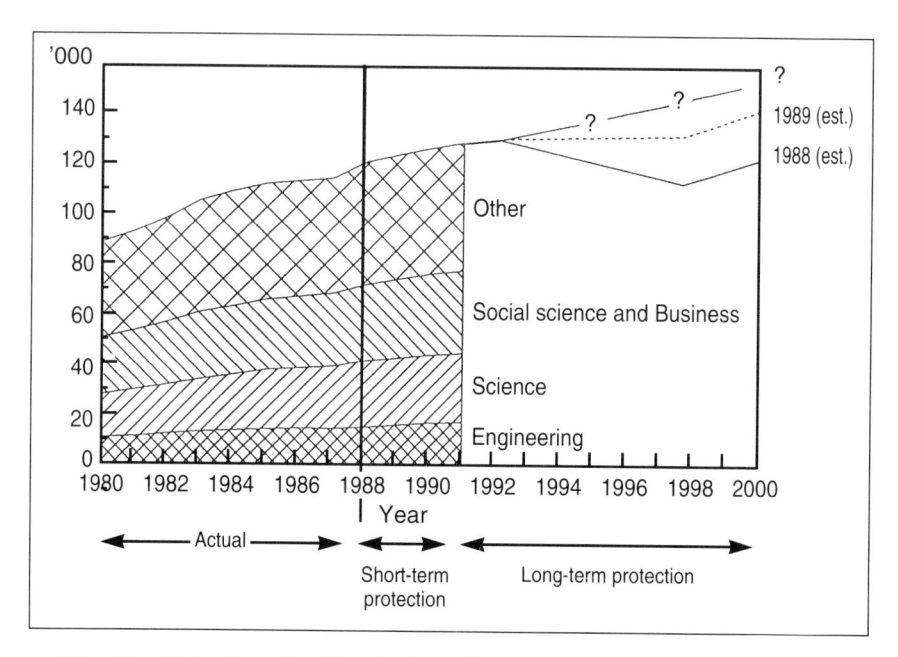

**Fig. 7. Actual and estimated graduate output, UK, 1980–2000.**
From Institute of Manpower Studies and Department of Education and Science figures

*The manpower context*

- A rising proportion of women.
- A slowly rising proportion of mature graduates.
- A rising proportion of graduates from non-traditional academic backgrounds, e.g. with a B.Tec.
- A rising, although still small, proportion from ethnic minorities.
- A falling proportion of engineering and technology graduates.[9]

This last point will be worrying to many HR Managers, given the likely demand for such graduates. In 1986/87 23·4 per cent of men and 3·8 per cent of women undertook a first degree full-time in engineering and technology.

## Demand-side trends

As Amin Rajan has pointed out, there are no labour demand forecasts available to set alongside supply-side forecasts within a consistent framework.[10] Relying on 'second order' estimates, he categorises the UK as being in 'proximate balance', i.e. the demand for and supply of labour are in broad balance, on a numerical analysis. However, quantitative and qualitative changes in occupational structure have led to significant changes in the demand for particular categories. This is shown in Fig. 8 with an analysis of the impact of deskilling or reskilling on particular categories. The significance of growth in the qualification-based, white-collar occupations and the emphasis on growth in part-time jobs are noteworthy.

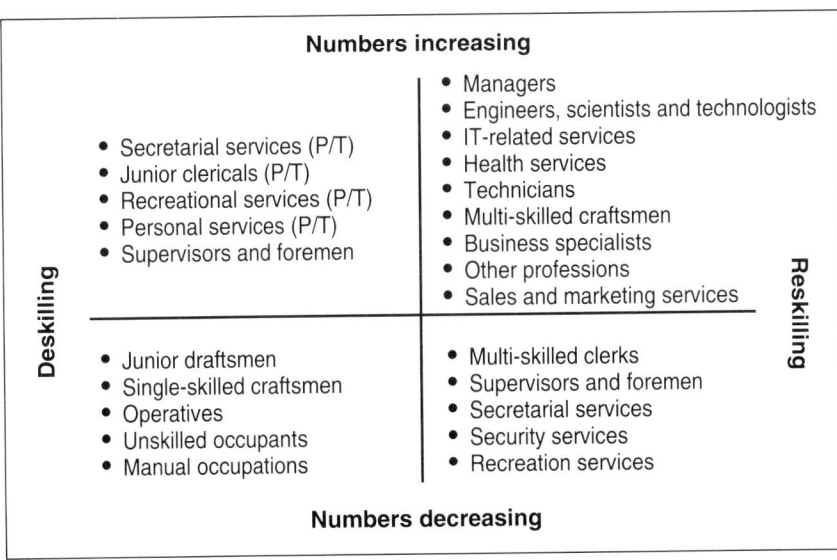

|  | Numbers increasing | |
|---|---|---|
| **Deskilling** | • Secretarial services (P/T)<br>• Junior clericals (P/T)<br>• Recreational services (P/T)<br>• Personal services (P/T)<br>• Supervisors and foremen | • Managers<br>• Engineers, scientists and technologists<br>• IT-related services<br>• Health services<br>• Technicians<br>• Multi-skilled craftsmen<br>• Business specialists<br>• Other professions<br>• Sales and marketing services |
|  | • Junior draftsmen<br>• Single-skilled craftsmen<br>• Operatives<br>• Unskilled occupants<br>• Manual occupations | • Multi-skilled clerks<br>• Supervisors and foremen<br>• Secretarial services<br>• Security services<br>• Recreation services |
|  | Numbers decreasing | **Reskilling** |

**Fig. 8. Quantitative and qualitative changes in occupational structure.**

From Amin Rajan, *Vocational Training Scenarios for the Member States of the European Community*, 1988, p. 92

Such an analysis is reinforced at sector level. In 1988 health authority recruitment targets suggested a need for nursing to take 46 per cent of all females leaving school in 1995 with five GCSEs or equivalent. Entrants with a good level of qualifications at the age of sixteen are also sought for 'technician traineeships, banking, building societies, the police, junior scientific support jobs, and some types of clerical work such as the Civil Service and local authorities'.[11] For HR Managers the following are just some of the categories of staff likely to be once again in scarce supply in the mid-1990s as the UK economy emerges from recession and the supply-side problems reappear:

- Computer programmers and analysts.
- Project managers.
- Development and design engineers.
- Software engineers.
- Electrical/electronic engineers.
- Actuaries.
- Accountants.
- Electrical/electronic craftsmen.
- Financial specialists.
- Teachers.
- Nurses.

Quantitative information is difficult to establish. For IT specialists there is more evidence. The trade union MSF has reported a growth in demand for IT products and services of 10–20 per cent per annum. The overall population of IT specialists was expected to grow at five per cent per annum to 1990.[12] Information technology specialists have been affected by unemployment in the early 1990s, although there is no reason to assume that demand will not increase again up to the year 2000 as IT functionality increases. Staff with networking and communication application skills are still particularly sought after, with a very buoyant demand for IT skills in finance and administration despite the problems of the UK economy.[13]

Other major medium-term occupational forecasts for the UK point to continuing demand for managerial and professional skills:

> The econometric forecasts suggest that between 1987 and 1995 there will be a 7 per cent growth in the number of jobs in the economy. It is anticipated that this growth will be spearheaded by business services, which are heavy users of graduates, to meet the growing demand by both individuals and firms . . .
>
> At an occupational level, there is expected to be a 17½ per cent growth in professional and related occupations between 1987 and 1995, an increase of over 900,000 jobs which will increasingly be filled by graduates. This growth will be due to a combination of sectoral growth and the rising demand for skills within organisations as a result of technological, organisational and product and service changes. Within this group there is expected to be a 21 per cent growth in scientific and

engineering occupations . . . A 12 per cent growth in managerial jobs is also forecast, an increase of 380,000 jobs . . .[14]

This model may need to be reworked to account for changes in the early 1990s, but the medium-term forecast is unlikely to change.

## Integrating supply and demand

HR Managers will find the above analysis of supply and demand of general interest, since it relates manpower trends to the time scales likely to emerge from the HR vision. There is a need, however, to develop specific organisation-related data. Multi-site organisations will need to study labour market data for each of their main locations. Some specialist skills will be in national short supply where the labour market will be the UK overall, or even, in some subjects, at an international level. There are six steps in this process of establishing the external part of an organisational manpower plan.

1. Establish what labour market your organisation is in. To do this, it is useful to analyse how many people were appointed in a particular calendar year, by age, sex and location. Trends in recruitment by age and sex can be compared to the national trends referred to above. The extent to which your recruitment is adapting to, say, women returners or older employees can be quantified in this analysis.

2. Next, you need to know where your employees live, and how large the organisation's catchment area is. County boundaries and/or post codes can be used for a convenient subdivision. Recruitment by age and sex can then be plotted in relation to catchment area. This analysis will also produce much useful data, including revealing any areas of underrepresentation, the extremities of the catchment area, and any differences in the age/sex profile by catchment area.

Areas of underrepresentation can often be explained by local competition in the labour market, by transport difficulties or simply by lower levels of population in particular areas. It is as well to know why areas are unrepresented. Without any obvious explanation, labour market targeting of an area could be very productive.

Not surprisingly, the analysis is likely to reveal that young men are more mobile from longer distances than young women.

3. Establish the supply-side trends in the catchment labour force, by age and sex, to the year 2000, and beyond if possible, depending on the time frame for the relevant vision and HR resourcing strategies. Department of Employment regional labour force projections will be of considerable assistance at this stage. Local county council information will often be of more precise value, and development agencies for the area can be of great assistance.

This analysis will show the percentage change in the labour force by age group and by sex. Figures for the increase in the total economically active population can be derived. The changing nature of the labour market in the areas in which you seek to recruit will be revealed in detail. Depending on the results of this analysis, you will want to explore further the factors that shape a labour force, including:

- The size of the population and its rate of growth/decline. Estimates on inward/outward migration are relevant here.
- The proportion of people in any age group in, or looking for, work.
- The net impact of commuting, i.e. which jobs particularly encourage people to travel long distances in order to be employed.
- Overall unemployment – the higher this is the less incentive there is for people to enter the labour market and look for a job.
- The range and type of work available.[15]

4. Examine education trends. This process includes:

- School polls: forecasting trends in the number of fifth-form students in schools in your catchment area.
- Examining the recent results of schools in your area by A level, GCSE, B.Tec. or other relevant subjects to predict future trends.
- School leaver destination: how many sixteen-year-olds stay at school or in further education, go into employment, join YTS schemes or become unemployed?

This analysis will enable you to predict the number of fifteen-year-olds entering the labour market with the required academic qualifications. As a result you may need to adopt new or different strategies towards school leavers. These issues are examined in chapter 5.

5. Analyse future labour demand in your catchment area for skills relevant to your business. If you are an employer of clerical labour, for example, you will need to study office space which is:

- Built and ready for use but still empty,
- Speculative, but ready for planned offices to be built,
- Office space left by companies moving to new premises.

This will give you a figure of square feet projected for office employment. Using an appropriate figure of square feet per employee, an estimate can be reached of projected extra office jobs. Economic conditions will, of course, influence whether this space is actually translated into jobs, but at least you will have an indication of the likely demand, given various economic scenarios.

Company relocation to your catchment area could have a major impact on demand-side analysis. This in turn is influenced by supply-side factors such as population growth, net inward migration, a young age profile, high education standards, and the availability of good-quality private and rented accommodation.

6. The final stage is to establish from the analysis whether demand will equal supply in your catchment area. Depending on the extent of the gap,

*The manpower context*

various strategies will need to be considered to manage any skills gap which may impact on your ability to deliver the relevant HR strategies for your organisation.

Nationally, therefore, the medium and long-term trends in the number of school leavers, and in the total economically active, are well known. The numbers of young people decline to 1994 but the overall size of the labour force increases. The increase is almost entirely accounted for by women returners. Education adds to the supply-side difficulties for employers, since a greater number of school leavers will remain in full-time education. Despite short-term unemployment, from 1992 onwards this scenario is likely to be compounded by difficulties on the demand side in many sectors, including managerial and professional jobs, and once again, IT jobs. However, supply and demand statistics must be examined by each organisation within its own catchment area. This six-stage plan of action will enable a manpower plan to be produced covering many of the key external trends of relevance to the HR vision and strategies.

Next, this chapter turns to an examination of internal trends within the organisation in the 'manpower audit'.

## THE INTERNAL LABOUR MARKET

The above analysis of external supply and demand has, of course, revealed only part of the resourcing context of the HR vision. The HR Manager already has in the organisation people of varying levels of ability and readiness for fresh challenges. These staff will have their own expectations of career development. There will be known retirements to contend with, and further the possibility of increased turnover. Staff resources may become available as business objectives change – then the issue of skills fit and mobility need to be considered. Underlying such manpower issues are more fundamental questions of productivity, organisation goals and structure. Can the current workforce produce more without the need to recruit extra skills which may be in short supply? Can key staff in one part of the organisation be freed to move to another if overlapping responsibilities in the former part allow such restructuring? Will separate business units in the same organisation support cross-unit promotion? These and other issues are addressed in the concept of the manpower audit. When this internal audit is combined with the external manpower context the HR Manager is well placed to develop both an effective diagnosis and the right remedies to correct any resourcing imbalance to meet the demands of business strategies in the future.

### Manpower audit

Firstly, there is the need to establish certain basic facts through a manpower audit. Most HR Managers will have such data within their manpower planning capability, and this should include:

1. A breakdown of staff by grade and by operating unit. Such a grade analysis assumes there is a common grading structure to enable such a tabulation. Fig. 9 shows one approach to this analysis. This is very basic

| Grade | Location/Business unit ............................ | | | | |
|---|---|---|---|---|---|
| | Production | Engineering | IT | HR | etc. |
| Executive A | | | | | |
| B | | | | | |
| Technical 1 | | | | | |
| 2 | | | | | |
| 3 | | | | | |
| Craft | | | | | |
| Semi-skilled | | | | | |
| Sales | | | | | |
| Clerical/admin. A | | | | | |
| B | | | | | |
| C | | | | | |
| Totals | | | | | |

**Fig. 9. Tabulating staff distribution by location, grade and function. Each organisation will define its own broad grading categories**

information which HR Managers will always be asked for. It will reveal concentrations at particular levels. When reproduced at monthly intervals it will indicate flows of staff between grades. It needs to be considered alongside information on current vacancies and on future needs. It is an important basis for future analysis.

2. A distribution by grade/sex using the same location/function split as shown in Fig. 9. This is shown in Fig. 10. Any equal opportunities monitoring programme will also need to establish these data. It adds an important dimension associated with changes in the composition of the workforce as the number of 'women returners' increases. The HR vision may also concentrate on equal opportunities, and this data base will be relevant to this aspect of the vision.

3. A distribution by *age*. Analysis of the labour force by age has always been a key component of manpower planning because of its implications for future resourcing. A predominance of key employees in the forty-five to fifty-five age group, let alone the fifty-six-plus age group, will sharpen the organisation's

| Location/Business unit ........................ | | | | | | |
|---|---|---|---|---|---|---|
| Grade | Sex | Production | Engineering | IT | HR | etc. |
| Executive A | Male | | | | | |
| | Female | | | | | |
| | Total | | | | | |
| Executive B | Male | | | | | |
| | Female | | | | | |
| | Total | | | | | |
| | etc. | | | | | |

**Fig. 10. Tabulation of staff distribution, including grade and sex**

focus on staff development among younger employees. Where internal staff development is simply not enough to fill all known vacancies a planned recruitment strategy will be necessary or other steps will have to be taken to resolve the imbalance. Other problems associated with this age profile can relate to career blocks if there is a preponderance of staff in the thirty-to-thirty-four or thirty-five-to-thirty-nine categories in key middle-ranking grades. This can have considerable implications for turnover among staff in the grades below, who may perceive their career aspirations in the organisation to be limited. This, of course, can have major implications for achievement of business and HR strategies. A typical way of analysing the age distribution of staff is shown in Fig. 11.

It is useful to combine age and sex by location and function in order to begin a more sophisticated analysis of the profile of the workforce. Any jump in the average age of men or women in specific grades needs to be analysed, since it may suggest a frustrating 'block'.

4. A distribution by *length of service*. Another important component of manpower planning; it is generally coupled with the analysis of labour turnover. Thus high turnover of short-service staff can suggest problems in induc-

| Location/Business unit ............................. | | | | | | | | | |
|---|---|---|---|---|---|---|---|---|---|
| Grade | Sex | Under 19 | 20–24 | 25–29 | 30–34 | 35–39 | 40–44 | 45–55 | 56+ |
| Executive A | Male | | | | | | | | |
| | Female | | | | | | | | |
| | Total | | | | | | | | |
| | etc. | | | | | | | | |

**Fig. 11. Tabulating staff distribution by location, function, sex and age**

tion, or in initial training, or possibly a problem in recruiting people with inappropriate knowledge and skills, or wrong expectations.

So far we have a snapshot of resourcing in the organisation at one point in time. It has concentrated on grade, age, sex and length of service. We therefore know something of the profile of the workforce, indicating blocks, imbalances, areas of underrepresentation and future resourcing gaps. As one writer put it in describing this 'diagnostic approach' to manpower planning, 'Before any manager seeks to bring about change, or reduce the degree of imbalance, he or she must be fully aware of the reasons behind the imbalance (or the manpower problem) in the first place.'[16] However, the HR vision unfolds over a five to ten-year time frame. Therefore to this snapshot of the workforce there is a need to add 'flow' data covering (1) recruitment, (2) promotions and (3) turnover. Each will be analysed in turn.

**Recruitment statistics**

It is useful to analyse new recruits over a defined period of time (say, on a calendar year basis) by grade and function for each location or business unit. Figure 12 shows a typical approach, using a similar basis to earlier figures in this chapter.

Analysing recruitment data by sex is important, given the trends referred to earlier. It enables the HR Manager to establish whether the organisation is attracting more women than hitherto. The frequent analysis of such data –

## The manpower context

| Grade | Sex | Production | Engineering | IT | HR | etc. |
|---|---|---|---|---|---|---|
| Executive A | Male | | | | | |
| | Female | | | | | |
| | Total | | | | | |
| Executive B | Male | | | | | |
| | Female | | | | | |
| | Total | | | | | |
| | etc. | | | | | |

Location/Business unit ..............................

**Fig. 12. Tabulating recruitment by grade, sex and function**

monthly is recommended — allows adjustments to recruitment policy to be carefully monitored.

Closely related to the recruitment figures is the analysis of known vacancies, by grade and function/business unit/location. In a context of market scarcity, vacancies should also be analysed by the time since the vacancy was first identified and acted upon. Such analysis can subdivide as follows for vacancies:

- Over four weeks.
- Over twelve weeks.
- Over twenty-six weeks.

At senior levels, with up to six months' notice being required before a new recruit can join the organisation, vacancies of over six months may occur. At more junior levels such longevity can suggest major resourcing problems which will require investigation and action. All vacancies over twelve weeks should, in general terms, be analysed in detail and action plans identified. Vacancies that can be sustained over long periods, e.g. over a year, must raise the question of whether the job is required to be filled at all.

## Promotion statistics

An analysis of historical data on promotions can be indicative of levels of future promotability, other things being equal. On the assumption that, for example, the quality of new recruits has not been reduced and that normal turnover is occurring at higher grades, the flow of promotions can be expected to fill future known vacancies at a similar rate to the past. However, other things are rarely equal. Recruitment standards may have been diluted; a temporary freeze on recruitment in a context of redundancies will have hit the flow of new staff; expansion may have created a higher number than usual of new recruits at a particular level. These factors need to be considered when reviewing data or promotions. A typical way of presenting these data is shown in Fig. 13.

Some HR Managers will want to go beyond this rudimentary level of analysis. For example, it is important to relate the promotion of males and females by grade to the total number of males and females in each grade. Particularly in relation to equal opportunities monitoring, promotions need to be considered with regard to the ratio of men and women in a particular grade.

| Grade from which employee is promoted | Sex | Location/Business unit ............................... | | | | |
|---|---|---|---|---|---|---|
| | | Production | Engineering | IT | HR | etc. |
| A | Male | | | | | |
| | Female | | | | | |
| | Total | | | | | |
| B | Male | | | | | |
| | Female | | | | | |
| | Total | | | | | |
| | etc. | | | | | |

**Fig. 13. Tabulating promotion by grade, sex and function**

## Turnover statistics

Analysis of employee turnover is another vital component of the manpower audit. Typically, this is shown as leavers expressed as a proportion of average employee strength during a given period – say twelve months. This can be misleading if used during the learning curve, and some specialists have suggested using twelve months' service as the base point for a calculation. Thus:

$$\frac{\text{Number of employees with twelve months' service now}}{\text{Total employed one year ago}} \times 100$$

is a more refined index of the extent to which fully trained staff are leaving.[17] More sophisticated approaches to labour turnover have also been developed and the interested reader is referred to *The Manpower Planning Handbook* by Malcolm Bennison and Jonathan Casson (McGraw Hill, 1984), in particular chapter 5.

There are other problems too. It can be misleading to include normal retirements in the 'leavers' figure, although early retirement may reflect the very problem you are trying to analyse. It can also be helpful to subdivide the analysis of turnover to 'avoidable' and 'unavoidable'. Typical components of each category are:

- *Avoidable*
  Better pay and prospects.
  Unsuited to the work.
  Poor performance.
  'Domestic reasons' or 'unknown'.
  Dislike of the work.

- *Unavoidable*
  Maternity.
  Normal retirement.
  Death in service.
  Spouse relocation.
  Further education.

Such a subdivision arises from a process of exit interview or exit questionnaire. These are a necessary but unreliable method of investigation.

Tabulating resignation by sex and length of service can be a revealing method of analysis, as indicated in Fig. 14. A similar analysis can be undertaken for each function or department. Similarly, resignations can be investigated by grade, sex and age. Completion of these tables on labour turnover will lead to a report on the meaning of the figures, analysed by unit, by department, by length of service, sex, age, and by reasons, where available.

Significant 'avoidable' losses of staff aged under twenty-five with over three years' experience can indicate a worrying loss of crucial resources which may have been ready for a supervisory or technical role. Each organisation will

| Grade | | Sex | Location/Business unit .............................. |||||
|---|---|---|---|---|---|---|---|
| | | | Years |||||
| | | | Less than 1 | 2 | 3–4 | 5–6 | 7 |
| | A | Male | | | | | |
| | | Female | | | | | |
| | | Total | | | | | |
| | B | Male | | | | | |
| | | Female | | | | | |
| | | Total | | | | | |
| | | etc. | | | | | |
| | | | | | | | |
| Overall total | | Male | | | | | |
| | | Female | | | | | |
| | | Total | | | | | |

**Fig. 14. Tabulating resignations by grade, sex and length of service for the overall location or business unit**

need to judge what a 'significant' level of turnover is. Some of the factors to be taken into account in evaluating the costs of turnover were well described in an IPM book by P. J. Samuel,[18] including:

- *Recruitment and induction costs*

    Advertising, interviewing and administration.
    Staff time.
    Non-productive time during induction.

*The manpower context*

- *Salary costs during training*

  Lower output during training period.
  Training staff costs, including supervisory time, and material costs.
  Lower material utilisation.
  Extra wear and tear on machinery or equipment.

- *Costs of regaining lost production time*

  Costs of additional overtime.
  Any costs of sub-contracting work to other companies.

- *Costs of excess stock*

  Costs of holding excess stocks to maintain supplies when turnover occurs.

There are many other items more difficult to quantify, including:

- Loss of customer goodwill, owing to vacancies or inexperience affecting customer service standards.
- Impact on the morale of the workforce generally.
- Impact on supervisors and managers who may be distracted from strategic roles to operational tasks whilst covering for vacancies.

With 'customer orientation' a likely key feature of the HR vision, high turnover can be an item of major significance.

Clearly, the length of the learning curve and of the time a vacancy is likely to remain unfilled will also be important in attempting to define a 'significant' level of turnover which calls for remedial action. It is, however, reasonably safe to predict that lowering the avoidable turnover of more experienced staff will be an important component of any HR vision. Analysis of the basic data will be an essential first step to defining the extent of turnover, and therefore the magnitude of any strategic responses to improve retention.

## PRODUCTIVITY

Finally, in this chapter on the manpower context within which the HR vision and associated strategies are implemented, there is a need to review the productivity of labour. The HR vision is likely to refer to the need for continuous improvement in work processes if organisations are to remain competitive. Unfortunately, as one writer in *Personnel Management* put it in July 1989, 'Productivity, and the use of productivity measures to bring about improvement in it, is often not seen as the Personnel Manager's domain, but it is an aspect of manpower which is crucial to the organisation's success . . . .'[19]

The Fawley agreements of 1960 in which increases in pay were awarded in return for defined changes in working practices are well known,[20] and led to a major review of productivity levels in the mid-1960s. This was also in the context of the Labour government's productivity, prices and incomes policy.

Economic circumstances maintained productivity measurement on the agenda in the 1980s. Increasingly, management action on productivity has been taken without 'trade-offs' in the form of higher rates of pay being available. Similarly, competitive pressures have led to cost reduction programmes, as indicated in chapter 1, particularly focusing on overtime costs, costs of stock, and manning levels generally. Purchasing operations have been carefully reviewed and cash management and financial accounting procedures tightened.

Within manufacturing and services a productivity review is generally a response to certain changing demands, including:

- Faster turn-round times on deliveries.
- Product and process changes.
- The need for improved quality.
- The need to reduce costs, including labour costs.

As one writer put it,[21] reducing labour costs involves the study of five main areas of work:

1 Identifying the productivity area of any element in production.
2 Reducing the frequency of performance at any stage of the job.
3 Changing the methods or equipment which personnel use in the work.
4 Eliminating idle time, overlapping work, overtime, and duplicated work.
5 Establishing standards of performance for departments, managers and staff.

There are many techniques of work measurement available to assist organisations focusing on productivity improvement. The basic questions to be asked are straightforward, irrespective of technique, and include:

- What specific improvements do I want to achieve?
- How do I quantify success?
- How do I monitor progress?
- Do I want to pay for the improvements?
- Who will manage the improvement task?
- What are the costs/problems?

Inevitably, trade unions will seek a share of any 'savings' in return for their co-operation in securing the productivity improvement. As part of the bargain, management has often argued that any additional payments must be self-financing; that no additional payment can be made until specific improvements have been achieved; and these improvements must be quantifiable. The exact division of any savings between the organisation and the workforce will depend on the circumstances of each case. Overall effectiveness in all cases will depend upon good-quality supervision.

It may also be necessary to review the way work is performed. Here the issues are associated with specialisation which at semi-skilled level can increase productivity dramatically, as well as with the levels of discretion and autonomy available to individuals in their job. If specialisation can increase productivity, it can also produce jobs with highly repetitive tasks which may in turn add to labour turnover.

As organisations grow there is a trend towards the creation of new specialisms – systems analysts, corporate planners, financial reporting specialists, and so on[22] – which puts added pressure on the recruitment and retention of the 'knowledge workers'.

## SUMMARY

The business strategies, the HR vision and the HR strategies need to be related to the external and internal manpower context. To ignore this is to present the vision in a utopian manner, unrelated to the practical resourcing realities confronting the organisation. Externally, medium and long-term manpower trends must be understood and plans initiated to manage their impact on the business. Short-term easing of labour market pressures in a recession must not deflect the HR Manager from developing resourcing strategies to cope with the medium-term trends. Internal resources must also be examined. HR strategies must fit internal resourcing, and there are basic manpower planning questions to be answered, including productivity questions, as a precursor to the successful development of HR strategies.

## REFERENCES

1 *Employment Gazette*, Vol. 97, No. 4, April 1989, p. 160.

2 *Employment Gazette*, Vol. 98, No. 1, January 1990, p. 9.

3 *Employment Gazette*, Vol. 98, No. 2, February 1990, p. 64. See also NEDO *Defusing the Demographic Timebomb*, London, 1989, p. 13.

4 NEDO, 'Restructuring the workforce to meet the demographic challenge', paper presented to an IPM seminar on Personnel Strategy in Changing Labour Markets, Oxford, April 1990, pp. 1–2.

5 AMIN RAJAN, *1992: a Zero Sum Game*, Industrial Society, London, 1990, p. 68.

6 *Employment Gazette*, Vol. 96, No. 5, May 1988, p. 269.

7 RICHARD WAITE and GEOFFREY PIKE, *School Leaver Decline and Effective Local Solutions*, IMS Report No. 178, IMS, Brighton, 1989, p. 45.

8 RICHARD PEARSON, GEOFFREY PIKE, ALAN GORDON and CLARE WEGMAN, *How Many Graduates in the 21st Century? The Choice is Yours*, IMS, Brighton, 1989, p. 9.

9 *Ibid.*, p. 90.

10 RAJAN, *op. cit.*, p. 89.

11 *Employment Gazette*, Vol. 96, No. 5, May 1988, p. 271.

12 MSF position paper on 'High Technology Skills Shortages' (unpublished), MSF, London, April 1988.

13 See IMS, *IT Manpower Monitor 1988*, and HELEN CONNOR and RICHARD PEARSON, *Information Technology: Manpower into the 1990s*, IMS Report No. 117, IMS, Brighton, 1986.

14 PEARSON *et. al.*, *op. cit.*, p. 82.

15 For more details see, for example, *The Cambridgeshire Labour Force 1981–2001*, Cambridgeshire County Council, Cambridge, 1989.

16 JOHN FYFE, 'Putting the people back into manpower planning equations', *Personnel Management*, October 1986, p. 66.

17 P. J. SAMUEL, *Labour Turnover? Towards a Solution*, IPM, London, 1971, p. 9.

18 *Ibid.*, pp. 15–16.

19 DAVID BELL, 'Why manpower planning is back in vogue', *Personnel Management*, July 1989, p. 42.

20 ALLAN FLANDERS, 'The Fawley experiment', in *Management and Unions*, Faber, London, 1975, pp. 51–65.

21 JOHN WINKLER, *Company Survival during Inflation*, Gower Press, Farnborough, 1975, p. 92.

22 See JOHN CHILD, *Organisation: a Guide to Problems and Practice*, Harper & Row, London, 1977, p. 30.

CHAPTER 5

# Resourcing strategies

Human Resources strategies for a quality workforce will inevitably major on resourcing issues. How can the organisation better attract high-quality recruits? What changes need to be made to the recruitment process to support the HR vision? What is the role of line management in the recruitment process? Resourcing strategies will not be just about recruitment processes. Medium-term manpower trends continue to suggest that HR strategies will need to target alternative sources of labour, including:

- Women 'returners'.
- School leavers.

This chapter begins with a detailed review of recruitment strategies and then examines the strategies to tackle these untapped resources.

## PROFESSIONALISM IN RECRUITMENT

In the late 1980s employers and their agencies spent almost £500 million on recruitment in the national, regional and specialist press.[1] Organisations might spend an average of £100,000 per annum on recruitment advertising, with some budgets running to £1 million. Barry Curnow, in *Personnel Management* in November 1989, reviewing the results of a survey of 1,000 personnel professionals, concluded that recruitment will be the factor that will most affect success in achieving business and corporate objectives in the 1990s. 'If it was true to describe the 1970s as the "era of industrial relations" and the 1980s as that of organisation culture and change management it becomes increasingly apparent that the 1990s will be the "era of the recruiter . . ."'[2]

HR Managers will have had to conduct the analyses described in chapter 4 to quantify the extent of any recruitment needs. If this is the era of the recruiter, there are commentators who feel that HR Managers have much to learn about recruitment. In his book *Recruitment in the 90s* Peter Herriot asserts; 'Decisions get made on totally inadequate and often prejudicial information. The organisation recruits in its own image – or, rather, in the image of its recruiters.'[3] Further, he says, organisations fail to provide the information candidates need; they don't know what to do with the candidate information they have, and the purpose of interviews is often confused. He recommends 'thorough professionalisation' of the whole process, underpinned by careful job analysis.

Those HR Managers investing heavily in psychometric testing, in the skills of interviewing, in training, assessment centres, and so on, may argue with the 'totally inadequate' statement. However, most will want to improve the objectivity of their recruitment, to improve the recruitment of quality staff and to assure the process is more cost-effective. But how?

Professionalism in recruitment starts long before the job analysis stage of the process, and uses concepts well known in sales and marketing. The main components are:

- *Market research.* What does the prospective employee (customer) know and feel about your organisation as an employer?
- *Segmentation.* The necessity to segment the geographical areas or job holders in which recruitment will take place.
- *Selling to and targeting* prospective employees against a background of business strategies and the HR vision; from overall name awareness campaigns linked to the corporate image through to specific programmes aimed at select groups.
- *Techniques* of recruitment, including open days, leaflets, posters and bus cards.
- *Job and skills profile.* Description of the job accountabilities, and the knowledge, skills and abilities (competences) required to perform the job effectively.
- *Recruitment support.* Brochures and other literature on the organisation and the job context; the physical facilities for recruitment.
- *Selection.* The precise mechanism, including tests to screen and choose candidates for a job.
- *Recruitment audit.* How do those recruited rate their experience? What actually happens to those recruited? For example, does their performance in the job match the results of any tests used in the interviewing process? What is the cost effectiveness of each recruitment mechanism?

Measurement is an important dimension to a professional recruitment process. Different forms of measurement can be used to evaluate each of the above stages. This chapter concentrates on these eight components of effective recruitment strategies to secure a quality workforce.

## Market research

HR Managers need to understand how prospective employees perceive their organisation, or indeed whether they know about it at all. Crucially, this information can be gained by specific age groups (say by fourteen-to-sixteen-year-olds), by specific geographical areas, by social class, sex, current working status, or qualifications. From such analyses HR Managers can form a detailed judgement about the views of prospective employees in the relevant labour market towards the organisation.

The main objectives of this labour market research are to:

- Measure the awareness and knowledge of prospective employees in a particular catchment area of your organisation and other major employers.
- Assess attitudes towards these organisations.
- Discover where people gain information from about these organisations.
- Find out what people in the area consider important in a job.
- Assist the organisation in its resource planning by providing a benchmark on which future surveys can be based.

Specialist research experience may be necessary in defining an appropriate sample size, especially as statistically valid conclusions are to be drawn from the analysis of subdivided data. A sample of at least 600 respondents will probably be required.

Typical questions for respondents in the fieldwork stage of this research will include:

- Give the names of any organisation in the area (as defined) that you know is employing people. (Measuring 'spontaneous awareness'.)
- (The names of organisations are read out.) Tell the questioner how well you know each organisation:

    Know very well.
    Know a fair amount.
    Know just a little about.
    Heard of known thing.
    Never heard of.
    Don't know.

    (This produces a 'familiarity index'.)
- (Showing the same organisation) How favourable or unfavourable are your opinions of each?

    Very favourable.
    Mainly favourable.
    Neither favourable nor unfavourable.
    Mainly unfavourable.
    Very unfavourable.
    Don't know.

    (To produce a 'favourable index'.)

Additional data on how your organisation is rated by the respondent can be added, bringing out particular aspects such as pay levels, career opportunities, training or location. Respondents can be asked from what sources they learnt about your organisation, who they work for at the moment, where they work, how satisfied they are at present and so on.

HR Managers will have to judge what standard or benchmark to set to weigh up these results. Over a period of time, comparative data can be compiled enabling trends to be monitored. These trends will most likely focus on:

- *Spontaneous awareness.* Some organisations will already have very high spontaneous awareness arising from their high-street presence or extensive corporate advertising. High name awareness may not correlate with awareness of the organisation as an employer. Fewer than one in ten respondents naming your organisation suggests low visibility, which may be a problem if external recruitment is necessary.
- *Familiarity index.* Combining 'know very well' and 'know a fair amount' will enable analysis of how familiar people are with your organisation. Familiarity broken down by age, sex or educational qualifications will provide very important data for the subsequent targeting of recruitment campaigns.
- *Favourable index.* Combining 'very favourable' with 'mainly favourable' will indicate whether people who are familiar with you actually favour you too. High familiarity linked with a low favourable opinion will require action. Comparison on favourability can be made with other organisations, to place your company in a rank order.

Other indices can be compiled around other questions, as required.

With over 600 in a sample, and subdivisions on the basis of age, sex and qualifications, a very detailed snapshot will emerge of awareness, knowledge and attitudes towards your organisation. Making use of these data is vital. If, for example, young people do not know you are recruiting – and you are – here is an audience to target. If people do not know, or know little, about your career opportunities – and you have many – this message can be refocused in your advertising. A rich source of data will be revealed which will lead direct to a more tailored recruitment process.

## Segmentation

As marketeers segment the customer base, so HR Managers will need to segment the labour market. This process can take three different forms:

- *Geographical segmentation.* An analysis of the recruitment catchment area for your organisation. Use can be made of post codes to subdivide a geographical area. Previous recruitment from these areas into the company would be the basis of the breakdown and could again be analysed by sex, age and qualifications. Any areas of geographical underrepresentation would emerge from this investigation.
- *Functional segmentation.* An analysis of the labour market by functional category or specialism. Thus if an organisation was recruiting newly qualified actuaries it would need to assess the number of graduates with relevant qualifications emerging from universities each year and the number of student actuaries in employment who might be targeted. Knowledge of the scope of IT resources would be necessary if you were recruiting

## Resourcing strategies

IT specialists. Functional segmentation is particularly relevant when recruiting in a national or international labour market.
- *Personal segmentation.* A wide variety of personal characteristics can be used for segmenting the prospective labour force, including age, sex, educational qualifications and number of children. For initiatives such as targeting older workers or women returners, analysing the labour market in this way will be critical. What is the point of targeting older workers if in your catchment area there are few to employ?

Information on population projections is normally available from county councils, development agencies or from the Department of Employment regional labour force projections.

### Selling and targeting

The market research carried out at the first of the two stages above may have revealed a general need to raise the image of the company as an employer. Direct recruitment advertising can influence overall image and, in this respect, links with corporate advertising. The main objective of any recruitment advertising will be to attract high-calibre staff who will join your organisation and long-term make a significant contribution to its objectives. Such applications are more likely to be attracted to organisations that are well known, established but expanding, with a recognisable identity, good career opportunities, and which offer training and a rewarding job. While pay ranks high in any list of the factors people consider important in a job, so do 'interesting and enjoyable work', 'job security' and 'opportunities for advancement'.

As an organisation advertises its corporate message so its profile is raised and in turn the public perception of the organisation is adjusted. The perceptions of those who work in the company will be influenced, too – hopefully, leading to more satisfaction with the organisation. This relates directly to components of the HR vision. It is vital to ensure that this communication process is part of a total communications plan, and that messages in different media are consistently and mutually reinforcing the overall theme.

Recruitment advertising therefore needs to match other forms of corporate advertising in style, tone, format and quality. The relationship between recruitment advertising and corporate advertising can be strengthened by the consistent use of the corporate logo, by type style, by a common 'sign-off line ('Simply the best' or 'A whole new world' or 'Putting people first'). Prospective employees will be able to see other corporate adverts such as on television and in the national press. When they see recruitment advertising using consistent themes it emphasises that they are seeing a professional organisation which can clearly co-ordinate all aspects of its business – in short, a good company to work for.

Recruitment advertising allows the organisation to impress customers and shareholders further, as the Tesco advertisement (Fig. 15) shows.

As David Wheeler, Director General of the Institute of Practitioners in Advertising, put it in *Personnel Management*:

> # You see wasteland...
> # We see customers and jobs
>
> Stimulating our growth are business orientated professionals with the ability to see potential, take decisions and act.
>
> In the front line of this process, our specialist Researchers are pioneers in the use and development of Store Location Analysis as a management tool. Utilising powerful modelling techniques, they provide not only guidelines for development strategy, but a detailed filter system for site evaluation and new store sales forecasting.
>
> With each new superstore representing an initial investment of several million pounds, and new openings planned at the rate of twelve per year, our Researchers are a major influence on multi-million pound decisions which are changing the face of retailing.
>
> Spearheading developments in other key areas are professionals in Buying, Marketing, Merchandising, Distribution, Finance, Property, Personnel, Computing, Technology and Store Management. Together they represent the specialist skills and expertise which make Tesco one of the most sophisticated and fast growing operations of its kind.
>
> The Tesco approach to business creates an ideal environment for professional talent.
>
> Look out for specific appointments in the press.
>
> **(TESCO)**
>
> **Tesco means Business**

**Fig. 15. Corporate recruitment advertising by Tesco Stores.**
Cited in *Personnel Management*, April 1988

Greater pressure to identify and attract the most able people at all levels has led to the development of recruitment advertising into a highly sophisticated activity. In many instances it is beginning to converge with what is generally known as corporate advertising. This is not surprising, since it is just as important, if not more so, to get over the ethos, objectives and flavour of the organisation to would-be employees as it is to impress customers and shareholders. Given that the organisation's recruitment advertising will be seen by many customers and shareholders, the emphasis today is on image building and corporate projection.[4]

Recruitment advertising, however, can allow the organisation to be much more precise in its targeting of specific audiences. It may provide the only opportunity to improve awareness among particular groups. For example, three distinct segments were identified above by geography, function or personal characteristics. If your organisation is in a particular catchment area, then use can be made of local newspapers. Surveys have identified the increased use of the regional press, partly because of the cost of national media campaigns but also because of the ability to target specific catchment areas.[5]

Particular functional specialists can be best targeted by use of the specialist press for recruitment advertising, such as *Insurance Post* for insurance specialists, *Computer Weekly* for IT specialists, *Personnel Management* for personnel specialists, and so on.

Finally, individuals can be targeted on the basis of particular personal characteristics. Lorraine Paddison, writing in *Personnel Management*, has quoted Rank Xerox, who were keen to broaden the image of the job of customer engineer, and to attract more women. One example of the company's advertisements aimed at attracting more women is shown in Fig. 16. She also quotes the example of Channel Four television, which recruited specifically for disabled staff. She concludes:

> Targeted recruitment works. Not only can it produce increased applications from the targeted group, it does not deter traditional applicants – an initial fear of many employers. As a result the overall response rate will often increase. However, it is no quick-fix solution to recruitment problems. Changing a company image and making a significant shift in the mix of the workforce takes time.[6]

The development of a creative style that is recognisable, presents the right message, and is consistent with corporate advertising, will require close co-ordination in the organisation between the public relations, marketing and HR departments. Advertising agencies can add value with strong and cohesive campaigns to build corporate identity and attract employees simultaneously. Few will be the readers of this book who have not been subjected to countless media presentations from agency personnel demonstrating their creativity and success in other organisations. Ultimately, as with headhunters, personal empathy between you and the agency staff will be vital, as will cost and track record. After the initial choice of agency, repeat business will depend on the delivery of high-quality applicants to fill your vacancies. While these targets can at least be set in advance and closely monitored, failure will be rationalised by the agency as down to the organisation. 'You don't pay enough, so what do

## RANK XEROX

### Is there one good reason why more Customer Engineers aren't women?

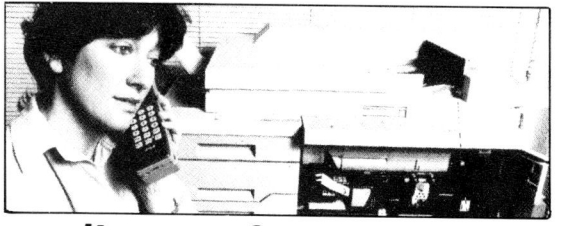

The job requires you to understand our customers' needs, decide priorities, and plan and organise your own time. To achieve this you will have the full back-up of a professional team, comprehensive training and the latest technology, including a mobile 'phone.

What do you need? You will need to convince us that you have a genuine interest and some experience in electro-mechanical engineering, supported by a City & Guilds/BTEC or equivalent qualification, plus self-motivation and good communication skills.

Depending on location and experience, you can start with earnings of c.**£10,000 — £13,000 p.a.** Generous benefits include family BUPA, excellent company pension scheme and a fully expensed company car. You will also be joining a Company which encourages and recognises personal and career development through our 'Career Map' structures.

Whilst encouraging applications from women, we are as keen as ever to hear from equally qualified men.

We currently have opportunities throughout **Central and Southern England** so why not give us a call?

Speak to Sandy Dines on 01 965 0606, or Neil Foulger on 0908 663355 for more information, or write to them at Rank Xerox (UK) Ltd, 438 Midsummer Boulevard, Central Milton Keynes, Milton Keynes MK9 2DZ.

Considering the job itself — absolutely not! That's why Rank Xerox is spearheading change to attract more women, as well as men, as Customer Engineers.

Join us and you will be the key interface with our customers for After Sales Support. This will involve you in visiting customer premises, diagnosing faults, repairing and installing our office equipment. In short — developing and maintaining customer loyalty, and sustaining our reputation as a quality supplier.

*We only discriminate on ability*
*These positions are open to both men and women*

**Fig. 16. Advertising aimed at recruiting women staff by Rank Xerox.**
Cited in *Personnel Management*, November 1990, p. 56

you expect?' will be a typical reaction to a miserable response from a recruitment advertising campaign. You will need to take all factors into account in a decision to stick with an agency despite poor response rates.

### Techniques of recruitment

Advertising in the regional, specialist and national press will, for most HR Managers, be the main method used to attract prospective employees. Effective recruiting strategies, however, demand further examination of other techniques which could be useful to the organisation. This includes open days, leaflets and posters, bus cards, radio advertising and cash rewards.

#### Open days

'Open days' have a number of advantages as a recruitment technique. They give to prospective employees the opportunity to meet company representatives and get a first-hand flavour of the organisation, the location, the job and the package. By deliberately creating an easy-going atmosphere where the individual can ask questions without feeling under pressure, hesitant candi-

## Resourcing strategies

dates can be converted into firm applicants. Equally, the organisation's representatives can learn more about the candidate, which could be very helpful in the subsequent screening.

This opportunity for first-hand assessment can be taken further by organising on-the-spot interviews for interested candidates. This speeds up the first stages of the recruitment process to a considerable degree. There are other advantages, too. Line managers and HR specialists can work together on the open days. Such line involvement adds commitment to the recruitment process and clearly signals, in a high-profile manner, the organisation's recruitment activities. Open days are best 'flagged' by insertions on advertisements or by radio advertising. There are costs involved, such as local hotel or in-company facilities, as well as the cost of printing material about the organisation and jobs. Large-scale material – posters and the like – can be reused. Overall, this is a cost-effective technique which is self-recommending.

### Leaflets and posters

Leaflet campaigns and posters in key locations can also be a useful adjunct to a recruitment advertising campaign. Leaflets, when placed into thousands of homes in the targeted catchment area, can be a very direct method of advertising. The leaflet can raise a name awareness generally which could have useful commercial spin-offs. There are disadvantages. Many leaflets will be deposited in empty homes, or into homes where no prospective employees live. Some people react adversely to 'junk mail' to which category your well conceived recruitment leaflet may unfortunately be attributed. There are distribution costs to be considered, often via the distribution outlets of local free newspapers. Overall, this is not a technique likely to produce many applications.

Giving out leaflets at carefully chosen locations can be more effective. With a trained eye, for example, individuals in the right age group can be presented with the leaflet, old-age pensioners just receiving a smile.

Direct mailing of recruitment literature to potential new recruits can be more effective. A list of potential recruits can be gained from existing staff, customers or other contacts. There are equal opportunities implications here which are covered under 'cash rewards' below.

Posters avoid distribution costs, but need careful positioning if they are to be read. An example of one successful poster campaign is shown in Fig. 17. This was targeted at commuters to London, emphasising the advantages of working locally.

### Bus cards

An inexpensive yet effective method of recruitment advertising that is surprisingly little used. A card placed upstairs on every other bus in a medium-sized town for two months can cost a few thousand pounds. With schoolchildren congregating on the upstairs of buses, this advertising is likely to be particularly useful as part of a campaign aimed at young people.

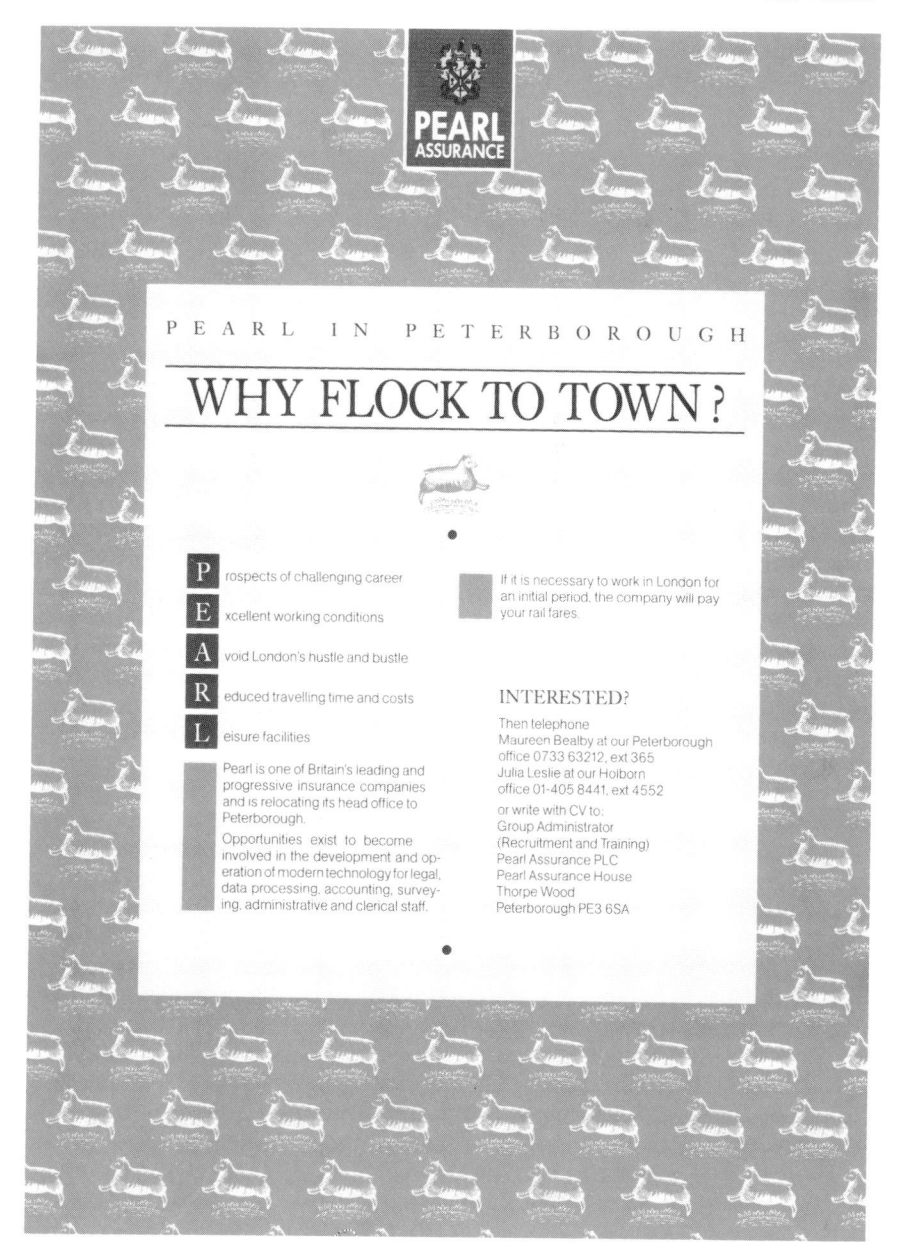

**Fig. 17. Poster advertising aimed at Londoners weary of commuting**

## Radio advertising

Advertising on local radio can complement a local press advertising campaign, creating a momentum and visibility not otherwise gained by reliance on a single medium. The average thirty-second 'sound bite' may cost you more than other techniques, and doubt exists over whether the relevant target population are listening to the radio as your advert appears. Radio advertising can, however, be useful in informing prospective employees about open days or recruitment fairs. As with many other forms of recruitment advertising, it helps name awareness and takes the product into the listener's home.

## Cash rewards

Some employers have tried to attract the right candidates by offering their existing workforce a cash sum if they introduce someone to the organisation who is subsequently offered a job. For example, the proposer of a successful candidate receives a taxable payment of say £500. It can be paid in two parts. The first (often a smaller amount) is paid on the first pay date after the candidate has commenced employment. The second, larger, payment is paid after the candidate has successfully completed a six-month or one-year probationary period.

From an equal opportunities viewpoint, care is needed before such an inducement is introduced. 'Word of mouth' recruitment, relying upon the existing workforce, can lead to the race and sex profile of that workforce being replicated. Ethnic minorities, for example, can be disadvantaged by this method of recruitment. If a cash reward is to be used, or indeed if reliance is to be placed on recruiting through the existing workforce, it should be part of an all-embracing recruitment campaign including use of local advertising, open days, the use of job centres and other techniques.[7]

There are, of course, other techniques not covered so far, of which the most important is the use of recruitment agencies, and headhunters. There has been a significant increase in the use of recruitment consultancies, employment agencies and executive search organisations. With this increased use of external agencies has come a fall in the reported use of job centres.[8] Recruitment agencies can bring expertise to the recruitment process and can be important in, for example, recruiting functional specialists. They can, too, take some of the work load from the recruitment department short list. For this and other services you may pay between 10 per cent and 33⅓ per cent of first year's earnings, depending on the service provided, the number of jobs to be filled and your negotiating skill. For large-scale recruitment, a 'no placement, no fee' basis of remuneration for the agency makes good commercial sense.

## Jobs and skills profile

Two important components of effective recruitment are a job description, and a clear definition of the knowledge, skills and abilities ('competences') a candidate must have to perform the job effectively. The competences can link recruitment direct to the HR vision.

Job descriptions will most likely exist in most organisations. They should provide an up-to-date summary of the principal responsibilities of the job. Key dimensions should be included, such as the number of people supervised and the annual budget. Too detailed job descriptions have been rightly criticised in recent years for 'freezing' the job, leading to claims for regrading upon even small additions. A focus on the principal accountabilities, of a more general nature, reduces this particular difficulty.

A definition of competences required to fill the job effectively includes definition of the skills, abilities and personal characteristics demanded. These should reflect only the critical components required to meet the job challenge. Such competences can be translated to action or behaviour, which can in turn be incorporated into a 'person specification' or interviewing checklist. The use of such competence analysis in the assessment of potential is described more fully in chapter 7 in relation to development strategies.

Armed with a job description and competence analysis, the HR Manager will be able to produce key information for the applicant, as well as being able to design any selection tests or assessment centre better. An example from WH Smith of the use of competence assessments for the definition of core skills to be used for graduate recruitment is shown below.

*Written communication*
Communicates easily on paper with speed and clarity
Presents ideas concisely and in a structured way
Uses appropriate language and style
Grammar and spelling are accurate

*Oral communication*
Speaks to others with ease and clarity
Expresses ideas well and presents arguments in a logical fashion
Gives information and explanations which are clear and easily understood
Listens actively to others

*Leadership*
Shows skill in directing group activities
Has natural authority and gains respect of others
Capable of building an effective team
Involves all team members, gives advice and help when required

*Team membership*
Fits in well as a peer and as a subordinate
Understands own role and the role of others within the team
Shares information and seeks help and advice when necessary
Offers suggestions and listens to the ideas of others

*Planning and organising skills*
Can make forward plans and forecasts
Can define objectives and allocate resources to meet them
Sets realistic targets and decides priorities
Devises systems and monitors progress
Makes good use of his/her time

*Decision making*
Evaluates alternative lines of action and makes appropriate decisions
Identifies degrees of urgency for decisions
Responds to situations quickly and demonstrates flexibility

*Motivation*
Shows energy and enthusiasm
Works hard and is ambitious
Able to work on own initiative with little detailed supervision
Sets own targets and is determined to achieve them

*Personal strength*
Is self-confident and understands own strengths and weaknesses
Is realistic and willing to learn from past failures and successes
Is reliable, honest and conscientious
Can cope with pressure and control emotions

*Analytical reasoning skills*
Can quickly and accurately comprehend verbal and numerical information
Able to analyse arguments objectively and to reach logical conclusions
Can present well-reasoned and persuasive arguments[9]

## Recruitment support

As with marketing and sales support, recruitment support means literature, including brochures, application forms, short guides to the organisation, copies of 'mission' statements and strategic objectives, leaflets on career and training opportunities, and other documents. All such supporting material needs to be professionally produced, with design features that support the advertising campaign. Thus logos and other identifiable trade marks on the recruitment literature will clearly and consistently reinforce earlier messages. This is a selling opportunity – candidates may be dissuaded at this stage by poor documentation.

The content of such documents must therefore be carefully thought through. Table 5 reproduces the results of a 1990 MORI poll on the attitudes of final-year undergraduates as to what kind of information they were most interested to find out from a recruitment brochure. The emphasis here on 'what the job will entail' (47 per cent), starting salary (36 per cent), and location (34 per cent), followed by training and career development policy, is probably an accurate reflection of the priorities of most prospective employees at all levels.

### Table 5. Attitudes of final-year undergraduates to information in a recruitment brochure (%)

| When you first pick up an organisation's recruitment brochure, what kind of information are you *most interested* in finding out? | |
|---|---|
| What the job will entail day-to-day | 47 |
| Starting salary | 36 |
| Where the company is located | 34 |
| Training policy | 27 |
| Career development policy | 20 |
| Opportunities for promotion | 19 |
| Degree/disciplines required | 16 |
| Long-term pay and benefits | 14 |
| Culture/style of management | 12 |
| The company's products/services | 10 |
| How much responsibility/how early responsibility given | 8 |
| Overseas work/foreign travel | 8 |
| Number of graduates taken on/vacancies | 8 |
| Size of organisation | 6 |
| History of the organisation | 6 |
| Physical working environment | 5 |
| Career histories of people with the company | 4 |
| Sample projects of people's work | 4 |
| Background information on individual locations | 3 |

Source: MORI, *Attitudes of Final-year Undergraduates 1990* (sample 1,001 = 100 per cent), cited in Philip Schofield, 'The difference a graduate recruitment brochure can make', *Personnel Management*, January 1991, p. 38.

Many commentators have urged organisations to design material which is 'candidate-friendly'.[10] Some organisations, such as Harrod's and British Airways, have separate locations with purpose-built facilities for recruitment. Such facilities can be given their own identity. Information desks, interview booths, a comfortable waiting area, knowledgeable and friendly reception staff would be key components of such a recruitment centre.

Some organisations take the marketing analogy further by colour-coding all recruitment literature, depending upon the job or training opportunity. Thus all jobs and training openings for A-level applicants would be colour-coded to delineate this type of vacancy from others. All job adverts and brochures would contain a brief description of the job itself and the skills required to perform it.

These are important elements in a professional and effective approach to recruitment.

## Selection

The selection stage can consist of many phases. Typically there will be an initial interview after certain candidates have been rejected on the basis of their application form. This is a good point at which to evaluate the effectiveness of the advertising or other recruitment techniques. A high number of unqualified or wrongly qualified applicants will suggest that the advertising was not explicit enough in what was required.

Following the initial interview, there will often be a second or final interview. At semi-skilled levels, or where large numbers of applicants need to be seen, reliance may, of necessity, have to be placed on one interview. At clerical, sales, technical and managerial levels interviews are increasingly being supported by selection tests or by assessment centres. Both forms of assessment add considerably to the data base available to managers on the basis of which selection decisions can be made. Given the costs of recruitment, and the implications of getting wrong candidates, this extra investment is reasonable if decision-making is improved.

There are many tests available on the market for the recruitment of staff at all levels and in most functions. The HR Manager must be satisfied that the tests are a valid predictor of skills/knowledge relevant to the job. 'Off the shelf' tests should be extensively 'trialled', comparing test results with actual job performance. Only when a clear correlation has been established, probably over at least a year, between job performance and test results should a particular test be incorporated into the selection procedure. Future checks will still be necessary to continue to ascertain that the tests remain relevant to the required job competences. Checks must also be made to ensure that the questions are not discriminatory and relate only to the job.[11]

It would be preferable, although more expensive, to design selection tests in-house that were specifically tailored to the requirements of one organisation and one category of jobs. The same process of trial and validation would be necessary.

Assessment centres can be a powerful mechanism in the selection procedure. Once again there is the key need to define the competences demanded by the job. These can be translated into specific exercises, tests, one-to-one interviews and/or group discussion designed to reveal the main competences. Each exercise will identify certain competences. Competences can be assessed, therefore, on a number of occasions throughout the process of the centre. One, or maybe two, days would be allowed, with trained assessors recording performance against the defined requirements. Feedback to the candidate is generally provided after the assessors have reached a consensus. There is a move towards greater openness with candidates in relation to assessment centre results, even with the candidates who are rejected.

The reader who as acted as an assessor – and there will be many – will, hopefully, agree with the use of the word 'powerful' above. Across a range of exercises and tests the 'bullshit' factor all but disappears and behavioural patterns can be identified. As with selection tests, the results of assessment centres should be subsequently compared with job performance. There are some down sides. They are time-consuming, especially for busy line managers. Since the assessors need to be credible, it will undoubtedly be 'busy' line managers who are nominated as assessors. Some individuals may 'freeze' on the day and not show their true potential. This is also true of interviews, and at least assessment centres approach candidates from different perspectives, which should assist individuals who dislike one style of assessment. The overall process of competence analysis, centre design, training and organisation may, for some organisations, prove too costly and complicated. In general, however, assessment centres are an effective component of professional recruitment.

Finally, having reached a judgement on a candidate in a way which has not, hopefully, put the applicant off, there is the matter of references and checking qualifications. One survey suggested that 22 per cent of organisations checked all qualifications, 54 per cent checked some and 24 per cent did not check any. Fifty-nine per cent checked all references and 38 per cent checked some. Both references and the checking of qualifications are part of the building of a data base prior to an offer of employment, and both stages need to be approached with a thoroughness equal to that of the earlier stages in the recruitment process.

### Recruitment audit

Auditing the recruitment process occurs at four levels.

1. Setting performance indicators for each stage of the internal recruitment process, and evaluating performance against these milestones. For example, four weeks could be provided between notification of a vacancy and first interviews; a further four weeks to a decision and a total cycle of twelve weeks from notification to the job holder commencing employment. More senior jobs will require longer time periods. Assessment centres may also influence the timing, but that can be allowed for in the performance standards. Significant variations from the established standards will need to be individually investigated, and remedial action initiated if necessary. Remedial action might include extra staffing for the recruitment section if turn-round times are not being met. One of the major causes of candidate demotivation is a slow turn-round of applications.

2. Assessing the total number of applications, the number of short-listed candidates, the number of candidates offered jobs and the number of candidates commencing employment for each different recruitment technique. The total cost of each technique, and hence the *per capita* cost of recruitment, should be added to this analysis. A typical framework is shown in Fig. 18.

Each separate campaign can be evaluated in this way. Poor performing techniques can be adjusted or dropped. The cost effectiveness of each technique can be explored, and low-cost, high-employment techniques

*Resourcing strategies*

| Source of application | Number of applications | Number of shortlisted candidates | Number offered job | Number commenced employment | Total cost | Cost per head appointed |
|---|---|---|---|---|---|---|
| Local press advert | | | | | | |
| National press advert | | | | | | |
| Specialist press advert | | | | | | |
| Leaflet drop | | | | | | |
| Radio advert | | | | | | |
| Bus cards | | | | | | |
| Open day | | | | | | |
| Recruitment fair | | | | | | |
| *Total* | | | | | | |

**Fig. 18. Analysis of recruiting effectiveness**

enhanced. In this analysis it is assumed that all candidates are of equally high quality.

3. Monitoring, as part of an equal opportunities policy, is an important component of the audit process. Areas where there is underrepresentation of, for example, ethnic minorities can be identified and the reason for any imbalance explored.

4. Conducting an attitude survey among staff who have been recruited. Concentrating on these staff in your organisation is more practical than following up those rejected or who have pulled out. The survey will ask questions about levels of satisfaction with each stage of the recruiting process. As with the market research in the first section of this chapter, the HR Manager can set targets for each part of the process. For example, 85 per cent must be satisfied or very satisfied with the quality of information provided before the job interview. Such audits should be conducted at least annually.

In the context of managing a quality workforce, effective recruitment will be increasingly a selling activity as well as a selection process. The HR Manager needs to attract high-quality candidates to fill vacancies, on time and in the right number. The consequences for the organisation of failure to fill those vacancies are great.

The HR Manager adopts techniques from marketing and sales, as well as refining proven selection methods, to recruit effectively. These include more research of the market place, segmenting the labour market, and selling to targeted groups. A wide range of recruitment techniques are available. Detailed job and skill profiles need to underpin recruitment, and job brochures and other literature must support the overall effort. Selection processes are vital to the quality of the end product, and four levels of audit enable the organisation to evaluate recruitment performance.

For HR and line managers, recruitment will be a high priority in the 1990s. Organisational success and meeting the HR vision will increasingly depend on the professionalism of the recruitment effort.

## UNTAPPED RESOURCES

Resourcing strategies, given medium-term changes in the labour market, may lead some organisations to re-examine two groups of potential employees: women 'returners' and school leavers. There are other groups to consider as well. For example, in the mid-1980s there was a focus on older staff.

The active recruitment of older people has been most noticeable in the retail sector. Rising unemployment has reduced the significance of these initiatives, although there are other reasons as well as demographic pressures for focusing on older workers. These include both the level of experience brought by such people to the organisation and the need to provide an age balance to the profile of the workforce. One recent report quoted the Dixon's group, Sainsbury's and Tesco as having found that older people tend to be high-quality applicants for jobs. The major qualities cited by those companies were:

- Their skills and experience.
- Their high regard for customer service.
- Their stabilising influence on younger staff.
- Their contribution to better overall staff retention rates.[12]

Dixon's were aiming to recruit staff over forty; Sainsbury's, part-timers aged fifty-five and over, with Tesco also seeking over-fifty-fives. Tesco's in particular reported that absenteeism, amongst their older employees was very low and stability was very high.[13]

This section will, however, concentrate on women in the workforce, and it is to this subject that we now turn.

### Women 'returners'

Despite rising unemployment, the increasing emphasis on women in employment is noteworthy. As the IMS put it:

> Decline in the number of school leavers, increasing employment participation by women, and exceptionally slow growth of the workforce as a whole is leading to a re-evaluation of the female workforce. Employers need to increasingly turn to women to avoid labour shortages. In this context, measures to increase the recruitment and retention of female staff are taking on a new importance.[14]

# Resourcing strategies

Chapter 4 has already shown the numbers of women who will return to the labour force up to the year 2000. By that date women will make up 45 per cent of the labour force. A substantial number of these will be in part-time occupations. Few will have jobs at senior management level, however.[15] Female participation in higher education is increasing. Several changes, including a greater number of one-parent families, and financial pressures prompting women to work add to the changing picture of family life in the UK. Certain aspects of the woman's role remain largely unchanged – for example 'shouldering the major responsibility for household chores and where appropriate child care'.[16]

What are the factors which influence a woman in the decision to return to work or not? There are many issues, including finance, child care facilities, the hours a woman would be expected to work, whether the woman is suited to staying at home, her career ambitions and whether she intended to have more children. The provision of child care facilities will be near the top of the agenda. Organisations looking to support women returning to work, as part of their HR vision, or looking to retain key women employees who want to combine their career with having children, need first of all to consider the child care options and what support the organisation should provide.

## Child care options

*Playgroups* bring children together to play, usually for two to three days per week for a few hours. Children are normally taken from the age of three upwards, and these playgroups are often run by a trained supervisor with voluntary helpers. As a result of the limited hours involved, these schemes cannot normally provide the type of care required if the mother is to resume her career, even on a part-time basis. Play groups allow the child an opportunity to socialise and give the mother some welcome relief from the responsibilities of child care.

*Child-minders* It is possible to find a 'nanny' or child-minder who will look after young children in her own home. Play facilities may be limited, but the nanny and child may develop a close and affectionate relationship. This may suit very young children in particular, say those under two years old. All social services departments should have a list of registered child-minders, and the personnel department should hold copies of such lists for their area. Adequate provision remains a difficulty. Equally important to the women will be the cost of financing a full-time child-minder.

Some organisations operate a child care subsidy to assist the woman who is using the services of a child-minder. For example, Cambridge City Council pay up to 75 per cent of basic fees, up to a maximum (in 1989) of £40 per week for full-time attendance with a registered child-minder approved by the council.[17]

Child-minders can fall ill, too. They may also decide they've had enough (despite your child being delightful) and the parent then has the problem of finding an adequate replacement.

*Nursery schools* typically operate from 9.00 a.m. to 3.00 p.m. and close for school holidays. Typically children will be accepted from the age of three. Nursery schools assist integration into primary school proper and help develop social skills at an early age. A day nursery will have the added advantage compared to a nursery school of opening throughout the working day, often closing only on bank holidays. They will also take children from a much younger age. Again the problems are availability and cost.

*Workplace nurseries (creches)* resemble a day nursery except that they are dedicated to an employer or group of employers. They may be on the same site as the job, which is reassuring to both mother and child.

Workplace nurseries are inevitably costly to set up. Much depends, of course, on whether the building is purpose-built or whether existing facilities are adapted for the purpose, and on the number of children to be accommodated. Running costs will also be influenced by the number of children less than two years old.

For the HR Manager, cost is not the only issue of concern on the subject of workplace nurseries. Inevitably, the number of places will be limited. Refuge Assurance, for example, has been reported as opening a nursery for twenty-six children. A nursery at Hillingdon Hospital offers forty places.[18] With up to fifty places on offer, and probably fewer in practice, how is selection managed for a large company with, say 2,000 staff who may be interested?

Brighton Borough Council is reported as having solved the difficulty by adopting the following criteria:

- Whether or not the employee has sole/main responsibility for his/her children.
- The income available to the employee.
- The problem of travel to alternative child care provision.
- Whether the employee comes within the categories of people who are underrepresented in the council's workforce as a whole or in particular sections of the workforce.[19]

Others more simply operate on a 'first come, first served' basis, or use length of service. The scheme could be targeted to those job categories where there were greatest scarcity problems. Yet this would be internally divisive and generally rejected for that reason.

With significant costs, and limited spaces available, organisations have increasingly explored community nursery ventures, possibly in association with the local authority. Appropriate premises can be utilised to create a network of nurseries, hopefully within reach of employers. With organisations paying on a *per capita* basis, high capital costs can be avoided.

*Out-of-school care* Generally parents themselves will have to find a way of coping with out-of-school care or care during school holidays. Programmes can be arranged in sports centres or some schools. However, for mothers utilising nursery schools the problem of arranging child care out of school hours remains a difficult one.

One 1990 study of child care found:

- One per cent of children in local authority day nurseries.
- Twenty-three per cent of children attending part-time nurseries, allowing mothers the opportunity to work limited hours.
- Forty per cent of three-to-four-year-olds at school, but enjoying no out-of-school care.[20]

Child care provision remains patchy, and workplace nurseries, even though the best solution for the mother, may not prove cost-effective for the organisation, especially those with multi-site operations such as district or branch offices each employing few staff. For these reasons, organisations have explored the use of child care vouchers. Luncheon Vouchers Ltd run a scheme in this area. The company buys a voucher up to the price fixed in advance and presents it to the employee. The employee arranges specific provision with a child care provider and pays partly or wholly by voucher. The voucher is then redeemed from the voucher company. The problem with such a scheme is obvious – there simply is not the availability nationally of quality child care provision. In short, there may be nowhere to spend the voucher.

Given these issues, it is not surprising that organisations have sought to encourage more women to resume a career after having children through the simpler approach of a 'career break'. It is this initiative which is explored next.

## Career break schemes

One summary explained career break schemes thus:

> Career break schemes were invented primarily for women. Female employees taking a three or five-year break to have children and cope with the pre-school years lost their place on the career ladder, and employers lost trained and skilled staff. The idea behind the early schemes was to keep professional women in touch, both with the organisation and with developments in their speciality, so that they could return to work at less of a disadvantage, and take up their jobs where they had left off.[21]

Career breaks and/or extended maternity leave arrangements are designed to encourage more women to return to work following the birth and early rearing of children. This makes sense as part of a retention strategy, given the investment of time and money in recruitment and training. There is also a strong equal opportunities dimension to such initiatives.

Companies can also gain an edge in recruitment by having a career bridge scheme. Many organisations take the practical step of consulting women who are on maternity leave about their views on a career bridge. Others set up workshops for women employees from which ideas on the management of child care and a career can be explored. Scheme design will concentrate on the following main elements:

- Eligibility criteria.

- The length of the break.
- The 'guarantee' at the end of the break.
- Benefits during the break, and on return.
- Keeping in touch during the break.

The details of each aspect are now discussed.

*Eligibility* The most common criterion of eligibility to the advantages of a career break is length of service coupled with a minimum number of hours worked per week. Two to five years' service would be a typical service-related stipulation. Certain organisations have added grade qualification, stating that eligibility is open only to those in particular jobs or grades. Whilst such a requirement enables the organisation to control the numbers on a career break, and to target only pre-defined key groups, such a criterion can be divisive. When women employees have been asked their views on this subject a great majority have stated that the career break should be available to staff of all grades. This is placing equal opportunities considerations above more commercial judgements about scarcity value and the need to retain key skills. Men and women are generally both eligible, although in practice few men will be able to participate.

Most schemes also contain an overall statement regarding performance, e.g. British Rail in their guarantee scheme state that employees must have 'a satisfactory performance record'[22] Others add career potential to the list. Again there are difficulties of definition, and the need to retain staff with key skills may not be synonymous with the need to retain staff with potential. Management must have the ability to rule out women who are poor performers from the benefit of a career break which may be up to five years long. Such cases will need to be carefully documented.

*Length of the break* Most career break schemes last for a maximum of five years, with a minority of organisations opting for longer periods up to ten years. Women who were consulted at Barclays Bank are reported as stating that a five-year career break was too long to be away from a career if there was to be future promotion.[23] Other samples suggest that two years or less would not be popular, either, because the first two or three years are seen as the crucial period of child care. Any time period between two and five years seems reasonable, with, critically, flexibility for the woman to choose within the five-year period exactly when she exercises her right to return. Such flexibility is valuable if the woman intends to have more than one child.

In practice the time when a woman can return will also relate to the availability of child care facilities either at the workplace or in the locality. If good-quality child care is not available, the woman will inevitably have to defer her return until four or five years after the birth of the child. This is another sound reason for the length of the break being at least five years.

*'Guarantee' of return* This is an issue that requires careful consideration.

*Resourcing strategies*

Should a contractual guarantee be given of a job after five years or not? What is it that is being guaranteed? Many managers will be understandably cautious about contractual guarantees looking five years ahead, given the rate of change and uncertainties of the 1990s. Others will ask why, without a contractual guarantee, a woman should take part in the career break scheme? This point is sharpened if it is a requirement of the scheme that the woman cannot work for another employer during the career break. For the woman to hold herself off the labour market for, say, five years only to be told, 'Sorry, there is no job,' seems unduly onerous.

Practice reflects the different views expressed above. Many of the major clearing banks guarantee a return to the same grade, but not to the same job. Other organisations – possibly where turnover is less or the business more volatile – have given a 'commitment' seriously to consider the woman on the career break for vacancies that arise. Those organisations that provide a guarantee have then to consider what happens if there is no suitable job available at the time the woman elects to return. There are at least three options:

- Pay lump-sum compensation. Redundancy scales could be used, or separate terms defined if the redundancy terms are inappropriate.
- Place the woman on a 'reserve' scheme pending a suitable opportunity becoming available.
- Create a supervisory job on a temporary basis, until a suitable vacancy occurs. As Leicester City Council put it:

The returner will be provided with suitable employment, wherever possible in the department and on the type of work they were doing immediately before they resigned. If there is no suitable vacancy the returner will be employed in a temporary supernumerary position and will be absorbed into the first appropriate vacancy that occurs. They will be entitled to reject up to three alternative offers of permanent employment. If three offers are rejected the Council will be under no obligation to offer further posts and the Council's obligations to the returner will cease.[24]

Companies with non-guaranteed return-to-work clauses or 'reservist' schemes do not obviously need to specify what happens if no suitable job is available. Such schemes cannot, however, be too rigid about working for other employers during the career break.

*Pay and benefits* Most organisations distinguish between the benefits available during maternity leave, or extended maternity leave, and those available during a career break. With a career break, all benefits normally cease. Upon return, benefits continue at the level before the break. Any improvements in conditions of service are honoured for the leaver, who is therefore 'no worse off' as a result of the career break. Continuity of service is normally provided, for example, in relation to pensionable service. Esso dealt with the pension issue as follows.

> At the start of the break, employees leave the Esso pension plan and have all the standard leaving options available to them. On returning to full-time work, employees can rejoin the plan. Providing their prior rights have remained within the Fund prior service will be linked to their current period of plan membership. Equally . . . employees may be eligible to buy back pension service for any periods of temporary work completed during the career break.[25]

The treatment of benefits during maternity leave of up to fifty-two weeks is generally different. As part of an equal opportunities and/or retention strategy, organisations are increasingly providing continuous service throughout the maternity leave. Specific benefits such as concessionary mortgage facilities will most likely be frozen during the period of leave and paid in full retrospectively upon return. Some organisations believe it wise to wait three or six months after the leaver has returned before making such payments. This is, however, more likely to demotivate staff, and evidence of abuse is rare. Trade unions are likely to continue to argue that benefits should be payable throughout the period of maternity leave. Given the inevitable uncertainty about whether the leaver will return to work or not following childbirth, organisations are likely to continue to defer benefits until the return is realised.

Special lump-sum payments are being made to leavers to further encourage their return after maternity leave or a career break. There is evidence, too, of organisations enhancing the level of maternity pay 'up front'. Such inducements are likely to increase in future as organisations continue to seek to encourage staff on maternity leave to return to work.

*Keeping in touch*   Most organisations maintain contact with the leaver during the career break. The following ways are typical:
- Staff briefings throughout the year.
- Regular paid training, with the duration and type of training varying according to individual needs.
- Staff publications sent to the member of staff on the career break.
- Appointment of a staff 'sponsor' with a brief to keep in touch with the woman throughout the break.
- Special events, often of a social or sports nature.
- A maternity club set up on company premises, primarily for social reasons, but enabling contact to be maintained.
- Career counselling, on return from the break. Women may lack confidence, having been out of work for years. Confidence can be restored by counselling and by other techniques, such as coffee mornings and work shadowing.

## Resourcing strategies

There are many other details to be considered, including the notification period for the right to return, the number of permitted breaks and the guidelines/information to be provided to staff. Despite the number of details to be resolved, career breaks and extended maternity leave schemes are welcomed by staff as providing much greater flexibility, enabling women to manage better the combination of child care and a long-term career.

Initiatives on working time, including part-time working, are covered in chapter 8.

### Other measures affecting retention

This chapter has concentrated on child care and career breaks in relation to women returners. There are other measures which can be taken which impact upon the retention of women staff. The Institute of Manpower Studies has summarised some of them in Table 6.

Special management training schemes for women are increasing in popularity. In addition, British Telecom has run a women-only engineering course since 1987.[26] Such programmes and others – as the table shows – are infrequent, despite a scarcity of skills in many areas and in many disciplines. HR Managers will be aware of the dangers of developing 'women only' programmes. Many people argue that training and career development need to be based upon ability, and special allowances for particular groups based on sex or race is, in itself, 'discriminatory'. Others will argue that without positive action women will not be able to overcome the 'gates, hurdles or obstacles' in the way. Continuing high turnover of female staff, or a recognition that skilled female staff are not realising their full potential, will raise the issue of women as an untapped resource higher up the managerial agenda in the 1990s.

**Table 6. Practices affecting retention of women, other than child care and career breaks (% of respondents)**

| | Sector | | | | | | |
|---|---|---|---|---|---|---|---|
| Practice | Chemicals | Metal goods | Rubber and plastics | Retailing | Hotel and catering | Local authority | All |
| Equal opportunity training: | | | | | | | |
| Managerial and personnel | 9 | 7 | 11 | 13 | 14 | 26 | 13 |
| Others | 5 | 4 | 7 | 8 | 5 | 23 | 9 |
| Personal effectiveness/assertiveness | 1 | 0 | 2 | 1 | 1 | 17 | 4 |
| Women-only courses | 1 | 0 | 1 | 1 | 3 | 16 | 4 |
| Women's groups/societies | 1 | 0 | 0 | 0 | 0 | 0 | 0·1 |
| Sexual harrassment measures | 1 | 0·6 | 3 | 3 | 0 | 17 | 4 |
| Self-defence courses | 1 | 0 | 0 | 1 | 0 | 5 | 1 |
| Well-women clinics/screening | 2 | 0 | 0 | 0 | 0 | 4 | 1 |

Source: IMS survey, 1990

## School leavers

A NEDO survey identified the following responses from employers taking initiatives in relation to young people (the figures are percentages):

- Improving links with schools and colleges   49
- Improving youth training   47
- Changing pay and benefits   35
- Improving career prospects   32
- New approaches to selection   32
- Reducing entry standards   17

Chapter 4 has already shown the decline in the number of school leavers entering the labour market in the mid-1990s. Rising unemployment in the early 1990s will have tempered the seriousness of this position for some employers. Others, especially those requiring school leavers with four or five GCSEs, will continue to find the labour market difficult, despite rising unemployment

In developing strategies the better to target school leavers for your organisation, it is useful to consider first the perceptions young people have of different companies, and what they are looking for in a career. Table 7 shows the results of one survey on this subject. The emphasis on interesting work and the starting salary is perhaps not surprising. Training is less valued by this particular sample than expected.

### Table 7. Factors young people consider when applying to employers

| Ranking | Factor | No. of first choices | Approx. % of first choices |
|---|---|---|---|
| 1 | Interesting work | 82 | 34 |
| 2 | Starting wage/salary | 42 | 17 |
| 3 | Prospects for promotion | 31 | 13 |
| 4 | Job security | 20 | 8 |
| 5 | Pleasant working conditions | 17 | 7 |
| 5= | Friendly people | 17 | 7 |
| 5= | Good training at work | 17 | 7 |
| 8 | Equal opportunities | 11 | 5 |
| 9 | Good pension scheme | 3 | 1 |
| 10 | Good sports and social facilities | 2 | 1 |
| 11 | Flexible working hours | 0 | 0 |

Source: Simon Bysshe, *Ways of Work*, 1990.

Employers need to open lines of communication to schools, schoolchildren and their parents. Opportunities to emphasise the 'interesting work' in your organisation can then be exploited. How is this to be done? There are at least four areas to explore:

*Resourcing strategies*

- Sponsorship, 'cadetship' schemes and work experience.
- 'Adopt-a-school'.
- Schools liaison.
- Career conventions and fairs.

Each is briefly discussed in turn.

## Sponsorship

Sponsorship schemes provide opportunities for young people at school, college or university to gain appropriate qualifications as well as valuable working experience within the organisation. As a sponsored student – or cadet – the following advantages normally apply:

- Paid work experience, generally arranged during holiday periods.
- Special training programmes arranged with the employer.
- Financial assistance towards the cost of textbooks, course fees and other expenses.
- Opportunities to meet employees and their managers to discuss the 'world of work'.
- Opportunity to use company facilities, such as the sports club.

Some employers will guarantee employment at the end of the period of sponsorship. Others will specify that the sponsorship provides an enhanced opportunity of permanent employment with the company. Subject to successful completion of the course, sponsored students will have a major advantage in gaining employment because of their special insight into the organisation gained during work experience.

Sponsorship programmes run in conjunction with colleges or universities can also provide a valuable opportunity for the employer to influence the course content. Table 8 shows, for example, the course content of a cadetship scheme run by Pearl Assurance and Peterborough Regional College as part of the B.Tec. National Diploma in Business and Finance. The ability of the company to define options for the cadets is noteworthy.

## 'Adopt-a-school'

This is an aspect of schools liaison which brings line managers directly into the recruitment activity. Particular line managers are asked to develop a special relationship with an educational establishment near their home or place of work. The contact line manager would get to know the teachers, give career presentations to the students and liaise as regards work experience or visits between the school/college and the company. This approach is an innovative one which works to the mutual advantage of all concerned.

## Schools liaison

More generally, employers will need to research the schools within their local labour market. This may be managed best in conjunction with the YTS

**Table 8. Example of course content in the cadetship scheme run between Pearl Assurance and Peterborough Regional College**

| First year | Second year |
|---|---|
| ***Compulsory subjects:*** | ***Compulsory subjects:*** |
| 1. *Organisation in its Environment.* | 1. *Organisation in its Environment.* |
| 2. *People in Organisations.* | 2. *People in Organisations.* |
| 3. *Information Processing.* | ***Options:*** |
| 4. *Finance.* | Pearl cadets will be expected to include: |
| ***Options:*** | 1. *Business Law;* |
| Pearl cadets will be expected to include Principles and Practices of Insurance as one of their options, and select one of the following: | 2. *Accounting;* |
|  | as two of their options, plus two of the following; |
| 1. *Sales and Selling Methods;* | 1. *Marketing;* |
| 2. *Employment Practice and Industrial Relations;* | 2/3. *a choice of two modern European languages;* |
| 3/4. *a choice of one of two European languages.* | 4. *International Trade.* |
| Students will be given counselling and guidance before making a selection of the options. | Students will be given counselling and guidance before making a selection of the options. |
| An integral part of the course is a one week residential trip to another member of the European community with an integrated assignment. | An integral part of the course is a one week residential trip to another member of the European community with an integrated assignment. |

programme. Once the schools have been identified, up-to-date information will need to be maintained on the names of school heads and teachers, and the names of careers officers. Information can then be targeted at the schools. It might include:

- Posters, containing general information not necessarily related to the organisation.
- Newsletters from the company aimed at schoolchildren. Again, information will be provided on topics of general interest, albeit with the company logo prominent.
- Packages of career details, and general data about the organisation.

These relatively low-cost initiatives can do much to raise the image of the organisation in the school. Regular contact between the teachers and the organisation will be valuable, assuming no 'adopt-a-school' scheme is operating.

*Career convention*
These are more 'hard sell' events where students or schoolchildren can approach an organisation direct. At such events it is vital that material is highly professional and up-to-date.

## SUMMARY

Resourcing strategies to meet business needs in the 1990s will mean personnel professionalism in recruitment as well as exploring sources of relatively untapped labour. Effective recruitment will utilise techniques familiar in marketing, including segmenting the labour force and market research audits. As regards untapped resources, the most significant concentration will be on women. This arises from the increase in the number of women re-entering the labour market in the 1990s, from the need to retain skilled women after childbirth, and the context of a higher emphasis on equal opportunities generally in the HR vision. Providing women with more flexibility to manage their careers and their families will be of vital importance. Extended maternity leave and career break schemes will help, as will working time flexibility (see chapter 8) and child care provision. There are difficulties for most organisations in providing in-company child care, but external providers are likely to increase. School leavers and older people represent other sources of labour, and organisations can take a wide variety of initiatives – including adopt-a-school – to tackle these areas.

## REFERENCES

1 DAVID WHEELER, 'How to recruit a recruitment agency', *Personnel Management*, April 1988, p. 63.

2 BARRY CURNOW, 'Recruit, retrain, retain: personnel management and the three Rs', *Personnel Management*, November 1989, p. 41.

3 PETER HERRIOT, *Recruitment in the 90s*, IPM, London, 1989, p. 28.

4 WHEELER, *op. cit.*, p. 63.

5 BARRY CURNOW (*op. cit.*, p. 44) reports 46 per cent of respondents in one survey reporting increased use of the regional press and an 18 per cent decline in national press usage.

6 LORRAINE PADDISON, 'The targeted approach to recruitment', *Personnel Management*, November 1990, p. 58.

7 CURNOW, *op. cit.*, pp. 44–5.

8 For more details see the company survey in 'Recruiting and retention: tackling the universal problem', IRS *Employment Trends* 447, September 1989, p. 5.

9 ROBIN JACOBS, 'Getting the measure of management competence', *Personnel Management*, June 1989, p. 35.

10 See PETER HERRIOT, 'Candidate-friendly selection for the 1990s', *Personnel Management*, February 1990, pp. 32–5.

11 The CRE code of practice on recruitment covers this point in more detail.

12 IRS *Employment Trends* 431, January 1989, p. 3.

13 PAT LENNON, 'Facing the demographic challenge', *Employment Gazette*, January 1990, p. 43.

14 HILARY METCALF, *Retaining Women Employees: Measures to Counteract Labour Shortages*, IMS Report No. 190, IMS, Brighton, 1990, p. 3.

15 See *Women Managers: the Untapped Resource*, Kogan Page in association with NEDO, London, 1990, pp. 2–3.

16 *Ibid.*, p. 34.

17 See Incomes Data Study No. 425, January 1989, p. 27.

18 *Ibid.*, pp. 23, 25.

19 *Ibid.*, p. 23.

20 GINNY NEVILL, ALICE PERNICOTT, JOANNA WILLIAMS and ANNE WORRALL, *Women in the Workforce*, Industrial Society, London, 1990, p. 45.

21 'Bridging the career break', IRS *Employment Trends* 432, January 1989.

22 As reported in IDS Study No. 425, *op. cit.*, p. 12.

23 LESLEY HOLLAND, 'Career break schemes', *Women and Management Review*, Vol. 4, No. 2, 1989, p. 8.

24 Quoted in *European Industrial Relations Review* 182, March 1989, p. 26.

25 IDS Study No. 425, *op. cit.*, p. 15.

26 *Woman Managers, op. cit.*, p. 65.

CHAPTER 6

# Reward strategies

The organisation's reward strategies are likely to be central to the HR vision. Recognising and rewarding achievement, for example, will be a frequent component. Through the reward system, too, the organisation can reflect changing business requirements. In this, performance-related pay will be a necessary initiative. Compensation and benefits are also vital to effective recruitment and retention strategies.

If pay and conditions are central to the recruitment and retention of quality staff, employment costs are also a very important component of total costs. In a recession there will be increasing pressure to control such costs. There are examples of organisations in which pay cuts have been introduced. Generally, and depending on the seriousness of the financial and trading problems, organisations will freeze future increases or award increases smaller than the prevailing rate of inflation. These short-term measures will ease staff costs but cause inevitable distortion in relation to wage and salary comparisons in the labour market. Short-term savings have to be weighed against potential medium-term increases in turnover of quality staff unless the organisation awards future increases at a higher level. Organisations cutting back in this way may well argue that there will be no medium term unless pay levels are controlled. For others less acutely threatened by the possibility of closure, this is another example of the short-term crisis versus long term vision which can, as previous chapters have shown, impact upon the management of a quality workforce.

For most employees, pay and conditions will be high on any list of concerns in respect of employment. The style and attitude of the immediate manager, the timing and nature of the next promotion, the possibility of redundancy and many other factors will also be on the list. Without dwelling on whether pay increases can act as a motivator, or as a reward for past effort, or both, organisations in both the public and the private sectors recognise the centrality of basic pay in the management of quality staff. With basic pay as a key variable, many organisations believe in paying at or above the market rate and even in a recession have relatively little problem in funding the policy. Pay flexibility is also a vital component of HR management in the future. However, pay flexibility in one area is potentially a differential problem in another. Equity and consistency were higher-priority concerns for HR Managers in the 1960s and 1970s. In the 1980s the commercial consequences of losing quality staff were viewed as a more serious problem than the loss of salary consistency arising from a pragmatic pay response. Bogus regradings, increasing minimum starting rates, in-grade 'promotions' and other salary manipulations were more easily managed in an era of individualism and declining union influence. Organisations now prefer to build flexibility into the job-evaluated salary structure than find devices to 'break' a rigid scheme.

Recognising that flexibility, adaptability and innovation are likely to be elements of the HR vision, this chapter concentrates on how reward strategies can support the vision, and on methods of maintaining flexibility in the salary structure itself. 'Cafeteria' remuneration has taken flexibility to considerable lengths, and this concept is explored in some detail. Before examining these aspects of a remuneration strategy, it is useful to begin with the bargaining framework.

## LEVELS OF PAY BARGAINING

In chapter 2 the trend towards managerial devolution of authority was discussed in a context of changing business strategies. Smaller business units with devolved powers in the private sector have resulted in a continuing movement away from national and central bargaining. At national level the introduction of negotiation on minimum rates provided companies with more options in relation to their own circumstances whilst preventing the competition from undercutting them. In the 1990s even this may be felt by many organisations to be too restrictive. National negotiations often set a floor for further domestic increases which may not be affordable. Equally important, quality staff do not perceive the company as granting improvements but give credit to the employers' association. This detracts from the quality of the relationship between management and staff and makes it harder to secure local 'trade-offs'.

Central bargaining poses similar problems. Local management discretion to respond flexibly to changing local labour markets can be too constrained. In a recession, pay awards centrally may also be greater than necessary to maintain market competitiveness in each location, with a detrimental impact on employment costs. As with multi-employer bargaining, it is also difficult to secure productivity improvements through central negotiations.

Much will as always depend on the structure of the organisation[1]. Organisations with different business units but located in the same geographical catchment area may prefer to retain a degree of corporate control over pay levels to prevent inter-company movements of staff or parity claims. Other companies will wish to retain as part of their HR vision a corporate philosophy on pay and conditions.

The Engineering Employers' Federation no longer bargains nationally, although the demise of national bargaining on minimum rate owes more to problems with working time than to salary flexibility. Employers' associations retain an important advisory role with regard to market rates and organisational options.

*Reward strategies*

In the public sector the pattern of centralised national bargaining is breaking down, partly as a result of structural changes, such as the decentralisation of the water industry in 1983.[2] In the 1990s major organisational reforms in education and the National Health Service are calling into question the pattern of national agreements. In 1990 the new post of Health Care Assistant in the NHS was introduced with no national rate.

Autonomous self-governing hospital trusts and autonomous colleges and school boards may use their new powers to shape their own salary policies. Some health authorities are paying supplements to nurses and other key staff. One 1991 study describing a strategy within the NHS for greater local control over pay determination defined three strands:

> first, greater flexibility within Whitley itself; secondly, the creation of new groups of staff such as 'healthcare assistants' who will be outside Whitley's remit and subject to local pay bargaining; and thirdly and most significantly, the development of NHS trusts . . . which will have the freedom to determine the pay and conditions of their own staff.[3]

There are, of course, dangers here, including the ability of local management to negotiate local rates effectively, internal divisiveness within the NHS leading to lower morale or later problems of an 'equal pay for equal value' nature. The risks seem to be less than the possible advantages of a more responsive organisation flexibly relating in a more cost-effective manner to local circumstances.[4]

The framework of national bargaining remains in local government, although there is reasonable flexibility within these arrangements. Union leaders in the public sector have strong reservations about the widespread introduction of salary flexibility, which is viewed as an erosion of the principle of national pay scales. This is seen as the best way of protecting and enhancing the salaries of the lower-paid. Reservations are shared by some on the employers' side within local government who are concerned that the development of local bargaining will lead to an increase in total employment costs through parity claims leading to wage drift. However, the greater devolution of responsibility to schools and colleges, the further development of competitive tendering, and pressure in the local labour market from private-sector flexibility, will all contrive to increase the use of local salary 'packaging' in local government. This flexibility will in turn put pressure on job evaluation schemes.

## JOB EVALUATION

Job evaluation schemes continue to be popular in both the private and the public sector. One 1983 IPM study identified the following objectives for job evaluation:

i To set a rate for the job irrespective of the attributes of individual employees.
ii To determine the relationship between jobs and to establish a systematic structure for wage rates at the level of the firm . . .
iii To determine, recognise, and pay for the requirements of a job . . .
iv To ensure that the resultant structure of pay levels meets both the organisation's expectations and employee expectations.[5]

Job size remains a 'felt fair' basis for defining a rank order of jobs for any group of employees in an organisation, and the importance of job size may continue to be recognised in the HR vision. It can at least be analysed in detail, and a framework of relevant factors can assist the analysis. Equally important, a base point is established from which changes in job size can be measured. Given a fair degree of openness, in which job holders and their managers define the scope of the job, the factors and job score are published and appeals are possible; the resultant grading structure can provide a consistent and defensible framework for creating a salary structure.

So far, so good. The widespread use of job evaluation schemes such as HAY in the private sector and other analytical schemes in the public sector would be justified against similar criteria. Increasingly, problems in the application of job evaluation are casting doubt on the validity of job evaluation in general. There are seven main problems.

1. Job content is changing rapidly, largely as a result of technological developments. This impact, already marked in the manufacturing sector and in design and development, has also become more significant in the service sector. Job holders are required to develop PC and software management skills. Jobs may be deskilled on the one hand; however, there will be a need for high-level technical skills to deal with one-off and more complex processing operations which would be beyond the scope of all bar the most sophisticated software. The impact of technology on administrative and clerical jobs has yet to be fully realised. It will have a significant impact on job size, as well as on job location.

2. Organisations are changing rapidly. Unusual will be the HR Manager who has not recently been through a reorganisation, or who does not expect one shortly, or both. Successive reorganisations are symptomatic of rapid changes in the business environment which require, as the HR vision will undoubtedly state, flexibility and adaptability. There are dangers that reorganisation can too easily be seen as a panacea by management under intense pressure to deliver. Whatever the cause, very often, as soon as a job evaluation exercise is complete, reorganisation requires a further major review of job size.

3. Labour market pressures within specific sectors have led to grade and salary revisions (of which more below). Individuals may be regraded without anyone looking closely at the job size factors which should underpin promotion. Salary responses to market pressures can avoid changing the job-evaluated graded structure, but such responses often create internal pressures as salary differentials are adjusted. Organisation or company-wide job evalua-

## Reward strategies

tion schemes which embrace radically different jobs are most susceptible to internal tensions in response to market pressures. Separate schemes which evaluate only, say, finance jobs or clerical jobs can be more easily adjusted, although boundary problems across different schemes will still arise.

4. As chapter 3 on the components of the HR vision described, there will be a trend towards self-management work teams. Further developments of semi-autonomous work groups which embrace, for example, in a team many different function and skill levels have further complicated traditional job evaluation. Greater interchangeability of job holders across different tasks, the blurring of boundaries between skilled and semi-skilled work, and changes in the role of first-line supervision, have all impacted upon job evaluation schemes. Business strategies and an HR vision emphasising a matrix style of organisation, with the emphasis on teamwork, will seek maximum flexibility in the deployment of staff. Job evaluation schemes can in this context be perceived as rigid and prescriptive.

5. The increasing reliance upon project management processes and organisation can create similar tensions. With job holders constantly moving between different projects as organisations adapt and respond to new strategic directions, so job size will vary considerably across projects. Management will want to maximise individual contributions, but those contributions will differ according to the required skill mix of each project. With job size varying between projects, and projects beginning and ending, 'traditional' job evaluation has difficulty coping with the pace of change. As a result, most job holders in this project management category (and increasingly many others) find themselves 'excluded' or 'not yet evaluated' or some other term which allows for the required flexibility.

6. Job descriptions can have the undesired effect of 'freezing' the job as described, moving against the flexibility required in the HR vision. Most job evaluation schemes have introduced shorter job descriptions in recent years, with a focus on principal accountabilities rather than an exhaustive list of tasks. However, 'It's not in my job description' remains a comment sometimes made as organisations adapt and innovate.

7. There are enormous pressures on line management time. Job evaluators have to be credible, knowledgeable and representative of the jobs being evaluated. Perhaps more than before, management time for job evaluation will be more limited and this despite a recognition that membership of a job evaluation committee can give unique organisational insights.

These problems overlap, and will be felt differently by different organisations. In summary, the rapid pace of change, managerial time pressures and the need for maximum flexibility have led to serious questioning of the role and validity of job evaluation. Recognising, however, that there are still advantages from a graded structure which is underpinned by job size to develop logical internal pay relationships, how can time demands be lessened, market factors accommodated and flexibility maintained? There are several possibilities:

## Computer-assisted job evaluation

This approach has been said to represent the next phase in job evaluation practice.[6] Evaluations are computer-generated, based on questionnaire responses. The questionnaire provided to job holders clearly needs very careful definition, since it must be able to differentiate job size across the range of jobs included in the exercise.

Computer-assisted job evaluation approaches are built upon an agreed system of benchmark evaluations. Organisations must choose firstly what system to use. The current grading structure can act as the framework but this is unlikely to be acceptable. HR Managers will need to review the usual range of options – ranking, paired comparison, analytical schemes, and so on, which is used by a trained committee to evaluate benchmark jobs. If this so far resembles conventional job evaluation, the next stage is different in that a questionnaire is fed into a computer. The software is designed to analyse the job against the pre-defined benchmark framework and define the correct slot. As Helen Murlis and Derek Pritchard put it, 'The major advantages which computer-assisted techniques provide are in the efficiency of the process, consistency, and the ability to decentralise the process substantially.'[7] Efficiency improvements arise from removal of the need for a job description, and the elimination of the need for an evaluation committee for most of the process.

More research and experience is required before judgements can be passed on about the validity of computer-assisted job evaluation. What if job holders do not feel that the questionnaire does justice to the complexities of their job? (Job evaluation committees are well able to interpret overwritten jobs.) How much time is spent on non-benchmark appeals? Might flexibility be reduced, since job evaluation committees are often able to maintain flexibility in a way impossible for a software system? Subject to dealing with these issues, computer-assisted job evaluation is at least tackling the issue of efficiency improvement in the job evaluation process as well as seeking greater clarity in what differentiates jobs.

## People, not jobs

Conventional job evaluation places great emphasis on the definition of the job size, rather than on the evaluation of the person doing it. Lesson No. 1 in all job evaluation courses, drummed into us with repetitive force. For many jobs which are machine-controlled or in some other way highly prescriptive, the impact of the individual on job size will indeed be very limited. In many other jobs, particularly in the clerical, managerial, sales, research and other fields, the individual can alter the job size by their own personal contribution. Of course, conventional job evaluation can cope with this, for example by regular re-evaluations. However, more flexibility can be included by using job evaluation of job size to set broad grading parameters, allowing managerial discre-

# Reward strategies

tion within this for individuals to be ranked according to their personal contribution, or skill level, as defined by specific competences. With line management discretion to rank the individual based upon agreed definitions, a further step can be taken to enable line flexibility in the management of quality skills. This can also assist the development of continuous learning if that is part of the HR vision.

## Market rate job evaluation

Normally, market factors are considered when designing the payment levels associated with a job-evaluated grading structure. Such pay levels are then subject to (generally) annual review to reflect changing market movements, the rate of inflation, ability to pay and other factors. It is possible to build market rate information into the scheme at an earlier stage. Michael Armstrong has defined seven stages in this process:

- Identify the jobs to be evaluated.
- Analyse and describe benchmark jobs in terms of job content.
- Obtain from salary surveys information on the market rates for the benchmark jobs, ensuring correct job-for-job comparison.
- Develop a salary structure for the benchmark jobs based on these data.
- Slot benchmark jobs into the salary structure.
- Check that the provisional allocation is correct in job size terms. 'If the job B is obviously lower in the hierarchy than job A it can be placed in the next grade down, but a 50 per cent overlap between the grades would enable the salaries of people in job B to advance to a level comparable with the market rates for similar jobs without the need to upgrade the job.'
- Allocate non-benchmark jobs.[8]

As always, there are advantages and disadvantages. Market salaries are well able to fluctuate rapidly, which could distort the overall evaluations. It is also very difficult to gain accurate market information on a job-for-job basis. Maintaining a separation between job size and salary levels can still provide salary flexibility without calling the graded structure itself into question.

Consideration of the market in relation to job evaluation provides a suitable link with the next section, a review of the components of salary structures. Getting this right will also be critical to successful management of key skills.

## SALARY STRUCTURES

Most HR Managers will be maintaining, for staff, salary structures consisting of minima-maxima for different grades. Such structures are becoming more common among manual staff, although job rates or structures with two or three initial steps before the job rate is reached remain widespread. Writing in the mid-1980s, Brewster and Connock[9] identified a number of changing emphases in the factors being rewarded in pay structures, and in the changing structural parameters of pay systems, as shown in Tables 9 and 10. Since this analysis more emphasis has been placed on quality, flexibility, group working and job knowledge/skill among 'staff' as well as manual employees.

### Table 9. The changing emphasis on which factors to reward

| Type of employee | Factor being rewarded | |
| --- | --- | --- |
| | Away from | Towards |
| Manual | Output | Machine utilisation<br>Quality<br>Flexibility<br>Group working<br>Job knowledge/skill |
| 'Staff' | Time<br>Service<br>Age | Direct incentive schemes<br><br>Merit/performance assessment |

Source: C. Brewster and S. L. Connock, *Industrial Relations: Cost-effective Strategies*, Hutchinson, London, 1985, p. 85.

### Table 10. The changing structural parameters of pay systems

| Type of employee | Structural parameters | |
| --- | --- | --- |
| | Away from | Towards |
| Manual | Single-factor schemes<br>Work measurement<br>Job rate | Multi-factor schemes<br>Performance assessment<br>Scope for individual progression |
| 'Staff' | Automatic progression<br>Fixed salary ranges<br>Fixed increment size | Variable progression<br>Open-ended salary ranges<br>Variable increment size |

Source: C. Brewster and S. L. Connock, *Industrial Relations: Cost-effective Strategies*, Hutchinson, London, 1985, p. 87.

Reward strategies for maintaining quality skills in a context of medium-term market scarcity for certain jobs are crucial and flexibility in the salary structure is vital. HR Managers will need to continue to consider the following components in the flexible management of a salary structure:

- Market-related salary scales.
- Salary minima and maxima.

*Reward strategies*

- Merit and performance-related pay.
- Market scarcity supplements.
- Incentives and share option schemes.
- 'Cafeteria' remuneration.

Each will be examined in turn.

## Market-related salary scales

HR Managers will continue to gather data on market rates to monitor comparative movements in the market. There are many approaches to this subject. Of considerable value is the use of a job evaluation scheme such as HAY, which is deployed in a large number of organisations. As a result, interrogating the HAY database can generate salary information for particular job scores. Comparisons can be drawn with industries or with specific sub-groupings within each industry. Medium and upper-quartile salary data will be most commonly sought from such a data base. Using job-evaluated data in this way at least attempts to overcome the difficulty of comparing job size, which can bedevil accurate market rate comparisons. Even in the use of schemes like HAY there are dangers, since there is an assumption that the HAY score in one organisation is equivalent to the HAY score in another. With the same guide charts in use this is theoretically the case. Organisations, however, will inevitably interpret the charts to produce results which reflect their internal value system. Correlation studies can be undertaken to check for consistency, and deriving market data from a proprietary job evaluation scheme in widespread use is probably the safest way to analyse comparative salaries.

There are many other specialist salary surveys to which organisations can contribute and from which relevant salary data can be obtained. There are, for example, surveys for computer specialists, legal executives and accountants. All require careful interpretation before conclusions can be drawn about market rate positioning. It is sometimes safer to be part of a salary club with organisations in the same sector, since detailed job-for-job comparison can be undertaken, and knowledge of the environment of each member of the club will add to its overall validity.

Market rate information can be used in three main ways. First, the information will be necessary to build a salary structure around a new job-evaluated grade structure. A policy decision will be required on where the organisation wishes to be positioned in relation to the market. Having identified median salary and upper quartile salary data for the mid-point of a job-evaluated points range, for example, precise positioning is possible. Many HR Managers will want to be located between the median and upper quartile. Costs will be an issue in relation to the current spread of salaries. There will be short-term costs in raising staff to the minimum of a range often referred to as correcting 'green circle' job holders, and longer-term costs, with staff moving to a maximum if it is significantly higher than the current maximum. In addition, care will be needed in ensuring that not too many jobs are above the new maxima, referred to as 'red circle' job holders, since for the job holder above the scale maximum this can be demotivating. Some may indeed be in your 'quality' category. The issues are shown diagrammatically in Fig. 19.

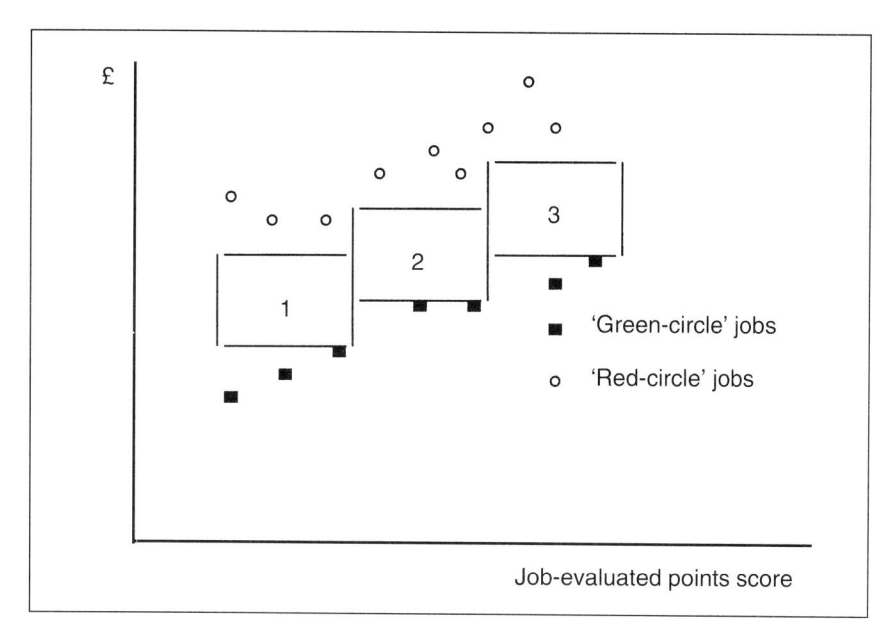

**Fig. 19. Salary structure with defined maxima and minima based on market rate data**

Second, market rate information can be used to check the continuing relevance of a current structure in market rate terms. This may be particularly appropriate just prior to an annual review, where the pace of salary movement over the preceding twelve months needs to be checked. Third, market rate data will be critical to the definition of a market supplement for defined categories of staff should the need for such an additional allowance be agreed. This subject will be explored in more detail shortly.

Overall, organisations need simply to maintain a high level of awareness about market rates. Policy decisions can then better be taken against not only the background of market data but also cost pressures, turnover rates, future plans for expansion or contraction, and other relevant factors.

## Salary minima and maxima

Although many manual employees will have job rates, possibly with one or two defined salary steps before the job rate, most non-commission-earning grades will have a defined salary range. Salary ranges can be up to 50 per cent wide. Indeed, narrower salary ranges can act as a major rigidity factor, preventing flexible responses to individual requirements. As a result, HR Managers come under pressure to 'break' the salary ceiling. So is it worth retaining a ceiling? Again, a balance is necessary between flexibility and control. In the absence of the ceiling, line management freedom to reward staff flexibly through salary progression will be constrained by budgetary control processes working against targets and standards for employment costs. Managers who abuse this flexibility will be held to account against such cost ratios. However, the effectiveness of this approach depends upon strategic controls being well defined, and on management information systems being in place to provide the data. If these systems are not well developed, salary ceilings will continue to act as an important control device. They can also serve to limit employee expectations. In their absence the 'average' employee may have unrealistic expectations of salary growth. They should rarely be upheld so inflexibly that key staff are allowed to leave, or become seriously demotivated for want of moving through a salary ceiling. Each case will need to be considered on its merits, and the ceiling bypassed only in cases justified by high performance or market pressure. Often both are, of course, linked.

As a result of market rate pressures, scale minima and/or maxima can be increased – sometimes by different amounts for different grades. In that case differentials may be affected, although organisations have increasingly successfully defended differential claims on market grounds. Extensions of salary maxima can also be linked to performance. For example, progression beyond the old maximum to a new maximum may be payable only to those performing at 'outstanding' or 'very good' levels under a performance management scheme.

## Merit and performance-related pay

By introducing or increasing the size of budgets allowed for merit payments within salary scales, organisations have built in greater flexibility both to reward higher performance and to respond to market rate changes. Poaching of high-performing staff is obviously more likely than of 'average' staff, and significant merit awards aimed at above-average and outstanding staff can assist a retention strategy. Moving from fixed service-related incremental progression to variable progression is also a key element of an HR vision to endow line managers with more authority to reward their own staff, again within strategic controls.

Performance-related pay is generally defined as providing salary rewards directly linked to individual performance against defined objectives. No cost of living review or service increment is payable under most such policies. The rewards of such a scheme can be significant — say, up to 20 per cent per annum of basic pay plus one-off bonus payments. As one spokesman of the National Westminster Bank put it:

> In summary, the objectives of performance-related reward are to create greater understanding of the bank's long and short term corporate objectives and to focus managers' attention on them; to relate the objectives of divisions, units and individual managers to corporate objectives and to provide managers with cash rewards more closely linked to personal performance and achievement.[10]

In this example of performance-related pay among its managers the bank linked salary progression with performance in a way typical of such schemes. Thus within each salary range there are three cut-off points — at the sixtieth percentile for fully satisfactory performers; at the eightieth percentile for 'good' performers and the hundredth percentile (i.e. the maximum) for outstanding performers. The distinction between the old and new pattern of incremental progression is shown in Fig. 20.

Such performance-related pay schemes are normally accompanied by a matrix of suggested payments based upon performance against targets and position in the range. These operate within a defined budget, which will vary each year, depending upon market-movements, ability to pay, rate of inflation and other factors. A typical matrix for illustration purposes is shown in Fig. 21. Scale increases may differ from the performance-related pay budget allocation.

Performance-related pay is now widely used in the private and public sectors. Merit rating is likely to be introduced into some parts of the education sector. Polytechnic lecturers have agreed to appraisal in national negotiations. One 1990 LACSAB survey of the effects of performance-related pay on local authorities is reproduced in Table 11. This shows 84 per cent of respondents believing retention was improved. LACSAB also enquired about the reason why 5 per cent of local authorities surveyed had not introduced performance-related pay. There were three main reasons:

- Performance could be raised through performance management procedures without a link with pay.
- The costs and management time were perceived as too great, especially at a time when line managers were under pressure from competitive tendering and Community Charge legislation.
- Opposition from politicians or trade union representatives arguing that the public service ethos counted for more than financial incentives.

Most HR Managers in the public or private sector will continue to see relating rewards to an individual's contribution to organisational goals as central to overall business effectiveness in the 1990s.

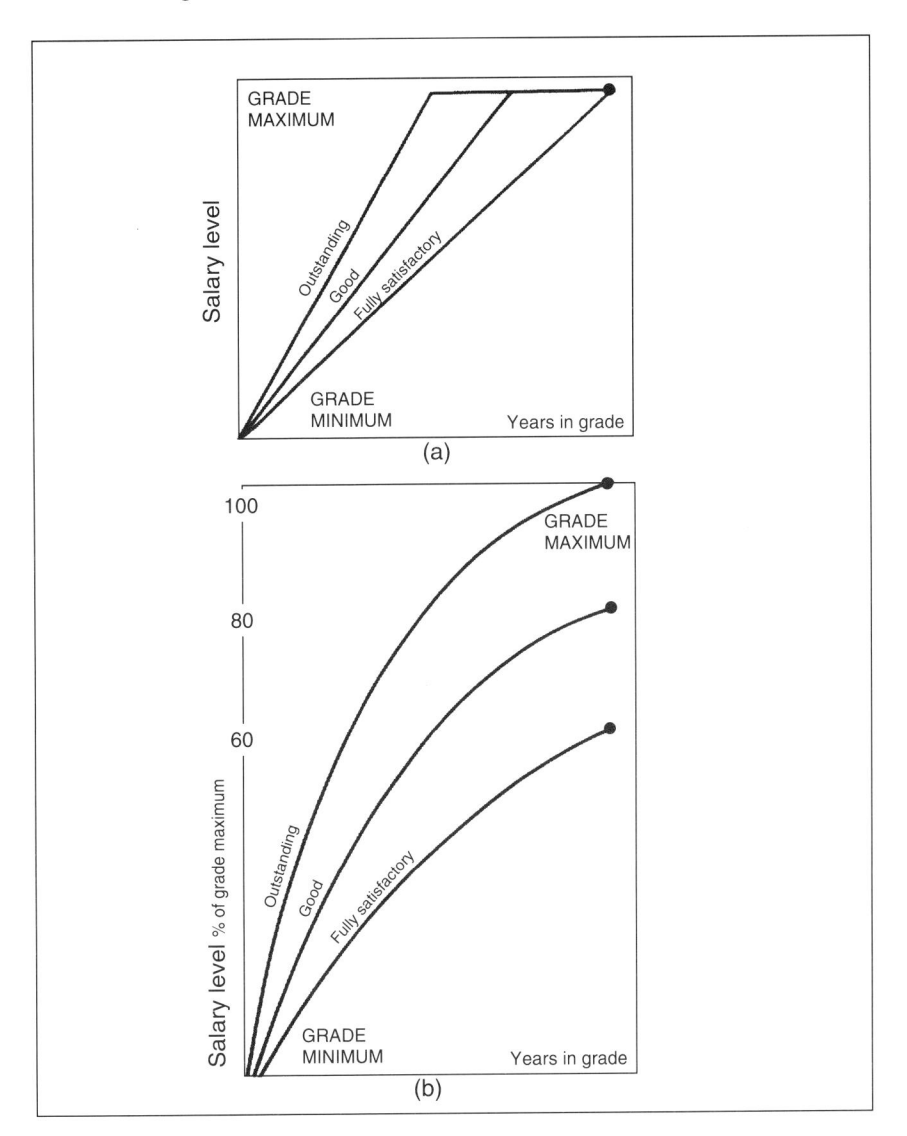

**Fig. 20. The (a) old and (b) new pattern of increments at National Westminster Bank.**

From Michael Goodswen, 'Retention and reward of the high achiever', *Personnel Management*, October 1988, p. 62

| Performance assessment | Position in range (%) | | | | |
|---|---|---|---|---|---|
| | 80 | 90 | 100 | 110 | 120 |
| Outstanding | | | | | |
| Very good | | | | | |
| Good | | | | | |
| Adequate | | | | | |
| Unacceptable | | | | | |
| Not assessed | | | | | |

**Fig. 21. Typical matrix of performance-related salary increases**

## Market scarcity supplements

Market scarcity supplements are monetary additions to basic salary for individuals defined as in the category of 'scarce skills'. The supplement can be consolidated or non-consolidated for pension purposes. It can be treated as a separate allowance or added to the salary range of the job holders affected. One specific point for debate is whether the supplement should be paid to *all* job holders in a job defined as scarce. What if a job holder is off sick and will not return for six months and you know that person will simply not be poached? Does it make commercial sense to award a market supplement in such a case? To do so would be to risk creating a general sense of unfairness in the organisation. Market supplements should be paid only to those individuals in the scarce job category defined by the line manager as personally marketable.

There is evidence of the systematic use of market supplements to basic salary. Supplements of 10–20 per cent of basic salary have been common for accountants, surveyors, information technology specialists, and design and development engineers. Three-quarters of London boroughs had introduced market pay supplements by 1987.[11]

Market scarcity supplements are paid to holders of jobs which are difficult to fill in the national or local labour market. There are four main problems in relation to such supplements.

- It may be difficult to define the circumstances in which a supplement is required. The most obvious reasons are turnover of key staff or great difficulty in recruitment. However, managers will not want to wait too long

## Table 11. Effects of performance-related pay (PRP) in local authorities (percentage of authorities)

| Proposition | Strongly agree | agree | Neither agree or disagree | Disagree | Strongly disagree |
|---|---|---|---|---|---|
| Motivated employees | 8 | 80 | 8 | 4 | 0 |
| Stimulated initiative | 3 | 76 | 16 | 5 | 0 |
| Led to concentration on short-term objectives | 8 | 36 | 36 | 18 | 3 |
| Led to concentration on measurable objectives | 15 | 54 | 22 | 7 | 2 |
| Increased efficiency | 3 | 68 | 29 | 0 | 0 |
| Reduced trust between managers and employees | 0 | 15 | 13 | 41 | 31 |
| Reduced staff levels | 0 | 5 | 21 | 36 | 38 |
| Improved recruitment | 5 | 70 | 23 | 3 | 0 |
| Improved retention | 10 | 74 | 16 | 0 | 0 |
| Led to good employees leaving the authority | 0 | 3 | 5 | 38 | 54 |
| Clarified work objectives | 38 | 54 | 5 | 3 | 0 |
| Increased labour costs | 24 | 24 | 21 | 26 | 5 |
| Increased work load on reviewing managers | 24 | 47 | 13 | 16 | 0 |
| Raised service quality | 5 | 57 | 38 | 0 | 0 |
| Raised level of output of services | 3 | 61 | 36 | 0 | 0 |
| Improved manager–employee relations | 3 | 45 | 47 | 5 | 0 |
| Created industrial relations problems | 0 | 8 | 18 | 50 | 24 |
| Weakened trade unions | 3 | 11 | 50 | 21 | 15 |
| Impaired team working | 0 | 13 | 24 | 42 | 21 |
| Fostered team working | 5 | 21 | 63 | 11 | 0 |
| Led to better relations with unions | 0 | 0 | 76 | 21 | 3 |
| Led to complaints that payments are unfair | 5 | 24 | 32 | 26 | 13 |
| Increased employee satisfaction with pay levels | 10 | 56 | 26 | 8 | 0 |

Source: LACSAB, *Performance Related Pay in Practice: a Survey of Local Government*, 1990, p. 7.

to prove the need for a supplement in this way. A judgement has to be made from market rate evidence and from recruitment evidence as to the necessity of a supplement.
- Supplements can be internally divisive. Great care is needed in defining the category to which a supplement applies, to avoid knock-on effects on other groups not in short supply.
- Market circumstances do change, as the rapidity of the onset of recession in the winter of 1990/91 demonstrated. Once a supplement is given it is difficult to remove it, despite such changes in market circumstances. If an individual in receipt of a supplement is promoted, the opportunity can be taken to remove the supplement, otherwise the level of supplement is frozen and will in time become a smaller element of total compensation.
- Basic pay probably includes a market element for certain key individuals. To pay the supplement on top of enhanced salary effectively pays a market factor twice. It may be necessary to remove from basic salary part of this market amount before adding the full supplement back.

The main advantage of such supplements is that they permit a specific response to market scarcity for defined categories of staff. Cost increases can be contained by careful definition. Supplements remain a major element in any remuneration strategy aimed at the recruitment and retention of key staff.

A final related component of pay which is also treated as a supplement is the regional allowance. Moving from the original definition of inner London as within four miles of Charing Cross to a wider South East 'Roseland' allowance, such allowances are expensive and apply to all within the defined zones. Inevitably boundary problems arise, and some companies pay allowances in large towns beyond the South East of England. Although an inevitable element in the recruitment and retention of staff in London and the South East, the level of these allowances has also been one of the factors prompting relocation from the region. More of this in chapter 8.

**Incentives and share option schemes**

Incentive schemes can also be a major factor in an organisation's ability to attract and retain staff and support components of the HR vision. This arises partly because the individual can have a measure of personal control over earnings. Sales staff, for example, knowing the level of new business commission, can calculate their earnings from achievement of various levels of production. The individual can then decide which level to seek. Rewards are related to achievement in a direct way, and payment should preferably follow closely after the achievement of targets for the incentive scheme to have most impact. For managers, too, bonus schemes operating alongside performance-related pay can add a further incentive to the achievement of individual or company objectives. There are certain dangers of 'double counting' here if the same performance is rewarded under both performance-related pay and an incentive scheme. Careful definition of the objectives is also required – usually targets are measured against profits, or return on capital employed. In the non-profit-making public sector, cost reduction targets or service standards can be utilised to build bonus plans. Decisions are also needed on when to pay bonus, who is included, and what to do with starters and leavers. Substantial bonus payments, which are waived should the individual leave the organisation, can in themselves act as a powerful retention device unless the receiving organisation can be persuaded to pay the lump sum as part of an introductory package.

Share option schemes can encourage closer identification between the employee and the company's objectives and received considerable political support in the 1980s.

Profit-sharing schemes can also encourage a similar sense of indentification with corporate goals. However, unlike individual incentive schemes, they are paid to all, irrespective of personal contribution. With no direct relationship between personal effort and reward, schemes are unlikely to motivate staff. As they are also unreliable, they are unlikely to have any significant impact on recruitment or retention, either. Companies pursuing profit-sharing as part of their remuneration strategy are likely to do so with the wider aim of encouraging employee interest in and commitment to improving overall company performance. Having shares in 'friendly hands' may also be helpful.

## 'Cafeteria' remuneration

The concept of 'cafeteria' benefits, or total remuneration packaging, has been much discussed in the UK but seldom applied. In the 1990s, especially as more attention is centred on the costs of employment benefits, there is likely to be an increase in the application of remuneration packaging. What is it?

Cafeteria benefits can sometimes mean a limited choice between a few benefits but it is more commonly used to describe the choice from a full 'menu' of different benefits at different levels, each with attached price tags.[12] The main advantages of this approach are:

- Basic salary and benefits are fully costed. The effect of increases on total remuneration can be identified and better controlled.
- Individuals have freedom of choice to shape their benefits within a defined range. Thus a manager who values a pension more than a company car can choose to enhance pension benefits by opting for a greater proportion of total remuneration in this form. Such choices can vary in time as individual circumstances alter. Employees are likely to be more committed to and motivated by a reward package they themselves have shaped.
- Employees can see and value their total remuneration. At present, in many cases, conditions of employment are simply taken for granted. Remuneration packaging makes such conditions a more visible and valued part of compensation.

- An employee who has no need, or a reduced need, for a particular benefit is less likely to be demotivated by a colleague who has the benefit if the employee knows that other benefits, or salary, have been taken instead at the employee's own choice.[13]
- Dual-employment couples, whose benefits such as private medicine may be duplicated, can balance their overall benefit package better.
- Flexibility in the package may be preferred by some key staff to the absolute levels of basic pay or particular benefits. Offering flexibility of choice may be more cost-effective to employers than raising salary or benefits generally to attract and retain key skills.
- International comparisons of total employment costs can be facilitated if the scheme is used across different countries. Suitable indexes for comparison of the cost of living will be needed.

Against these undoubted advantages there are the inevitable disadvantages:

- Experience in the USA and Australia shows that the schemes can become very complex. Large guidance manuals are required for each individual to explain each benefit and the choices available. Employees need to spend a considerable amount of time analysing and absorbing this information, and some may even then not understand what the scheme offers.
- The HR function will need staff to administer and explain the total remuneration scheme. This may require extra head count unless tasks are reducing elsewhere.
- There are tax complications in the UK. Different – and sometimes advantageous – tax provisions apply to certain benefits, such as cars. Employees choosing one benefit against another may find their tax bill higher. A more uniform fiscal system in the USA and Australia has minimised the difficulty.
- Moving employees from one part of the organisation with total remuneration packaging to another without it makes comparison and administration difficult.
- Individuals may regret their choice, and become demotivated, especially if there is little room for amendment of choices in the short term.

Very attractive in concept, total remuneration packaging is a powerful retention strategy. Indeed, once managers have chosen their preferred remuneration package to suit their own needs, it is more difficult for them to leave unless a similar configuration of benefits is offered elsewhere. If this approach becomes more established in the UK it is likely to spread fast, because companies will need, for labour market reasons, to be able to offer similar flexibility. For the moment, complexity and tax difficulties are holding back any wider application.

Most remuneration packaging schemes start by costing all the items in the package to arrive at a total cost. Basic salary is often then sent at a pre-defined minimum level. For example, say 60 per cent of total remuneration must be taken as basic salary. The remaining 40 per cent can be chosen from the 'menu'. In the menu are typically:

*Reward strategies* 107

- Car options.
- Private medical options.
- Life insurance options.
- Personal loan options.
- Disability options.
- Education assistance.
- Relocation assistance.
- Pension options.
- Buying or selling holidays.
- Mortgage subsidy options.

Whilst there are schemes with over forty different conditions on the 'menu', it is also possible to restrict flexibility to a limited number of items. In the UK, NHS hospital trusts are reported to be considering such flexibility for middle managers and above. Staff would be able to decide whether 10 per cent of their salary should go into a superannuation scheme or into a car leasing programme or simply be paid in cash.[14] Indeed, in the UK the choice of car or salary may be the simplest and most obvious first step in the direction of total remuneration packaging.

## CONDITIONS OF EMPLOYMENT

Total remuneration packaging has already referred to conditions of employment, and this final section briefly reviews the different elements crucial to the management of key skills.

For manual staff, a major development in recent years impacting upon their recruitment and retention has been harmonisation of conditions. Defined as the process of reducing or eliminating differences in the basis of particular conditions of employment, the ultimate outcome is the concept of 'single status' where differences in all basic conditions of employment across different sectors of the workforce have been eliminated. Harmonisation strategies have improved the morale of manual staff, with consequential advantages of recruitment and retention, as well as improved workforce utilisation and improved employee attitudes. There have been cost implications, and differential claims from staff unions have had to be managed. Nevertheless these moves towards harmonisation, along with income security derived from measured day work schemes, remain of importance to the management of manual staff.

As to conditions of employment generally, the following benefits are worthy of separate discussion.

### Cars

A popular and vital element in the management of key skills, despite tax changes in recent years. A car is a visible sign of seniority and, with all expenses paid (generally with the exception of private mileage), a company car can remove the financial uncertainty over a major area of expenditure for the average family. This is, however, an emotive subject – and a costly one. Flexibility, as usual, is critical to the successful management of company cars. Schemes which prescribe a fixed range of cars may be appropriate for, say, middle management. At more senior levels, freedom of individual choice within defined invoiced limits is essential. These invoiced limits can be adjusted annually and can relate to seniority. Providing an interest-free or low-interest loan to staff who need a car can also provide maximum freedom of choice and remove some of the administration difficulties often associated with car provision.

## Private medicine

The 'psychological barrier' against private medical schemes appears now to have been removed, and the increasing application of private medical schemes looks likely. Totally funded schemes for management staff can be complemented by discount arrangements for staff overall.

## Mortgage and housing assistance

Various types of housing assistance exist in both the private and public sectors. It can be aimed at all staff or at those being relocated to high-cost housing areas. The assistance may take various forms, including salary supplements, one-off payments and (in local authorities) equity sharing. Specific arrangements can be made for housing assistance for new staff only, such as a subsidy towards mortgage costs for new graduates. Concessionary mortgage schemes as such are common in financial services and usually offer reduced interest rates for a defined amount of advance. The remainder above this concessionary limit can be at public rates, or on a sliding scale of interest rates ultimately arriving at the public rate. These schemes can be a very attractive element of an individual's total remuneration, albeit costly for employers. Some employers provide mortgage subsidies directly linked with a contractual requirement that the employee must stay with the organisation for a defined period. For example, in education, the mortgate subsidy scheme:

> aims to assist staff recruited from lower-cost housing areas, including first-time buyers, who purchase a property within twelve months of joining the County Council. The subsidy is provided for the first five years from the date of purchase and is paid on the understanding that you will stay with the County Council for at least six years.[15]

## Pensions

The components of a pension scheme likely to be of most significance in a recruitment and retention context are:

- The level of employee contribution. Non-contributory schemes in financial services remain understandably popular.
- Offering extra years' pensionable service – subject to Inland Revenue restrictions. This can be a very powerful recruitment and retention device, especially for older recruits who have moved jobs earlier in their career and who may not have taken out a personal pension.
- Final scheme salary. Assuming basic salaries increase annually, basing pension on final salary can act to retain staff to maximise final salary, and therefore pension. Manual staff will prefer a 'best three years out of the last ten' formula.
- Lump-sum death-in-service benefits are increasingly valued for the protection offered to the family in the event of death of the employee. Four times basic salary on death in service is increasingly common.
- Temporary and permanent disablement benefits, whereby enhanced pension is available as a result of sickness, can act as a helpful cushion, with major advantages to the family and the disabled employee.

## SUMMARY

Reward strategies will be central to the achievement of the HR vision. While increasing basic pay remains the most common employer response to collective or individual difficulties of recruitment and retention, remuneration policies have been developed to provide greater flexibility within defined strategic controls. Levels of bargaining have been devolved increasingly to local managers better able to respond to local labour market circumstances. Job evaluation schemes have to be capable of responding flexibly to the rapid pace of technical and organisational change, as well as providing scope to respond to changing labour market conditions. Salary structures need similarly to emphasise flexibility, whether in the form of salary progression, in the definition of scale minima and maxima or in the use of market supplements. Total remuneration packaging ('cafeteria' rewards) takes this flexibility much further and is likely to form an increasingly vital part of reward strategies for quality skills in the 1990s.

## REFERENCES

1 For more details see COMMISSION ON INDUSTRIAL RELATIONS, *Industrial Relations in Multi-plant Undertakings*, Report No. 35, HMSO, London, 1972, and A. W. J. THOMSON and L. C. HUNTER, 'The level of bargaining in a multi-plant company', *Industrial Relations Journal*, Vol. 6, 1975.

2 See *Public Sector Bargaining*, IDS Study No. 303, December 1983, pp. 36–7.

3 DAVID FILLINGHAM, 'When bargaining is a life-or-death issue', *Personnel Management*, Vol. 23, No. 3, March 1991, p. 37.

4 See also ROGER SEIFERT, 'Prognosis for local bargaining in health and education', *Personnel Management*, June 1990, pp. 54–7.

5 IAN SMITH, *The management of Remuneration: Paying for Effectiveness*, IPM, London, 1983, p. 68.

6 HELEN MURLIS and DEREK PRITCHARD, 'The computerised way to evaluate jobs', *Personnel Management*, April 1991, p. 53.

7 *Ibid.*

8 MICHAEL ARMSTRONG, *Principles and Practice of Salary Administration*, Kogan Page, London, 1974, pp. 77–8.

9 C. BREWSTER and S. L. CONNOCK, *Industrial Relations: Cost-effective Strategies*, Hutchinson, London, 1985, p. 78.

10 MICHAEL GOODSWEN, 'Retention and reward of the high achiever', *Personnel Management*, October 1988, p. 61.

11 *Recruitment and Retention of Employees in London Local Government*, Report No. 2 produced by the Greater London Employers' Secretariat and reported in IDS Report No. 504, September 1987, p. 29.

12 CAROL WOODLEY, 'The cafeteria route to compensation', *Personnel Management*, May 1990, p. 42.

13 See RICHARD COOKMAN, 'Employee benefits for managers and executives', in ANGELA M. BOWEY (ed.), *Handbook of Salary and Wages Systems*, Gower Press, London, 1975, p. 366.

14 *Personnel Management Plus*. Vol. 2, No. 2, February 1991, p. 1.

15 From 'Statement of benefits from . . . Education Authority'.

CHAPTER 7

# Development strategies

Achieving business strategies and successfully implementing the HR vision will require well thought out yet flexible development and training strategies. In particular, there will be new requirements on managers – in managing change, in managing technology, in thinking strategically. The need for increased adaptability, flexibility, innovation, customer orientation and productivity, however, impacts upon all employees in the organisation. If these and other related elements are the main components of the HR vision, long-term training and development strategies will be necessary to grow the skilled workforce to meet the vision of the future. These strategies may, too, increasingly embrace 'reversion' as well as promotion within the organisation. Of this, more below. Handscomb and Norman in their book *Strategic Leadership – the Missing Links* saw training and development strategies as one of three key components of strategic leadership, which began with:

> a deeper and more determined sense of strategic mission or purpose will be required. Second, a close integration of operational and strategic management and their effectiveness must be secured. Third, significant investments in manager and management team development will be required to establish essential conscious competence in areas such as strategic decision-making, opportunity and risk management and innovation – including lateral thinking and team leadership of realistic strategic implementation plans.[1]

Sir John Cassels has echoed the view of many specialists in his claim that a quality workforce can be achieved:

> by good management, good personnel management and a range of things of that kind, but in my belief training and education are central to the process. It is not sensible to think possible the idea of a quality workforce which is not well educated and well trained.[2]

The problems to overcome are substantial. Chapter 4 commented on the large number of school leavers entering the labour market with no educational qualifications at all. Turning to managers, the 1987 report on *The Making of Managers* gloomily concluded that:

There can be little doubt that, by comparison with other countries in this study, Britain has neglected her managerial stock. With some notable exceptions her companies have asked too little from their would-be managers and given them too little in terms of education, training and development. Quantity does not guarantee quality, but in . . . statistical terms we should probably need to be doing ten times as much as we now are as a nation . . .[3]

Some of the statistical comparisons which formed the starting point of the survey are as follows:

Why do 85 per cent of top managers in both the USA and Japan have degrees, while the only available comparative figure in Britain suggests 24 per cent?

Why are there over 120,000 qualified accountants in Britain, but only 4,000 in Germany and 7,000 in Japan?

Why, on the other hand, does Britain graduate only 1,200 MBAs a year while the USA produces 70,000, Germany none and Japan only 60?

Why, however, do 54 per cent of the directors on the management boards of Germany's 100 largest companies have doctorates, not in management but in some discipline such as engineering, science or law?

Why do most well-educated Germans not join a business until 27 years of age while the Japanese and the British start at 22?

Why do the large corporations in France spend 3·6 per cent of their wage bill on training of all types (with 30 per cent of that going to management training) when their law only requires 1·1 per cent?

Why do 42 per cent of the top 500 companies in America and many big organisations in Germany and Japan devote more than five days' off-the-job training per year to each manager?

Why do many Japanese companies need a formal manual for what they call OJT (on-the-job training)?

Why is a management career so sought after in all four countries?[4]

This chapter views development and training strategies as vital to achieving both organisational objectives and the HR vision. It will concentrate on the following subjects: (1) competences for the future, (2) assessing potential, (3) performance management, (4) career management and (5) training strategies. Competence analysis is a critical starting point, since training and development

*Development strategies*  113

activities stem from this framework of the skills, knowledge and personal abilities necessary to meet the future needs of the business. These competences will underpin methods of analysing potential, including assessment centre methodology. 'Performance management' is the label provided here for the overall process of setting key results and objectives and appraising performance. Such schemes are fundamental to achieving organisational objectives and allow a detailed focus on individual training and development needs. 'Career management' focuses on succession planning approaches, and the link between the analysis of the strengths, weaknesses and potential of staff and organisational resourcing requirements for the future. Finally this chapter concludes with a review of training strategies, particularly the changing technical training needs of staff at all levels of the organisation. Managerial training needs will be reviewed separately in this part of the chapter.

The starting point is competence analysis.

## COMPETENCES

At management level, a competence has been simply defined as 'an observable skill or ability to complete a managerial task successfully'.[5] Important dimensions of task effectiveness can be observed by interviewing effective managers, by using 'critical incident' techniques, by a 'repertory grid' or by more formal surveys. The concept has been given considerable weight by the publication by the Training Commission and the Council for Management Education and Development (CMED) of the main components of management competences. This classification was stimulated in turn by the problem expressed in the *Making of Managers* report already referred to, as well as the John Constable/Roger McCormick report *The Making of British Managers*, also published in 1987. The CMED work on competences forms the basis for developing 'criterion-referenced standards of performance for managers and supervisors. It is intended that the standards will be used to develop a system of nationally recognised qualifications.'[6]

The setting up of the National Council for Vocational Qualification (NCVQ) supported this aim by seeking to establish a National Vocational Qualification framework. The Training Commission developed a wider definition of competences which is worth quoting:

> Standards development should be based on the concept of competence which is defined as the ability to perform the activities within an occupation. Competence is a wide concept which embodies the ability to transfer skills and knowledge to new situations within the occupational area. It encompasses organisation and planning of work, innovation and coping with non-routine activities. It includes those qualities of personal effectiveness that are required in the workplace to deal with co-workers, managers and customers.[7]

Before describing the possible contents of future-based competences, it is important to note the advantages and disadvantages of this technique.

## Advantages of competence analysis

- It focuses on the future requirements of the business, linking clearly with business strategies.
- By looking to the future, the HR Manager can better understand the 'gap' between then and now, and plan accordingly.
- It is relevant to all aspects of the HR Manager's role, providing data to underpin recruitment, training, appraisal, assessment of potential, succession planning and reward strategies.
- It is systematic, based on observable behaviour, providing a thorough and more objective analysis of job requirements at different levels for the future than many other techniques.
- It is participative: key line managers and job holders can share in the development of the competence analysis. As with other HR processes, this is likely to lead to line commitment to the outcome.
- Competences can provide a clear signal to staff as to the most effective and least effective skills and behaviour required.
- The language of the organisation is used. As with tailored job evaluation schemes, it is more effective to base HR processes on the values of the organisation.

## Disadvantages of competence analysis

- In a rapidly changing business context, competences can quickly become out of date.
- There may be difficulties in finding staff able to articulate the future skills, knowledge and personal requirements of their job. Competences may therefore reflect only the present requirements.
- To be meaningful across a range of jobs, competences may have to be defined generically. This level of generalisation may reduce their practical worth.
- In finding 'core competences', specific competences required for specific specialisms may be underplayed even though the technical skills may be vital to effectiveness in the specialism concerned.
- Weighting of the competences may be necessary, given that the skill, knowledge and personal abilities required in a job will not all be equally important. This can mean the competence analysis becomes more complex than is desirable.

The technique certainly has disadvantages, then, and psychologists can argue at length about precisely what competences are, how they are structured, etc. To the HR Manager they offer a systematic approach to translating the HR vision and the needs of the future requirements of the business into practical statements of what is required at particular job levels. As they can be

*Development strategies*

## Senior managerial competences

Much in-company work has been undertaken in this area. McBeath summarised the objectives of management competences:

> When we talk about competences, we are asking questions about what people need to be able to do and about how they need to behave in order to be effective, normally in one job or a category or level of jobs . . .[8]

He identified three 'primary' objectives:

1 To provide maximum guidance in the specification required for any managerial position which is about to be filled.
2 To provide maximum guidance on the specification you are likely to need for your managers on into the future, as this will influence the recruiting you do now and the development programmes which follow as you endeavour to prepare individuals for those future roles.
3 To help you understand the difference between the 'now' and the future so that you can manage the change.[9]

What managerial competences are emerging? One set of 'new key capabilities' for senior managers is as follows:

- Strategic vision, and skills in opportunity identification.
- Conscious competence in strategic development.
- Corporate consciousness, priorities and skills.
- Identification with strategic customers and their needs.
- Awareness of importance and relevance of the available technology throughout all facets of the business.
- Vision to identify, access and introduce new technologies.
- Well practised in analytical management processes to allow focus on business results.
- Acceptance and support of strategy-driven style of management.
- Effectiveness in planning and managing change.
- A commitment to ongoing personal development.
- The introduction of intellectual challenge in senior-level decision making and taking.[10]

In a study of senior management core competences in both Shell International and BAT Industries, Victor Dulewicz said:

> Senior managers in both companies require cerebral competences such as strategic vision and a broad awareness ('helicopter' ability), and high powers of analysis and intelligence, the ability to relate to people through influencing, communicating, listening, motivating and delegating and the capacity to withstand extended pressure. Most importantly, they need the ability to get results through decisiveness and courage, a high level of achievement, motivation and well developed financial and business sense.[11]

Between these two lists the HR Manager will see the direction of senior management competences even though each organisation will need to review its own circumstances.

Senior managers operating at international level will, as chapter 2 showed, continue to increase in numbers in the 1990s. Competences for international managers have been defined as follows:

> *Competencies of the Well Developed International Manager: a Review.*
> International organisations which have adopted a strategy of placing expatriates in top management positions at host country locations should select and train individuals who have both technical and contextual competence. The technically competent manager knows the industry, the functional/managerial responsibilities, and the role of the subsidiary in the organisation's global strategy. The contextually competent manager is able to:
>
> - Intellectually and emotionally understand the value orientations and associated dimensions of both home and host countries;
> - Speak with conversational proficiency the host country's language;
> - Translate, adapt, integrate, and operationalise functional managerial responsibilities according to local conditions. This includes, but is not limited to, management style, reward system, time orientation, work design, and organisational structure;
> - Recognise the importance of local religious customs, local climate conditions, local history, as well as various political and regional alliances;
> - Understand the necessity of introducing technological advances at an appropriate pace.
> - Contribute to a global optimum, rather than a local optimum. In some sense, this means making choices which benefit the overall organisation even if they come at the cost of short-term personal interest. According to Doz and Prahalad '[he/she] is committed to overall corporate performance, rather than local results'.
> - Understand the difference between technical information (i.e. discipline or function-relevant information) and social information (i.e. culturally relevant information), and act as a boundary-spanning interpreter of both information types for home and host country personnel and decision makers.

## Development strategies

- Balance strategies for exerting control (i.e. attempts to keep the environment from changing in ways which will adversely affect the organisation) and strategies for increasing flexibility (i.e. means of increasing the firm's adaptability to a changing environment) when confronted with increasing uncertainty.[12]

Certain themes consistently emerge from reviews of senior management competence, including:

- Having strategic vision.
- Strong customer orientation.
- Results-oriented.
- Able to manage change.
- Technological awareness.
- Flexible.
- Very able communicator, especially on corporate vision.

### Competences for managers and supervisors

The Advisory Group to the Training Commission[13] developed a model of the competence dimension of a manager which is reproduced in Fig. 22. Each dimension is defined as follows:

- The first dimension identified was related to managing resources and systems. This dimension included the management of people, finance and the operational systems for which managers have responsibility.
- The second dimension recognised that the performance of these functions is affected by the environment in which the manager works, and so a

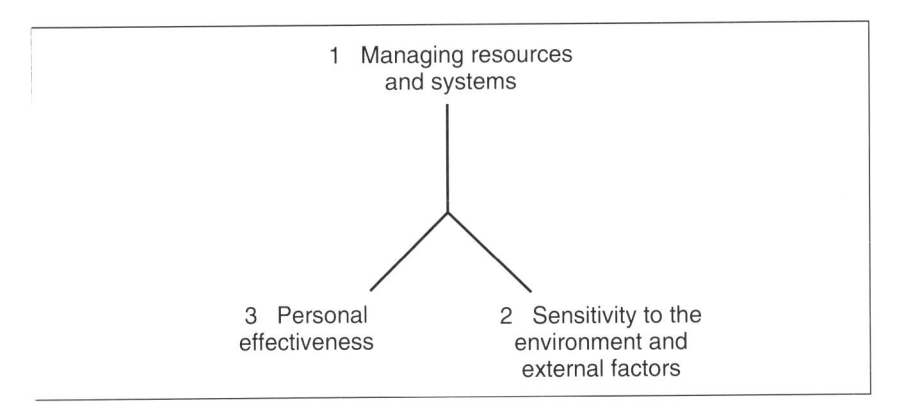

**Fig. 22. A model of the competence dimensions of a manager.**
From Department of Employment, HMSO, London, 1989, p. 4

sensitivity to external factors was an essential characteristic of all-round management competence.
- An important third dimension of personal effectiveness influences the ways in which individuals operate in different contexts: how they interact with others, the extent to which they can work as part of a team; their approach to decision-making; and a propensity to identify major opportunities.

Two other listings of managerial competences are reproduced below. The first was developed by Professor Harry Schroder and used at the National Westminster Bank. The second was derived from research at Henley Management College, based on a study of sixty-seven managers from a wide range of organisations.

There are similarities between these listings of generic competences – for example, the common emphasis on 'achievement/results orientation'. There are some surprising differences, too. For example, the Schroder definition does not appear to cover 'strategic perspective' despite this becoming a significant feature of middle management as well as senior management competences. The lists are included here to give HR Managers a sense of the direction of core competences. As with other levels, they need to be validated in relation to the circumstances of each organisation.

*Eleven high-performance managerial competencies*

*Information search*
Gathers many different kinds of information and uses a wide variety of sources to build a rich informational environment in preparation for decision-making in the organisation.

*Concept formation*
Builds frameworks or models or forms concepts, hypotheses or ideas on the basis of information; becomes aware of patterns, trends and cause/effect relations by linking disparate information.

*Conceptual flexibility*
Identifies feasible alternatives or multiple options in planning and decision-making; holds different options in focus simultaneously and evaluates their pros and cons.

*Interpersonal search*
Uses open and probing questions, summaries, paraphrasing etc to understand the ideas, concepts and feelings of another; can comprehend events, issues, problems, opportunities from the viewpoint of another person.

*Managing interaction*
Involves others and is able to build cooperative teams in which group members feel valued and empowered and have shared goals.

# Development strategies

*Developmental orientation*
Creates a positive climate in which individuals increase the accuracy of their awareness of their own strengths and limitations and provides coaching, training and developmental resources to improve performance.

*Impact*
Uses a variety of methods (e.g. persuasive arguments, modelling behaviour, inventing symbols, forming alliances and appealing to the interest of others) to gain support for ideas, strategies and values.

*Self-confidence*
States own 'stand' or position on issues; unhesitatingly takes decisions when required and commits self and others accordingly; expresses confidence in the future success of the actions to be taken.

*Presentation*
Presents ideas clearly, with ease and interest so that the other person (or audience) understands what is being communicated; uses technical, symbolic, non-verbal and visual aids effectively.

*Pro-active orientation*
Structures the task for the team; implements plans and ideas; takes responsibility for all aspects of the situation.

*Achievement orientation*
Possesses high internal work standards and sets ambitious yet attainable goals; wants to do things better, to improve, to be more effective and efficient; measures progress against targets.[14]

*Supra competences: short definitions of twelve independent performance factors*

Intellectual

1 Strategic perspective  Rises above the detail to see the broader issues and implications; takes account of wide-ranging influences and situations *both* inside and outside the organisation before planning or acting.

2 Analysis and judgement  Seeks all relevant information; identifies problems, relates relevant data and identifies causes; assimilates numerical data accurately and makes sensible interpretations; work is precise and methodical, and relevant detail is not overlooked. Makes decisions based on logical assumptions that reflect factual information.

3 Planning and organising  Plans priorities, assignments and the allocation of resources; organises resources efficiently and effectively, delegating work to the appropriate staff.

## Interpersonal

4 Managing staff — Adopts appropriate styles for achieving group objectives; monitors and evaluates their work; shows vision and inspiration; develops the skills and competences of staff.

5 Persuasiveness — Influences and persuades others to give their agreement and commitment; in face of conflict, uses personal influence to communicate proposals, to reach bases for compromise and to reach an agreement.

6 Assertiveness and decisiveness — Ascendant, forceful dealing with others; can take charge; is willing to take risks and seek new experiences; is decisive, ready to take decisions, even on limited information.

7 Interpersonal sensitivity — Shows consideration for the needs and feelings of others; listens dispassionately, is not selective, recalls key points and takes account of them; is flexible when dealing with others, will change own position when others' proposals warrant it.

8 Oral communication — Fluent, speaks clearly and audibly, with good diction; in formal presentations, is enthusiastic and lively, tailors content to audience's level of understanding.

## Adaptability

9 Adaptability and resilience — Adapts behaviour to new situations; resilient, maintains effectiveness in face of adversity or unfairness. Performance remains stable when under pressure or opposition; does not become irritable and anxious, retains composure.

## Results—orientation

10 Energy and initiative — Makes a strong, positive impression, has authority and credibility; is a self-starter and originator, actively influences events to achieve goals; has energy and vitality, maintains high level of activity and produces a high level of output.

11 Achievement-motivation — Sets demanding goals for self and for others, and is dissatisfied with average performance; makes full use of own time and resources; sees a task through to completion, irrespective of obstacles and setbacks.

*Development strategies*

12 Business  Identifies opportunities which will increase sales or
    sense   profits; selects and exploits those activities which
            will result in the largest returns.[15]

## Competences for all staff

Linked with the development of National Vocational Qualification are major initiatives being taken in all industries in the UK to establish employer-led standards of competence for functions up to supervisory level. In the insurance industry, for example:

> These tasks and functions are broken down into specific requirements and identify the skills, knowledge, understanding and required performance of individuals in order for them to do the tasks required of them . . . These standards are written as average standards of performance and may be only a minimum attainment by most employers. The standards can, therefore, be used as building blocks . . .
>
> Once the required skills, knowledge and understanding are attained by individuals, the standard work takes it one step further and tests the individual's ability to apply that knowledge or skill at the workplace – 'on-the-job assessment' is the key.[16]

The National Council for Vocational Qualification has already accredited many vocational qualifications for several industries, based upon the successful achievement of defined competence standards. One example of a 'unit of competence' of considerable likely relevance to the HR vision is 'maintaining quality of service to customers'. One component of such competence is defined for the insurance industry in Fig. 23.

Such competence-based assessment can play an important role in raising performance standards as well as instructing staff through receipt of a recognised vocational qualification. It contributes to the creation of a 'learning culture', which may well be part of the HR vision.

Hoechst UK developed a uniformly applicable competence schedule to improve the processes of:

- Internal and external recruitment.
- Developing the context of in-house training courses.
- Developing a system of rewarding effort.
- Developing a system of identifying potential for growth.
- Developing a system of identifying individual training needs.
- Establishing individual development programmes.

Thirty-nine competences have been developed, clustered as follows:

*Company-specific competences*

'Knowing the company tunes and how to play them on the company piano'

Ability to use company-related knowledge, effectively

Company-relevant competences

*Personal commitment*

At its lowest level, being punctual and attending regularly. At its highest levels, actively seeking out additional responsibilities, developing self, personal mobility, accepting new tasks

Personal competences

*Functionally specific comptences*

'Knowing how to play any companies' tunes on their instruments'

Ability to use a range of professional craft, clerical, manual or managerial skills effectively

Transferable competences

*Self-direction*

At its lowest level, doing urgent things quickly and allocating appropriate resources to important things; appropriateness of prioritization. At the highest levels, acting in own role appropriately for its departmental and organizational contexts

Job-context competences.[17]

The references to seeking out additional responsibilities, developing self, accepting new tasks, 'doing urgent things quickly' seem to capture well the direction of the HR vision for many organisations.

Other organisations have sought to develop performance standards in the context of 'total quality' programmes or as part of Performance Management schemes. These may not be competence-related but have the same aim of identifying the factors that help people do their changing jobs better. Total quality improvement programmes will focus on zero defects, on right-first-time, on eliminating 'non-conformance', on team work as part of problem-solving.

To summarise, competences can focus on the skills, knowledge and personal characteristics required for the quality workforce to do its jobs effectively. Organisations can signal via core competences the traits they seek to develop, representing their HR vision for all staff. There are disadvantages, but the range of uses for the HR Manager and line managers generally is wide. For these reasons, competences are likely to continue to guide development and training strategies in the 1990s.

## ASSESSING POTENTIAL

Enabling staff to achieve their full potential is likely to be a key component of the HR vision. How is this to be achieved? How are individuals to be differentiated in terms of their potential? Potential for what?

Chapter 5 noted the need for improved recruitment processes to achieve

## Development strategies

| UNIT OF COMPETENCE: | 6.1 Maintain quality of service to customers |
|---|---|
| ELEMENT OF COMPETENCE: | 6.1.1 MAINTAIN SATISFACTION OF EXTERNAL AND INTERNAL CUSTOMERS |

PERFORMANCE CRITERIA:
All customers dealt with in the manner prescribed by company and departmental standards
All complaints or incidents of poor service reviewed and remedied within company time scale
All problems, complaints or incidents of inadequate service brought to supervisor/manager's attention
All customers given answers to their complaints
All complaints affecting external customers brought to customer service officer within prescribed time scale
All customer notification of above-average service brought to attention of staff member

| ACTIVITIES/SKILLS: | RELATED KNOWLEDGE: |
|---|---|
| Identify needs of internal and external customers<br>Implement standards of behaviour to meet customers' needs<br>Train staff to correct standards of behaviour towards customers<br>Monitor performance of self and staff<br>Seek customer feedback<br>Deal with inadequate performance<br>Deal with incidents and complaints | Company standards of customer care<br>Behaviour patterns affecting customer<br>Human interaction theory |
| NOTES:<br>Competence assessed over a sufficient period of time to cover a wide variety of staff's attitudes to customers<br>Knowledge may require to be tested through simulated cases | TASK MANAGEMENT/PERSONAL EFFECTIVENESS:<br>Own approach to customers (internal and external) sets example to staff |

**Fig. 23. Core competence in customer service.**
From the Insurance Industry Training Council

more effective results. As with recruitment, assessment of staff could also be improved. The more clearly defined the future job requirements the more clearly can individuals be matched to those requirements. The above analysis of competences is clearly relevant to the continuous process of identifying potential.

Overall, assessments should as far as possible be:

- Systematic.
- Continuous.
- Multi-faceted.

*Systematic* in that assessments of potential should start with a review of current and past performance in the job. Successful performance in the current job is certainly one important indicator of future effectiveness in higher jobs. Not the sole indicator, of course, since people can 'plateau' but remain successful in their current job. To be systematic in potential appraisal calls for a methodology to capture the individual's strengths and development needs.

Hopefully the components of this methodology will be related to the changing business requirement for skills and knowledge in the organisation.

*Continuous* assessment means that at least once a year all members of staff at all levels should be reviewed and questions asked about their potential. Individuals do develop at different paces, and in different circumstances. The annual review should be sufficient to identify potential, although it could be six-monthly in the cases of, say, new graduates.

*Multi-faceted* in that the assessment of potential, as with performance, should review all aspects of the individual's progress, and it should be undertaken by more than one assessor. Relying on the views of one manager can be unduly narrow, allowing for greater subjectivity than is desirable.

Potential appraisal schemes therefore have the following objectives:

- To provide a systematic basis for identifying staff with potential to progress to higher levels in the organisation.
- To improve and expedite the job experience, development and training of such staff.
- To improve the quality of appointments at the designated level.
- To improve the recruitment and retention of quality staff by demonstrating a commitment to career development and training.

Various techniques can be used to meet these objectives, including:

- Potential appraisal.
- Assessment centres.
- Psychological profiling.
- 360° assessment.

Each will be reviewed in turn.

## Potential appraisal

Potential can be appraised by line managers producing a list of staff with the ability, in their view, to move on up the organisation. The line managers will, hopefully, have a clear vision of what is required. Hopefully, too, the HR Manager will be involved. Various mechanisms can then be generated to check out such staff, including discussions, project teams and testing. In small organisations such flexibility and informality in the appraisal of potential may be very effective if frequent working relationships mean that an accurate picture of the individual's performance and future potential can be gauged. In large organisations reliance on this informal style may be too subjective. It may be demotivating to quality staff to be bypassed in the assessment of potential if the manager being asked to make the judgement is either unaware of the employee's true potential or, worse, aware of it but deliberately suppressing the knowledge.

## Development strategies

More reliable in large organisations is to rely on an annual appraisal by the line manager against defined competences. A detailed appraisal analysing 'effective' or 'less effective' behaviour against the range of desirable competences for a given level in the business will at least ensure that decisions on potential can be justified. A number of staff not identified as having potential may still be able to become more effective in the current job via training, and this will also be analysed at this stage. If an individual feels he or she should have been nominated for promotion (assuming the organisation is open in these matters), then there is a systematic analysis underpinning the decision which can be communicated to the employee.

Openness in potential appraisal is a tricky subject. Informing staff they have potential for promotion can result in unduly raised expectations, especially if in the flatter organisation of the future the opportunities for promotion are reduced. Potential may also reduce in time, leaving the organisation with the task of removing someone from consideration for promotion who was previously informed they were eligible. However, a covert approach runs even greater risks. Staff will be aware of events occurring – for example, to ask someone to attend a one-day series of psychological tests or attend a training course will be suggestive of a plan of action. Quality staff may even leave the organisation, believing that no one had recognised their potential. It will be too late to tell them after they've left that they were high on the list for promotion!

On balance – and each organisation needs to make this judgement for itself – it is preferable to be open in informing staff in broad terms that their potential is recognised and being considered. No specific information as to 'next job' should be given until the job can be clearly delivered.

Line managers are in the best position to nominate staff as having potential. Nominations from the line should not be based only on a recommendation arising from the process of performance appraisal. This only gives evidence of how well an individual is currently performing in a certain job. It does not provide enough information on how the individual would perform in a higher-level job. This is where analysis of the individual's strengths and development needs against defined future competences is of most value. Nominations from line managers need to be verified, by senior line managers and by the HR Manager. Assessment centres can be useful in this process, and this subject is discussed next.

## Assessment centres

Assessment centres have been in use for many years in British companies, and there is no need here to describe the technique in detail. In summary, the following advantages and disadvantages can be identified when the technique is used as part of potential review:

## Advantages

- May provide detailed information on how participants perform in a variety of different contexts, including in-tray, one-to-one interviews and group discussion.
- Information is provided against defined competences, since the exercises are designed to identify the required skills, knowledge and personal characteristics required to be effective in the future.
- The information emerging includes strengths, potential and, critically, development needs.
- Line managers' involvement as assessors adds to their commitment to the process of reviewing potential and sharpens their own skills in assessing staff.
- There is a visible process of systematic potential review which is important to staff retention.
- Feedback to individuals on the centres can be detailed and immediate.

## Disadvantages

- The credibility of the assessors is critical — for senior line managers, who will be most credible, it can be a very time-consuming process.
- Setting up and running centres can be costly, particularly if consultants are employed to define the required competences and design the exercises.
- The competences may get out of date — centres must be regularly reviewed.
- Without pre-screening, 'unpromotable' applicants may be wrongly nominated.
- Attendance at a centre itself raises expectations which may then prove more difficult to reduce.
- Centres can be seen as highly competitive, with conspicuous winners or losers.
- If candidate feedback is not well handled, or is delegated to people who were not present at the centre, individuals can be demotivated, producing centre casualties.

These disadvantages can be overcome, particularly through clear objectives for the centres, through pre-screening of candidates, through careful definition of critical success factors in the jobs at the designated level against which the exercises can be carefully designed, through positive and open feedback highlighting for all the development and training needs arising. To emphasise this last point, many centres have been retitled 'development centres'.

Those HR Managers who are themselves assessors will know how powerful this technique can be in clearly differentiating the potential of staff. The example of British Petroleum is useful here. A team of general manager assessors from an assessment board observe individuals in a variety of group and one-to-one situations. The competences are used as a basis for identifying development needs and to establish potential for promotion to managerial

*Development strategies* 127

positions. Figure 24 shows by way of illustration two of the BP competences, the positive and negative indicators that the competences are being met and the possible development suggestions arising.

## Psychological profiling

The use of psychological tests can be part of the assessment centre or used separately to analyse potential. There has been a considerable increase in the use of psychological tests. One recent survey showed 74 per cent of a sample of medium and large organisations using ability or aptitude tests.[18]

Most likely, tests are being used in a cautious manner, particularly for senior-level external appointments. In such cases the consequences of failing to appoint the right person are very great and all sources of data need to be used. Psychological testing can be a useful adjunct to the interviewing and headhunting process.

Used as part of a potential review process, psychological tests can also add value. Care is needed in choosing the appropriate tests, in providing careful feedback, in avoiding quick, overgeneralised judgements of psychological type and in avoiding too heavy a reliance on such techniques.

## '360° assessment', etc.

This American term simply means seeking views on potential from all round the employee. This would embrace not only the manager but peers, subordinates and even those outside the direct workplace who have knowledge and experience of the job holder.

'Matrix' assessment is practised in the UK – mainly in American-owned companies. Other organisations are likely to tap various sources of data informally to build up as comprehensive a picture of the individual's potential as possible. Formally building-in the views of peers and subordinates is a course of action likely to prove contentious unless the culture of the organisation embraces openness and inspires honesty and frankness in discussing individuals at all levels.

There are other techniques, including self-assessment. Indeed, the best people are most likely managing their own career, having the will to win, self-confidence and leadership qualities already causing them not only to be noticed but to be empowered to seize opportunities to make an impact on the organisation. However, such obviously high-potential staff are relatively rare. For most organisations there will be a need to rely on managerial assessment of potential, using a pre-defined process which seeks to identify quality staff with business-related skills and personal characteristics desirable for the future. Before considering the training and development options for these staff, the related aspect of performance management should be reviewed.

**Personal Drive** Self-confident and assertive drive to win, with decisiveness and resilience

| 1 | 2 | 3 | 4 | 5 |
|---|---|---|---|---|
| Decisive even under pressure, assertive and tough-minded in arguing his/her case, very self-confident, shrugs off setbacks | Will commit him/herself to definite opinions, determined to be heard, can come back strongly if attacked | May reserve judgment where uncertain, but stands firm on important points, aims for compromise, fairly resilient | Avoids taking rapid decisions, takes an impartial co-ordinator role rather than pushing own ideas | Doesn't pursue his/her points, goes along with the group, allows criticism or setbacks to deter him/her |

+ indicators
- tough-minded driving style/pushes to get own way
- persistent in arguing points
- concerned to get solution he/she owns
- can confront others where important
- makes clear decisions when required
- commits self to definite opinions
- resilient to setbacks
- enjoys challenge, can accept mistakes
- maintains confidence

− indicators
- rather soft or 'nice'
- doesn't pursue his/her points
- doesn't like confronting others
- inclined to give way if attacked
- lets others make the decisions
- backs off from giving definite view
- reacts emotionally to setbacks
- anxious, worried about mistakes
- lacking confidence, appears uncertain

## Development needs

if score 'high' ⟵ medium ⟶ if score 'low'

| Possible strengths | Possible needs | Possible strengths | Possible needs |
|---|---|---|---|
| Tough-minded, results-oriented Comfortable with decision-making Faces conflicts Strong-willed Great faith in self Will take charge Determined to achieve Comfortable in competitive settings | Overly dominant One-way, selfish Overly direct, aggressive Needs to be in control Problem functioning as team player Resistant to others' ideas Over-confident Sees everything in terms of win/lose | Sacrifices own interests for good of whole Tactful Manages conflict situations Open to influence People work with, not for Comfortable in collaborative settings | Overly deferential Doesn't challenge enough Viewed as being passive Difficulty in making decisions Avoids confrontation or competition Occasional outbursts which no one can handle |
| 'Tough battler' | Only seen as 'tough battler' | 'Friendly helper' | Only seen as 'friendly helper' |

## Developmental suggestions

Read the situation; what sort of approach required – competitive/collaborative?
Encourage feedback from others/strengthen your ability to receive suggestions from others
Watch for signs that you are taking over, being *over*-assertive, *over*-competitive – learn to back off
Get more involved in situations requiring collaboration – cultivate ability to be a creative listener
Go on a course like the workshop for influencing skills
Don't interrupt so much – learn to respect the reasoned argument of those with whom you disagree

Take more initiatives, get things started
Stand up and be counted
Know what you want
Believe in what you are saying
Find situations involving a moderate level of conflict/competition
Raise the ante for yourself
Go on a course like the workshop in influencing skills
Work on needs, like necessity to be well liked by others and become more comfortable in handling conflict

**Fig. 24a    Example of a competence assessment at BP: (a) Personal drive.**

Cited in *Personnel Management*, August 1989, p. 38

**Team management** Ability to stimulate a productive team climate. Able to manage interaction of people with different perspectives, conflicting views

| **1** | **2** | **3** | **4** | **5** |
|---|---|---|---|---|
| Provides process leadership to promote team spirit and enthusiasm builds others, commitment to achieve super-ordinate goals | Encourages others to contribute, will act as a facilitator for the group, builds alliances between people and groups | Balanced approach, will suggest methods and procedures for how to tackle the task | Tends to overstate the importance and value of one's own contribution, will reluctantly involve self in group | Prefers individualistic, self-centred approach, will tend to be indifferent to others and will do nothing about it |

**+ indicators**
- uses humour to reduce tension
- tries to get agreement on principles
- behaves as a member of team and can get others to contribute
- draws out quieter members
- directs discussion by carefully timed interventions
- encourages an open flow of communication between members
- process-oriented, facilitative

**− indicators**
- attacks others, raises tension
- individualistic, not interested in group approach
- behaves unilaterally, e.g. as the decision-maker
- ignores quieter members
- impulsive in his/her interventions
- becomes impatient with openness between members
- task-fascinated

## Development needs

if score 'high' ⟵ medium ⟶ if score 'low'

| Possible strengths | Possible needs | Possible strengths | Possible needs |
|---|---|---|---|
| Establishes lively, inspiring environment Actively involved in work of group Open communication Stimulates others to participate in group problem-solving Facilitates creative approach Manages interaction Will develop participative decision-making procedures | Bogged down by the needs of the group Conformity Over-involved, loses objectivity Delays when decisions are required quickly Internal focus | Determination Resilience Challenging Individualistic | Perceived as aloof and distant, i.e. unapproachable, overly aggressive, caustic, self-centred May induce quasi-adversarial atmosphere Intolerant of mistakes |

## Developmental suggestions

Encourage individual expression
Sometimes encourage competitive as well as collaborative behaviour
Look externally rather than be preoccupied with internal cohesion
Keep a clear focus on tasks as well as process

Assume leadership for a group project; concern yourself with group process as well as agenda
Emphasise showing concern and support for subordinates
Solicit views from others
Develop trust in subordinates' capabilities
Look for win/win solutions
Keep the praise-to-criticism ratio at 5:1; make more use of 'strokes'
Encourage positive, experimenting atmosphere
Build enthusiasm in your group

**Fig. 24b   Example of a competence assessment at BP: (b) Team management.**

Cited in *Personnel Management*, August 1989, p. 39

## PERFORMANCE MANAGEMENT

Performance appraisal has long been a key feature of HR management in the UK. Appraisal schemes have in more recent years been extended to semi-skilled and skilled staff, albeit from a very low base. MacKay and Torrington (1986) have shown that 30 per cent of manual employees, 62 per cent of clerical and secretarial, and 70 per cent of supervisory staff are appraised.[19] In the late 1980s the emphasis moved from performance appraisal to performance management. Whilst setting clear and measurable objectives was always a major part of earlier schemes, the emphasis was more on the *appraisal* of past performances. Under performance management there is a dual emphasis: on setting key accountabilities, objectives, measures, priorities and time scales for the following review period and appraising performance at the end of the period.

There are four main reasons for this change of emphasis:

- The competitive pressures described in chapter 2 have resulted in a higher priority being given to performance improvement. This has led to the clearer setting of objectives, standards and priorities.
- It has been recognised that the corporate mission and strategic objectives can be more effectively implemented by linking them directly to key accountabilities and individual objectives. This rigorous association between corporate and individual objectives helps to ensure that the organisation is in practice moving in the direction developed by senior management in the mission.
- The renewed emphasis on quality has led to the refinement of quality standards, which can then underpin performance management processes.
- The increasing use of performance-related pay. As chapter 6 has shown, this is a major feature of reward strategies designed to recognise and remunerate achievement. To ensure its effectiveness, clear objectives, measures and time scales are necessary from which judgements about the individual's contribution can be made.

One case study worthy of inclusion here sought also to support the development of different behaviour and new values appropriate to the changing world of a major building society. Their performance management system:

> is a structured process for cascading down an organisation a clear understanding of *what* has to be achieved at each level and by each individual (in the form of well defined and agreed objectives and performance standards) whilst also creating a commitment to how it is to be achieved in terms of the key behavioural skills required for success.[20]

Figure 25 illustrates the approach. The use of behavioural criteria in this context links performance management clearly to the HR vision of the organisation.

*Name* J. R. Bloggs   *Job:* Manager, Operations   *Date:* June 87

Job purpose: Plan, direct and control the regional and branch operations to meet the Society's annual profit and growth objectives

| Key accountability | Measure | Objective/ Standards | By when |
|---|---|---|---|
| 1 Direct the regional operations to ensure that all planned targets are achieved within agreed budgets and timescales. | Monthly management reports regarding<br>Lending:<br>Life commission:<br>Investment balance: growth:<br>Other products: | £Z million<br>£Y,000<br>£X million<br><br>as agreed | Monthly and/or annually |
|  | Budget variance reports | Revenue:<br>£P million<br>Capital:<br>£Q,000 |  |
| 2 Develop and implement plans to ensure that all staff in the field operations are conversant with the Society's complete product range and are competent to deliver the required level and quality of service to customers. | Review of branch and individual training plans (quantity/quality) | Agreed standards of training | Annually |
|  | Quality service observations<br>Customer surveys | Written reports on unit performance | Periodic |
| 3 Ensure that branches and agencies operate in a manner consistent with Society policy and procedures. | Internal audit reports<br><br>Regular management reports | Agreed standards of compliance/ accuracy | Periodic annual |
| **BEHAVIOURAL CRITERIA**<br>Decisiveness<br>Interpersonal sensitivity<br>Persuasiveness<br>Planning and organising<br>Management control | Leadership<br>Problem analysis<br>Initiative<br>Judgement<br>Work standards |  |  |

#### Examples of behavioural criteria definitions

**Decisiveness:** readiness to make decisions, render judgements and take actions.

**Persuasiveness:** ability to make a persuasive, clear presentation of ideas or facts. Convince others to own, expressed point of view.

**Judgement:** ability to evaluate data and courses of action to reach logical decisions. Unbiased, rational approach.

**Planning and organising:** ability to establish efficiently an appropriate course of action for self and others to accomplish a goal.

**Fig. 25. Performance management at Birmingham and Midshires Building Society.**

The society now appraises its 300 most senior staff using a combination of agreed performance objectives and behavioural criteria. Shown here is a set of objectives and criteria for a fictitious job, intended only to illustrate the approach the society adopts.

Cited in *Personnel Management*, December 1988, p. 37

Typically, performance management schemes have the following objectives:

- To ensure a common understanding of the job holder's key accountabilities and standards of performance; their priorities and how they relate to the organisation's overall strategic objectives.
- To provide regular two-way feedback between manager and job holder on progress, with a view to improving performance.
- To identify training and development needs required to improve present and future performance.
- To create a shared commitment to the achievement of objectives and performance standards.
- To provide a fair basis for performance-related or merit pay increases where these are directly linked to individual performance.

The performance planning process is the key to performance management, and should be completed prior to the commencement of each review period. It should focus on the strategic objectives and standards for the unit of which the job holder is a part before establishing:

- The job holder's key accountabilities in general terms.
- Specific objectives for the following review period.
- A statement of priorities.
- A process for measuring performance or progress against objectives. Monetary objectives can be used. For more junior staff in the organisation other indices such as quality standards can be identified.

There can be difficulties in managing such systems. Clarity of objectives for each level in the organisation is clearly essential, but may not always be present. The manager needs training in setting objectives.

The link with pay can, as most HR Managers will know, prove contentious if different standards are felt to apply across different departments. The HR Manager has a key role in maintaining consistency. Nevertheless, as a driver of change in the required business direction, performance management schemes can make a vital contribution to organisational effectiveness.

## CAREER MANAGEMENT

The processes described so far all have relevance to career management, which is defined in this context as the identification, effective development and training of the right people to fill the job opportunities arising in the future. Competence analysis can support career management through clearer definition of the qualities required to fill the job opportunities. Potential assessment identifies the people who can move up or transfer laterally within the organisation and performance management provides information on how people are doing in their job. As has been said already, this is a major clue to future

## Development strategies

potential. Performance management schemes may also provide information on the individual's own career preferences and mobility, and this needs to be taken into account in career management.

Not all quality staff will seek promotion, and organisations need to ensure that these staff are fairly rewarded, with effective schemes in place to satisfy individuals' need for achievement to be recognised. Sales staff in particular may prefer not to be moved away from direct selling, which is almost inevitable as sales staff progress hiearchically. Research and development staff, similarly, may dislike the managerial functions which need to be undertaken as they progress in the organisation. To avoid this problem, many organisations have developed technical career paths, allowing scope for promotion without moving away from the individual's preferred specialism. The notion that career management implies 'promotion' is understandable, but is not referred to in the above definition. The preferred concept of 'job opportunities' includes promotion but also embraces lateral movement and reversion to lower-graded jobs in the organisation.

As managerial demands become more complex and rapidly changing there will be increasing numbers of people who will either be unable to handle them or who will prefer to revert to their original specialism. Organisations will need in future to create a climate within which such reversion is seen as acceptable. Harmonising conditions of employment, as chapter 6 showed, has assisted in the process by removing the obvious status connotations associated with particular grades. Organisations will need to go further. Raising the status of, for example, sales, research, manual and clerical jobs by re-emphasising the contribution made by these categories can begin the process of transformation whereby reversion to these grades from a supervisory or managerial level will be seen as increasingly acceptable, even desirable. In sales jobs there is generally scope for an individual's earnings to relate to individual effort, which means that a manager reverting to a sales job can probably match or exceed his previous earnings. In other cases 'red-circling' mechanisms which protect individual earnings may be necessary short-term for managing reversions.

There are significant issues of culture here, especially for the UK workforce, which is more status-conscious and hierarchical than in many other countries. Raising the status of various work groups such as sales and craft staff will therefore be a longer process. It may be an aspect of the HR vision but it will need determined management action to progress. Recognition schemes, communication of 'wins' from these work groups and other empowerment strategies, including the introduction of project-based or matrix organisations, will all assist in the process.

So career management embraces reversion as well as lateral moves and promotion. Of strategies for managing reversion very little is currently said – much more will be written in the 1990s. Concentrating now on career management in its more traditional definition, there generally needs to be a succession planning process which provides the framework for training and development activities. Succession planning cannot be too precise – HR Managers will know how rarely their succession plans are actually implemented precisely as intended. As chapter 2 has shown, massive changes are occurring in business strategies, particularly changes arising from the deregulation of particular markets and from joint ventures and acquisitions. Organisational changes can markedly affect succession planning. Devolution, too, has an impact. As one recent study of succession strategies for the future puts it:

> The stream of mergers, acquisitions and international alliances which have taken place since the mid-1980s has destroyed much of the older order and resulted in new structures and organisational demands. Many companies, for example, are now made of 'sub-businesses' each of which has different and often conflicting management needs. These needs are difficult to predict in advance, thus creating executive jobs with future parameters and demands that are often unknown. In the face of moving markets, involving shorter product life cycles, shorter consumer time spans, rapid changes in technology and unpredictable demand, the planned and orderly approach dictated by traditional succession policies may be difficult or impossible to achieve.[21]

It is not just the pace of organisational change that is impacting upon succession planning. Some individuals may be less keen in future to accept the rigours arising from promotion, especially to senior management positions. There are 'quality of life' elements here. Similarly, the main obstacles managers perceive to relocating are 'family ties', which can impede succession plans across business units where they involve geographical mobility.[22]

Finally, as chapter 3 indicated, the organisational implications of pursuing the changing business strategies and the HR vision are likely to be a flatter organisation with fewer middle management positions. This has a profound effect on traditional succession planning.

Fortunately there are some more positive developments. The growth of project management has led to the increasing use of multi-functional project teams. These provide excellent development opportunities for high-potential staff as well as challenging job assignments for others not necessarily on a fast track.

When, then, should now be emphasised within career management generally or succession planning in particular? There are five priorities:

1. Succession plans must relate closely to the changing business strategies, and to organisational developments. They must anticipate changing organisational roles such as project management opportunities, developments towards a matrix organisation or decentralisation. Organisational barriers to effective succession should also be addressed. In a devolved business this will be a key strategic issue for the corporate HR Manager.

2. In a context of rapid business change and uncertainty, generalised succession plans aimed at creating a high-quality pool of talents should be drawn up. This provides maximum flexibility without detracting from the investment in development and training for the future.

## Development strategies

3. Succession planning should become more of a partnership between the individual and the organisation. There is no 'job for life' or guaranteed promotion. Organisations can provide the framework for individuals to grow — individuals through their own self-development will contribute to their career management.

4. Lateral job opportunities and reversions will be increasingly important features of succession plans. This is especially relevant to staff over the age of forty-five, when the assumption has often been that development stops. One classification of career development over age which shows the danger of stagnation over the age of forty-five is shown in Fig. 26. 'Growth in the job' can be encouraged through payment systems, for example those which directly reward the acquisition of skills or knowledge. Movements towards semi-autonomous work groups, or the 'matrix' organisation, may increase the lateral opportunities within the work team. Project teams will provide similar challenges. Development goals can be set for all staff without the necessity to offer hierarchical promotion. 'Job rotation' has been often discussed but rarely implemented. Rotating across functions is in practice even rarer. This may involve changing managerial 'patronage' and can be difficult to action. More

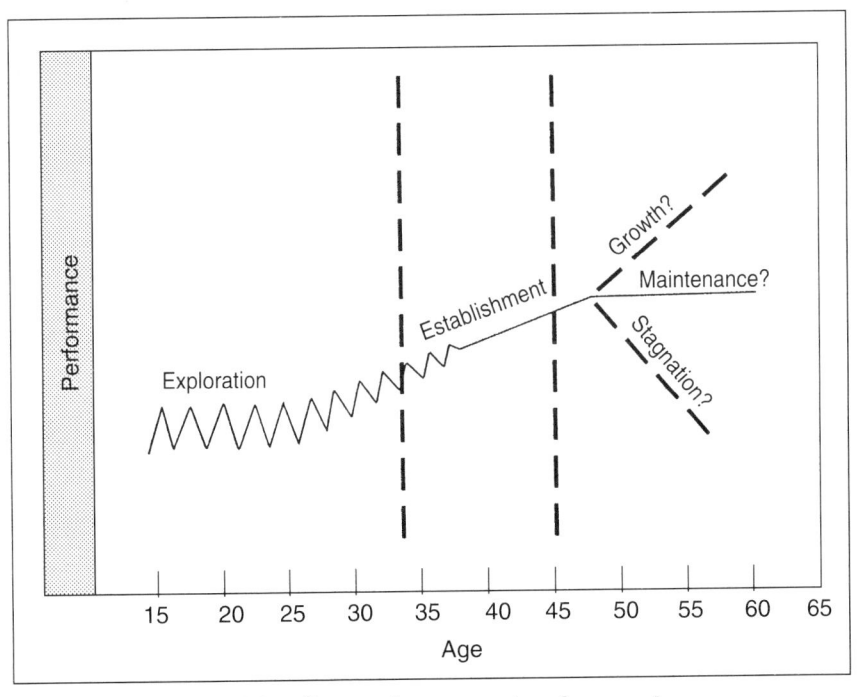

**Fig. 26. Stages in career development.**
Cited by Paul Evans in *Personnel Management*, December 1986, p. 29

likely, individuals' early careers will have provided single functional development which limits subsequent broadening. As certain roles – say marketing, finance or IT – become more specialised the organisational risks of cross-functional moves can also become too great, unless the individual has had relevant early career experience in other specialisms. The succession planning implication is the need both to plan *early* career exposure to different specialisms so as to facilitate later lateral movement and also to create the organisational climate in which boundary crossing is acceptable. Future general managers will require this type of career planning, too.

5. The focus of training and individual development will be the job itself. As Alan Mumford has said, 'Learning from doing the job was the most frequent, pervasive and intimate experience of learning.'[23] The importance in learning of 'development experience' on the job is well recognised by most HR Managers. Providing challenging assignments, the opportunity to produce a clear outcome and thereby to judge success or failure and to learn accordingly, to work with new people, to work with a boss who can input knowledge and skills, to participate in strategic thinking processes, to undertake a role requiring managerial skill, and so on, are all key elements in learning from experience. There is a need in such developments to recognise beforehand the development possibilities, and to review frequently what experience has in practice been gained. Creating such opportunities and providing such guidance for the right people will be a crucial role for succession planning if future competences are to be achieved.

The trend towards greater flexibility in succession planning, and a refocus on lateral growth in the job does not replace 'fast track' schemes or one/two-stop succession plans of the traditional type. This latter approach is still relevant, especially for emergency succession.[24] However, the emphasis, consistent with changing business strategies, organisational development and the HR vision, will be on flexibility in succession planning, on the importance of early development opportunities which provide diversity of experience, on partnership between the individual and the organisation, on 'growth in the job', on lateral movement and on reversion.

## **TRAINING**

The statistics quoted at the beginning of this chapter do not flatter management training in the UK. Yet there has been a radical improvement in recognition by the line managers of the value of training. A survey of training activities in 1986–87 showed that 125·4 million days of training were provided, split between 64·7 million off-the-job and 60·7 million on-the-job. On average, each employee received seven days' training a year, and spent over £800 on training per employee.[25] The statistics can be too reassuring. More than half the employees surveyed received no training at all. In addition, providing training does not guarantee the objects of the training have been met. Nevertheless the position is more encouraging. It was not long ago that

## Development strategies

levy/grant systems were in force to stimulate training activity, and Training Boards were felt to be necessary to provide further encouragement. If training is now more readily accepted as directly contributing to enhancing competitive advantage, there remain many problems, including:

- Too great a reliance, particularly at management level, on off-the-job programmes. Whilst these can be valuable in providing participants with key knowledge and skills, the relevance to job competences is often questionable. 'Useful experience, enjoyed it – not sure how it relates to my job,' may be a typical comment following attendance on a training course. In particular, individual managers attending a programme may receive a short-term benefit, but this can be eroded quickly if peers and the boss have not received similar training and cannot reinforce the changed behaviour encouraged by the training.
- Training needs analysis may not be sufficiently related to the required current or future competences. Reliance on performance appraisal can often provide too generalised comments from line managers, like 'Needs more management training'. The HR Manager will need much more precise information, but it is time-consuming to collect. More systematic alternatives to assess training needs reveal the depth of the problem, but the HR Manager is faced with producing workable programmes from the analysis. Finding the generic training needs leads to practical programmes, but these may not satisfy the specified requirements of individuals, or the organisation.
- Briefing and debriefing mechanisms are often not developed enough. Participants still do not always know why they are nominated for a programme, or what specific behavioural changes are sought following the programme. Debriefing following the course is crucial to identifying the necessary follow-up action but, again, this stage may be short-circuited in practice.
- There has been a concentration on knowledge training in the UK covering, say, products or management techniques. There is still too little skill training in areas of critical importance to the effectiveness of the employee. This has been noticeable among sales staff, for example.
- Training can remain for many a one-off event – attendance at a course externally or internally, then nothing for years. The concept of continuous learning partly through self-development and partly through on- and off-the-job training embracing open learning approaches remains undeveloped in the UK, despite encouraging initiatives in many organisations.
- Front-line managers do not yet admit the centrality of training to their role. How many supervisors are spending five hours a week or more every week throughout the year on training their work group? This type of daily or weekly on-the-job training is vital to overall effectiveness, as Japanese companies, for example, have shown.
- Evaluation of training remains patchy, and there is still an over-reliance on 'immediate evaluations'. Systematic attempts to follow-up training are

relatively rare. HR Managers may become too attached to particular programmes they have designed, despite individual and organisational requirements having moved on. Flexibility in training, and in much else, is important to maintaining its overall vitality.

The way ahead has been described in various recent reports. The study by John Constable and Roger McCormick, *The Making of British Managers* (1987), recommended:

1. A major promotional effort should be undertaken by the relevant government agencies and large companies to promote the value of management development and to publicise best practice.
2. Chief executives should see continuing management development as a major area of their responsibility. It should be a regular item for boardroom discussion and an important aspect of long-term corporate plans.
3. The implementation of strategic initiatives should be accompanied by well developed management achievement incentives.
4. Employers should seek to create personal development programmes for all managers.
5. Individual managers should be encouraged to 'own' their development programme.
6. Employers should establish strong links with external providers of management training with a view to both influencing the design of programmes and obtaining maximum use of expertise.[26]

This focus on a personal development plan for every manager was also included in recommendations in the report *The Making of Managers*[3]. The report recommended setting out a Development Charter which might include:

- A corporate development plan.
- Five days' off-the-job training/education for every manager.
- A personal development plan for every manager.
- Tuition reimbursement for approved self-education.
- A system for experience-based learning or 'integrated development'.

This report also recommends open learning and 'corporate learning programmes in which the core of key managers is helped (by expert outsiders) to assess the organisation's strategic capability in its markets and to decide on necessary steps for improvement (a British version of Japanese corporate thinking).'[27]

There are many case studies quoted in these reports which point the way. One will be referred to here – the Boeing Corporation's management development objectives. They state:

> The Management Development Programme will emphasize self-development by all managers, on-the-job development of all managers, personal attention of each manager to the development of his subordi-

nates, and the interjection of these individual actions with organisational management development under an overall system.[28]

The main components of training effectiveness emerge from these studies. They include:

- A clear link with changing business strategies and the HR vision.
- Specific objectives based upon careful analysis of both the changing business and individual needs.
- An individual training plan for all, since in the quality workforce everyone will have continuing learning objectives.
- An emphasis on self-development and personal 'ownership' of training.
- Strong day-to-day line management involvement in training.
- A concentration on on-the-job learning, with clarity in training objectives and feedback on results.
- A hierarchy of off-the-job training programmes to provide skills and knowledge to meet well researched training needs.
- Effective briefing and debriefing.
- The use of 'open learning' systems.

In this book much emphasis has been placed on adaptability, flexibility, innovation and customer orientation as likely components of the HR vision. Training can play a major role in achieving these elements of the vision.

- Abbey National introduced training in interpersonal skills and customer service. 'The emphasis here is that everyone has a customer. Training has undertaken most of the changes that have taken place over the last three years, namely training in business, appraisal and customer service.'[29]
- IBM (UK) Ltd launched a four-day residential course entitled 'Fit for the Future' aimed at working on ways of improving job performance through personal development. The programme is reproduced below:

  This four-day residential course, designed and used by IBM UK Ltd, does not aim to teach or develop specific skills. It offers participants an opportunity to step aside from the pressures of daily activities to do some intensive planning at a personal level which should enable them to make conscious choices about issues such as career options, personal motivation, ambitions and current priorities.

  Prerequisites
  At least one training course which develops interpersonal skills in a group environment.

  Participants must be committed to their own personal development and feel ready to go through a self analysis process.

  Not in the middle of a highly demanding work or personal situation.

  Prepared to share thoughts, feelings and aspirations in a group setting.

Objectives
'Fit for the future' uses techniques which are unfamiliar to most participants to enable them to:

- Build an inventory of personal strengths, values and patterns of motivation
- Recognise the missing factor when they are demotivated or without direction
- Be flexible and creative in their approach to work and career
- Value and use the strengths and differences of others
- Be able to recognise and reduce inner tensions and physical stress
- Re-evaluate aspirations and working style
- Implement an action plan incorporating changes arising from personal insight.

Method
This course can only be of value if both participant and participant's manager are willing and enthusiastic about working on ways of improving job performance through personal development.

Participants need to have an open and flexible attitude and be prepared to look inward for the learning that is offered.

Follow-up training is offered nine to 12 months later to evaluate and develop the personal action plan.[30]

- Boot's the Chemist have a 'quality initiative' programme 'which focuses on TQM principles and brings development activity centre-stage, involving everyone in a structured way in learning and identifying with a new approach to quality and the customer.'[31]

Training can be particularly valuable in culture change programmes because a consistent message can be communicated to large numbers of employees quickly. In performance improvement, in communicating strategic change, in quality enhancement, in developing IT awareness and other technical skills, and so on, the role of training in implementing the HR vision is vital.

## SUMMARY

Development strategies lie in the heart of the organisation's ability to implement changing business strategies and the components of the HR vision. Many of these components can be expressed in terms of competences – what is required to do the job effectively in the future. These competences will be a key ingredient in ensuring that subsequent training and development programmes are actually geared to what the organisation will require in the future. Processes of potential assessment, performance management and

# Development strategies

career management will rely on these competences. Each of the three processes has a role in ensuring that organisational objectives are met. Training is of key importance, especially when it relates closely to organisational and individual needs, users' personal development plans, open learning techniques and a focus on on-the-job training opportunities as well as off-the-job mechanisms to achieve training objectives. Managers in particular will not in future be able to rely on technical competence, but will need strategic vision and other personal qualities if they are to be successful. The HR vision will represent these trends, and be supported in turn by development strategies as described in this chapter.

## REFERENCES

1 RICHARD S. HANDSCOMBE and PHILIP A. NORMAN, *Strategic Leadership: The Missing Links*, McGraw-Hill, Maidenhead, 1989, p. 4.

2 SIR JOHN CASSELS, quoted in 'Towards a quality work force', *RSA Journal*, Vol. cxxxix, No. 5418, May 1991, p. 378.

3 *The Making of Managers: a Report on Management Education, Training and Development in the USA, West Germany, France, Japan and the UK*, NEDO/MSC/BIM, London, 1987, p. 13.

4 Starting point of the *Making of Managers* survey, cited by CHARLES HANDY in *Personnel Management*, May 1987, p. 8.

5 ROBIN JACOBS, 'Getting the measure of management competence', *Personnel Management*, June 1989, p. 33.

6 DEPARTMENT OF EMPLOYMENT, *Clarifying the Components of Management Competences*, HMSO, London, 1989, p. 1.

7 'The Training Commission's occupational standards programme', annex 3 of *Clarifying the Components of Management Competences, op. cit.*, p. 14.

8 GORDON McBEATH, *Practical Management Development: Strategies for Management Resourcing and Development in the 1990s*, Blackwell, Oxford, 1990, pp. 116–17.

9 *Ibid.*, p. 120.

10 HANDSCOMBE and NORMAN, *op. cit.*, p. 129.

11 VICTOR DULEWICZ, 'Assessment centres as the route to competence', *Personnel Management*, November 1989, pp. 57–8.

12 MICHAEL FINNEY and MARY ANN VON GLINOW, 'Integrating academic and organisational approaches to developing the international manager', *Journal of Management Development*, Vol. 7, No. 2, 1988, pp. 20–1.

13 *Clarifying the Components of Management Competences*, op. cit., pp. 4–5.

14 Cited by TONY COCKERILL in *Personnel Management*, September 1989, p. 55.

15 Cited by VICTOR DULEWICZ in *Personnel Management*, November 1989, p. 58.

16 ELIZABETH LUCAS, *Notes on the Standard Setting Process*, Insurance Industry Training Council, January 1991.

17 BARRY ALLEN, 'Corporate strategy and individual development in Hoechst UK', in MIKE PEDLAR, JOHN BURGOYNE, TOM BOYDELL and GLORIA WELSHMAN (eds.), *Self-development in Organisations*, McGraw-Hill, Maidenhead, 1990, pp. 124–5.

18 DAVID BARTRAM, 'Addressing the abuse of psychological tests', *Personnel Management*, April 1991, p. 34.

19 L. MACKAY and D. TORRINGTON, quoted by BARBARA TOWNLEY, 'Selection and appraisal: reconstituting "social relations" ', in JOHN STOREY, (ed.), *New Perspectives on Human Resources Management*, Routledge, London, 1991, p. 98.

20 JOHN MUMFORD and TONY BULEY, 'Rewarding behavioural skills as part of performance', *Personnel Management*, December 1988, p. 35.

21 LYNDA GRATTON and MICHAEL SYRETT, 'Heirs apparent: succession strategies for the future', *Personnel Management*, January 1991, p. 38.

22 See TRUDY COE and ANDREW STARK, *On the Move: Manager Mobility in the 1990s*, BIM, London, 1991, p. 8.

23 ALAN MUMFORD, *Developing Top Managers*, Gower Press, Farnborough, 1988, p. 16.

24 For further information on succession planning see WENDY HIRSH, '*Succession Planning: Current Practice and Future Issues*', IMS Report No. 184, IMS, Brighton, 1990.

*Development strategies*

25 TRAINING COMMISSION, 1988. For further information see J. BRAMHAM, *Human Resource Planning*, IPM, London, 1989, p. 36.

26 JOHN CONSTABLE and ROGER MCCORMICK, *The Making of British Managers*, a report for the BIM and CBI, April 1987, p. 22.

27 *The Making of Managers, op. cit.*, p. 18.

28 *Ibid.*, p. 38.

29 ALLAN WILLIAMS, PAUL DOBSON and MIKE WALTERS, *Changing Culture*, IPM, London, 1990, p. 147.

30 Cited by COLIN LEICESTER in *Personnel Management*, March 1989, p. 55.

31 EDGER WILLE, 'Should management development just be for managers?', *Personnel Management*, August 1990, p. 36.

CHAPTER 8

# Creating the right environment

The importance within an HR vision of creating the right working environment is now increasingly recognised. Dismissed by many commentators in the 1970s and 1980s as a mere hygiene factor, where people work and how they work – their pattern of working time – can help retention, improve communications and productivity, and lift morale generally. The place of work in particular can be an anachronistic reminder of features of an organisation's past. Chapter 5 emphasised the key link between company image and recruitment effectiveness. An eye-catching professional advert may have its effect nullified if the applicant arrives at dingy, old-fashioned premises. Staff working day by day in drab surroundings cannot help but be affected by them. Who has not witnessed the lift in spirits occasioned by moving into new offices or new manufacturing premises? It is very real. Similarly, the location of work can improve morale, absenteeism, timekeeping generally, and turnover rates. The relocation of many people out of London in recent years has been influenced by a number of factors, including costs. However, on moving from London, turnover rates can improve significantly, partly because staff avoid the long, tiring and expensive daily chore of commuting. While not all will warm to the 'quality of life' viewpoint arising from living in country districts, those HR Managers who have experienced relocation from a large conurbation will know that this is an important dimension for many staff. It is likely to feature more prominently in people's minds as housing costs, transport costs and crime rates continue to rise in large cities.

Employees are seeking, too, greater personal freedom in defining their working hours. Women 'returners' are, as chapter 5 has shown, very interested in working time flexibility to facilitate child care and the resumption of their careers. Staff generally are seeking to balance their personal and working lives better, and flexibility in the pattern of working hours is central to achieving this concern. Another major issue in this context is the desire for working time flexibility to look after elderly relatives. Demographic changes will ensure this is a pressing issue for many staff in the 1990s and beyond.

If maintaining a quality workforce requires the examination and implementation of strategies on the working environment and working time, the competitive and cost pressures on organisations in the 1990s must also be a fundamental consideration. This chapter will not advocate working time flexibility, or relocation, or improving the working environment, solely from an employee's perspective. Each of these areas has implications for the cost-

*Creating the right environment*

effective management of the organisation. It is possible to achieve both operational improvements as well as employee benefits from creating the right environment. This chapter explores these issues in the following order: working time flexibility; relocation; working environment.

## WORKING TIME FLEXIBILITY

There are several approaches to increasing working time flexibility, including: annual hours; flexi-time; part-time working (including part-time shift working); and job sharing. Each will be reviewed in turn.

### Annual hours

Organisations faced with variability in the supply of work have begun to implement annual hours contracts. Such variability in work requirements can arise from a seasonal pattern of demand. It can be seen most clearly in the food and drink sector, with, for example, summer or Christmas buying peaks. Other reasons for variation in work inputs are environmental factors (manufacturers of tumble dryers, for example, sell more of them in the winter) or budgetary cycles, which can influence, say, public-sector spending patterns.

With most employees working a fixed weekly number of hours, typically thirty-five, thirty-seven or thirty-nine, upward variability in work demands is traditionally met by overtime or building for stock. Downward variability may be countered by lay-offs under a guaranteed week agreement; more likely, 'waiting time' will simply occur. Organisations can also staff for lower work demands and recruit temporary staff to meet seasonal patterns. Semi-skilled temporary staff can cost between £500 and £1,000 each to recruit and train if lost output during the learning curve is taken into account.

Building for stock, where it is possible, will add to costs and has the added disadvantage that consumer tastes or technology may change in the short term, leading to the product being obsolete when it is pulled from stock to meet demand. Overtime working, too, can be costly[1] and over-reliance on it can reduce future flexibility to respond to further changes. It can and does become institutionalised, with detrimental effects on unit labour costs. Each organisation will also need to study the implications of overtime working on quality, absenteeism and accident rates. In manufacturing the average number of hours' overtime for those working it has stayed around nine a week for many years. Put another way, a third of the manual workforce in the UK works a six-day week throughout the year. Clearly, despite the cost and other implications, this is a pragmatic and preferred way for organisations to respond to changing work requirements.

So why develop an annual hours contract? It is useful to begin with a definition. Philip Lynch summarises thus:

The concept of annual hours is a simple one. Once the yearly hours of work are agreed between employer and employee it is then a matter of deciding how many of these hours should be committed to a rota schedule and what form it should take. Some of the hours may be held in reserve to be used when the employer and employee agree, or they may all be used within the schedule. The rota schedules themselves may be fixed or variable. All the hours outside the annual hours commitment are by definition leisure hours and no distinction need be made between different forms of leisure time, for example, annual holidays and rest days. The result is a very flexible framework for the organisation of working time.[2]

The emphasis is firmly on the employer identifying the underlying variability of work across the week/month/year and agreeing with employees a suitable annual hours arrangement to match working time better to these operational requirements.

Varying basic hours of work can be handled in many different ways. For example, by varying the length of the working day or the number of days/shifts worked across the year. A typical example here is the tumble dryer manufacturer Crosslee, which introduced a working week in the winter months of forty-three hours and in summer of thirty-two hours. This equated to a thirty-nine hour working week throughout the year. Figure 27 shows the pattern of sales and the way flexibility of working time adjusted production levels.

Another consumer goods manufacturer with similar seasonal work demands introduced variability in the length of the working week, from thirty-four hours to forty-two and a half hours. Figure 28 shows the effect on production (a) before and (b) after introducing variability of working time. Overtime working, commercial stock holding and the deployment of temporary staff will still be required to meet the peak of trade demand. However, as Fig.28(b) demonstrates, there is a much better alignment between production and trade requirements under the annualised arrangements.

Having identified the possible approach to an annual hours scheme, consideration must briefly be given to the various elements of such a contract, including: the period of notice; handling overtime; handling holidays/sick pay; and payment.

## Periods of notice

As the focus is on variability across the year, where possible the working time requirements should be set out in a 'year plan'. This could operate on a calendar year basis, but does not need to. As it is unlikely that the supply of work can be predicted so far ahead with any degree of accuracy, management will need to reserve the right to vary the schedule. Although, in many instances, such variations would be desirable at very short notice in order to ensure that services/output are most responsive to customer requirements, in practice such responsiveness is difficult to realise in a formal way with large

*Creating the right environment* 147

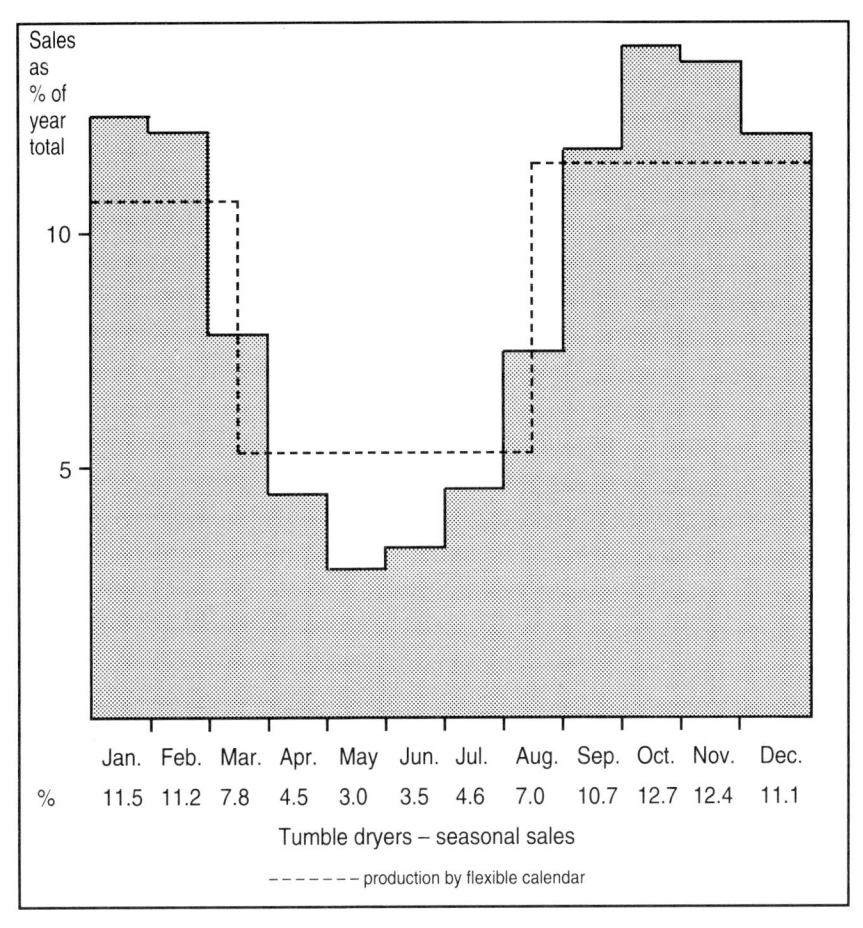

**Fig. 27. The sales and production pattern at a manufacturer of consumer durables.**

From *Industrial Relations Review and Report*, 17 February 1987

| | Jan. | Feb. | Mar. | Apr. | May | Jun. | Jul. | Aug. | Sep. | Oct. | Nov. | Dec. |
|---|---|---|---|---|---|---|---|---|---|---|---|---|
| % | 11.5 | 11.2 | 7.8 | 4.5 | 3.0 | 3.5 | 4.6 | 7.0 | 10.7 | 12.7 | 12.4 | 11.1 |

Tumble dryers – seasonal sales
– – – – – – – production by flexible calendar

groups of employees. Individuals may always be prepared to respond flexibly at very short notice. For the operation of an annual hours contract, however, employees and their trade unions may demand a longer notice period prior to introducing variations on the 'year plan'. This is a matter for discussion with each organisation, and the notice periods will differ depending on the importance of volume responsiveness to changing customer requirements, the predictability of the supply of work and the extent of flexibility in working time sought under the contract.

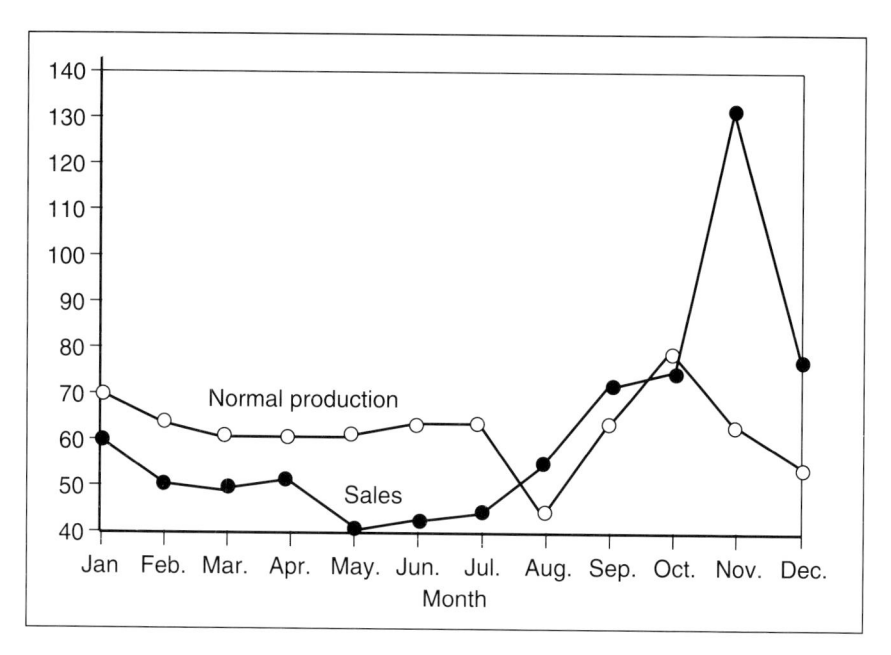

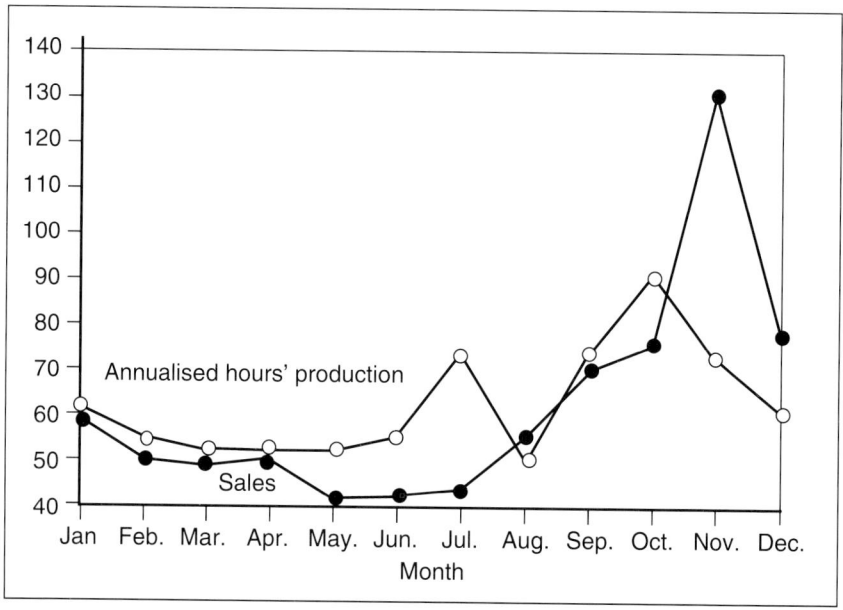

**Fig. 28.** Annual hours worked at a manufacturer of consumer durables: level of output (a) before the introduction of annual hours, and (b) after annualisation

## Creating the right environment

### Overtime

This is a major issue for both management and employees. For management the annual hours contract, by flexibly relating basic working hours to operational requirements, can, as has been stated, cut overtime costs. For employees overtime is an important aspect of take-home pay, one which may be virtually guaranteed for those who wish to work it. How is this conflict to be resolved? With difficulty, certainly, but there are negotiating possibilities. Undoubtedly trade union representatives will seek to maintain the payment of overtime premiums for hours worked above the current daily standard – say, 7·8 hours. Management will argue that the overtime premium is payable only for hours above the upper limit set in the schedule – say nine to ten hours per day. One possible compromise would be for overtime premiums to be paid for hours worked above those planned in the schedule. Thus if six hours are planned but 7·5 hours worked, 1·5 hours would be payable at the relevant overtime premium. This has the effect of imposing a discipline on technical and commercial management to set the plan at the appropriate level. Where the position is unpredictable such that 'discipline' is impossible to maintain with any accuracy, a more flexible approach allowing the carry-over of hours from one period to another is desirable.

### Holidays/sick pay

Assuming holidays are taken from the hours set in the schedule, handling such holiday taking will depend on the current definition of days of holiday within the organisation. Where a holiday is defined as a fifth of the standard working week – e.g. 7·8 hours for a thirty-nine hour week – then one option is to maintain this definition, even if the length of the standard working day varies considerably. In this approach, a holiday on a day scheduled for six hours' working would still count as one 'day' of holiday entitlement. This option has the obvious disadvantage, however, of encouraging the taking of holidays when longer days are being worked – and this will be in the period of greatest operational demands, when holiday-taking would most likely be discouraged. Jointly determined rules may then be required to minimise holiday-taking in the high period.

The alternative approach involves calculating holidays on an annual basis, in hourly units. Thus an entitlement to twenty-five days' annual leave in an organisation working a thirty-nine-hour week (7·8 hours per day) would provide 195 hours of holiday per year. Holidays of six hours, nine hours and so on would be aggregated towards this annual target. This sounds complicated, and many managers will understandably wish to avoid such an approach for administrative reasons. In this approach too, rules may still be needed to limit holiday-taking during the periods of extensive working. Such rules could include:

- Specifying a maximum number of days of holiday to be taken per month in the high period.
- Fixing days of holiday in the slack periods.
- Creating a 'window' during which holiday-taking is encouraged.

*Payment*
Variability in the length of the basic working day or week need not result in variation in basic pay levels. Difficulties may arise, however, in respect of starters and leavers, and in organisations with performance-related bonus arrangements. When 'new starts' join an organisation in the slack period, and receive the benefit of shorter working periods or shift-free days, and leave before the period of extended working, should some attempt be made to 'claim back' this advantage? A 'swings and roundabouts' effect may operate across the year, with employees also joining or leaving in the high period. If it is felt to be too coarse to rely on this averaging effect, then adjustments to pay will be needed, at the point of leaving, to take into account actual hours worked compared with payment received.

Turning to organisations with a variable bonus arrangement, while this presents little problem for periods of shorter or longer working days, it may be necessary to generate an 'average' bonus payment for shift-free days. Such averages are not unusual, and often apply to periods of holidays.

*Annual hours as a retention strategy*
Significant savings were established in the examples quoted above in overtime costs, the cost of holding stock and in the reduced deployment of temporary staff. Equally important from the viewpoint of retention strategies is the popularity among employees of such approaches. This factor arises from the increased opportunities for leisure time that occur in annual hours approaches. The longer hours are matched by 'shift-free' days, sometimes Fridays, sometimes aggregated in the slack period to form longer periods of free time. Such blocks of time off can be very popular, especially if the slack time occurs in the summer months. Not so attractive to employees of ice cream manufacturers! Personnel managers who have sought to introduce twelve-hour shift working on a 'four shifts on/four shifts off' basis will also know the popularity of this type of shift working. There are disadvantages for employees, including a potential loss of overtime earnings. However, experience suggests that the opportunities of involving employees in deciding the pattern of work and the extra blocks of free time can outweigh for the work group overall the disadvantages of loss of overtime earnings and, perhaps, such domestic difficulties as may arise in managing the working time variability. For management the cost savings, allied to greater responsiveness to customer needs, can significantly improve productivity. It can also be a major catalyst to the introduction of wider reforms.[3]

## Flexi-time

Whereas annual hours arrangements are employer-initiated, to reduce costs and improve responsiveness, flexi-time arrangements have generally been introduced as part of a recruitment and retention strategy. Typically, em-

## Creating the right environment

ployees are free to vary their personal starting and finishing times provided they work during a defined core period. Overall, an agreed number of hours must be worked within a set period. Employees may be allowed to build up credit hours over the contractual norm which are 'carried over' to be taken as 'flexi-days' in subsequent periods.

Flexi-time schemes are popular with staff and allow them a measure of discretion over working time.[4] Specifically, travel and domestic arrangements can be better managed under a flexi-time scheme, and as was noted above the opportunities to gain extra days' leave can be very motivational. Of course, there are disadvantages to employers. They can be summarised thus:

- Staff may, to the frustration of others (especially customers), be legitimately missing at times when impromptu meetings are called, or important events occur, outside core hours.
- Schemes which allow accrued hours can, if uncontrolled, lead to enormous numbers of hours theoretically owing to staff. As a result, most schemes are removing or limiting accrued hours.
- Control over starting and finishing times can slip unless supervisors are carefully monitoring the scheme. Electronic checking has assisted overall control in recent years.
- Flexi-time schemes are difficult to apply to certain groups, including managers, and manual workers, especially where the manual tasks are machine-controlled. Applying flexi-time only to 'staff' can be internally divisive and lead to boundary problems.

Flexible working hours schemes remain popular[5] and are likely to be retained, especially as new technology impacts upon clerical jobs. Flexi-time arrangements can be more advantageous in a context of VDU working or in other jobs where there is little scope for discretion in the pace or content of work.

Flexi-time schemes, however, may now include certain features which attempt to deal with some of the disadvantages:

- Defined minimum staffing levels are introduced for all time bands.
- Core hours may be extended.
- The necessity always to respect the 'needs of the business' is re-emphasised. Managers may therefore override the flexi-time scheme should circumstances demand it.
- The maximum number of debit/credit hours is limited, often to eight. These can only be carried forward one accounting period, and cannot be taken as a full day.

Despite such tightening, flexi-time schemes remain popular because they assist staff in transport and commuting arrangements, child care and other domestic responsibilities.[6]

## Part-time working

Part-time working continues to increase in the UK. As one IDS study in mid-1990 put it, 'The number of employees working part-time in Britain continued to grow throughout the 1980s, expanding by almost a million between September 1981 and December 1989.' The proportion of part-time employees as a proportion of all employees grew from 19·1 per cent in 1978 to 24·2 per cent in December 1989. Eight in ten part-timers are women, and more than two-fifths of women employees work part-time.[7]

Why part-time working? There are at least seven main reasons:

- Employers can match working hours to operational requirements better.
- The personal circumstances of key staff can be accommodated through part-time working. This will be particularly relevant to women returners.
- The productivity of part-timers is generally higher than that of full-timers (hardly surprising, since work is undertaken in more concentrated time periods).
- The absence levels of part-timers are generally lower – domestic requirements can more easily be fitted into the free periods in the part-time schedule.
- A pool of trained employees is available for switching to full-time work, or extending working time temporarily.
- Difficulties in recruiting full-time staff have prompted organisations to recruit and train part-time staff. 'Women returners' are more likely to be atttracted to an organisation if the hours of work are suitable, which will generally mean part-time working.
- Part-time working can cut overtime costs, since it makes it possible to avoid paying premium rates.

Part-time working in clerical activities is typically on a 9.00–13.00 : 14.00–18.00 hours basis. In principle, however, part-time working between 06.00 and 22.00 can be managed by a variety of combinations as shown in Fig. 29.

The forms of part-time working are many and varied, including:

- 'Twilight' shifts: 17.00–21.30 hours (Monday–Friday or Monday–Thursday).
- Two six-hour shifts: 06.00–12.30 and 12.00–18.30.
- Three four-hour or three five-hour shifts, e.g. 07.00–12.30 (thirty-minute break), 12.00–18.30, 18.00–00.30, 00.00–06.30.
- One week on, one week off. Two weeks on, two weeks off.
- 'Minimum–maximum' contract, e.g. twenty hours' minimum, twenty-five hours' maximum. (The extra five hours are at the discretion of the manager or supervisor and subject to a defined period of notice.) An offer letter is illustrated as follows.

*Creating the right environment* 153

*Minimum/maximum contract: offer letter*

Dear

Your hours of work will be a minimum of ........ hours per week, worked to the following times:
........ a.m. to ........ p.m. Monday to Thursday
and
........ a.m. to ........ p.m. Friday.
On each of these days there will be a break of ........ minutes. Under the terms of your Contract of Employment you may also be required to work a further ........ hours per week. The necessity to work these extra hours will be determined by management, and you will be given five working days' notice of the requirement. These extra hours may be worked in a block of separate units. You will not be required contractually to work above ........ hours per week, although there may be opportunities for overtime on a voluntary basis from time to time.

Your standard working week will therefore vary between a minimum of ........ hours and a maximum of ........ hours. Payment of salary will be at the rate of £ ........ per hour for all hours worked.

- 'Displaced' working week or day, e.g.
  daily: 10.00–18.00 (not 09.00–17.00); weekly: Tuesday–Saturday (not Monday–Friday).
- Saturday/Sunday contract.
- Friday/Saturday/Sunday contract.
- Friday or Saturday or Sunday or Monday *only* contract.

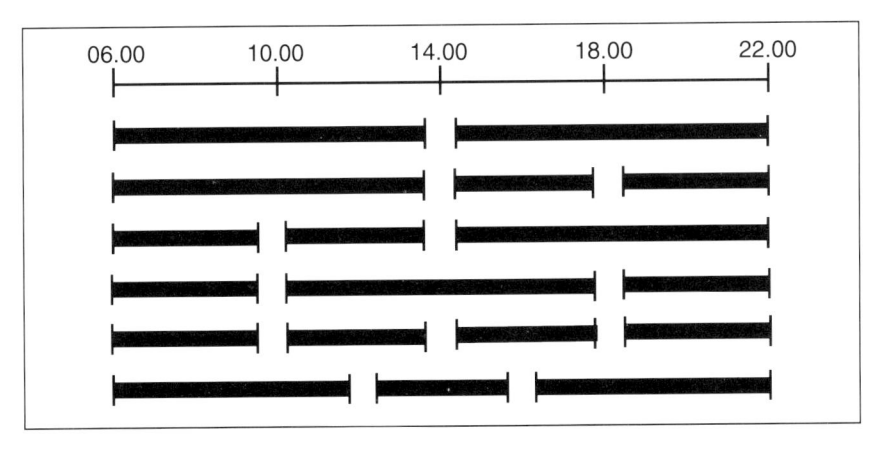

**Fig. 29. Part-time working: sixteen-hour working between 06.00 and 22.00 hours can be achieved by a variety of part-time combinations**

There are problems in part-time working. As one study put it:

> If part-time work is used in the lower end of the labour market there exists the possible danger of aggravating the polarisation into primary and secondary labour markets . . . the fact remains that he/she is in a weaker position on the labour market. . . . The 'second-class' stigma attached to much part-time work needs to be removed if real options are to be opened up.[8]

The 'second-class' stigma mentioned here is a danger, despite movements towards equalising *pro rata* terms and conditions of employment. There are also well known difficulties in recruiting for certain part-time hours. Generally, however, as both a flexible employer response to changing operational requirements and as a recruitment and retention device with real relevance, part-time working has considerable importance in creating and maintaining a quality workforce.

## Job sharing

Closely related to part-time working is job sharing. More frequently discussed than implemented, it offers a number of advantages and disadvantages:

### Advantages

- Opportunity to cover all holiday absence in a contractual way.
- Opportunity to cover long-term sickness, and possibly short-term sickness, in a contractual way.
- Absence levels may be lower, with commitments covered by periods off work. (The absence levels of part-timers are less than those of full-timers anyway.)
- Performance levels are likely to be higher because of shorter periods at work.
- Can use job-sharing partners to expand output quickly if required.
- Job-sharers are likely to be more co-operative and responsive to change.

### Disadvantages

- Marginal extra recruitment costs.
- Some extra training costs – both at the point of recruitment and subsequently as products/technology change.
- Job-sharers may be incompatible.
- Job-sharers may be perceived as 'second-class' employees.
- Communications become more complex.
- If one sharer leaves there may be difficulties in replacing her/him with compatible partner.

## Creating the right environment

- Allocation of overtime between partners and between job-sharers and full-time staff will need careful handling.
- It may not attract male unemployed because of the relationship between part-time salary and state benefits.[9]

For staff, job sharing offers similar advantages to part-time working, with possibly the added status of being in a divided full-time job and of working as a partner with a close colleague. Employers need to consider carefully which jobs can be shared. In practice, recruitment and retention issues will be the main reasons for introducing job sharing, as limited job share measures, for example amongst midwives, nursing staff or health visitors in the NHS have demonstrated.[10]

## RELOCATION

The onerous and costly business of commuting long distances to and from work has been a factor behind certain working time changes referred to above. Relocating all or part of the organisation can significantly reduce travel to work, cost and time, and is one of the more welcome dimensions of relocation from an employee's viewpoint. If, however, this is a plus, there are more worrying features which can result in the loss of key staff. This section reviews why and how organisations relocate, and examines the main issues.

### Why relocate?

Difficulties in the recruitment and retention of quality staff are likely to be an important reason for relocating, but not the main reason. The latter will include:

- Running out of space in the old location.
- The difficulties of the current location in handling new technology, or a newly required work layout.
- The costs of remaining in the current location, especially with city-centre rents and the need for other payments such as a London allowance.

The decision to relocate is a complex one, with enormous ramifications for the business. The decision must balance the cost of the move itself (including costs of the new premises as well as costs of relocation and redundancy payments for those not relocating) and the disruption to the business as staff relocate or leave, against the space problems, recruitment and retention difficulties facing the organisation and the cost of *not* relocating. Many organisations have relocated in recent years, and one estimate is that 10,000 jobs will move each year from central London.[11] Organisations relocating include the Department of Employment (800 posts from London to Runcorn, Sheffield and Bootle), BP Oil (700 from London to Hemel Hempstead), Lloyd's Bank (1,400 from London to Bristol), TSB Trust Company (200 jobs from Andover to Newport, Gwent), Shell Chemicals (from London to Chester), Pearl Assurance (from London and regional offices to Peterborough, affecting around 1,500 jobs).

Others have announced their intention to relocate., Some of the above organisations placed considerable emphasis on recruitment and retention difficulties. For example:

> In recent years, the TSB Trust realised that growth in the Andover labour force would not match the rate of growth in the Company's business and its demand for clerical staff. By 1986 it had also become clear that the number of school leavers would decline over coming years. The limit on the number of staff Andover could provide was estimated to be in the region of 2000 and this maximum would be reached in 1989/90 . . . Consequently the Company decided to relocate its operation to a more favoured location.[12]

Similarly, National Provident Institution, which relocated from Tunbridge Wells to Cardiff, said, 'We did our sums and realised the growth in the market meant we had to expand. But it was clear from our labour force projections that we would not get that growth in Tunbridge Wells.'[13]

Despite higher unemployment and a short-term easing of such recruitment problems in the early 1990s, medium-term projections for the labour force coupled with the powerful cost and space factors will continue to ensure that relocation remains a force in the 1990s.

## Managing the Move

'As with the domestic move, relocation is an event that scores high on the Richter scale of grief.'[14] It is vital that three key organisational steps are first taken to manage the relocation.

1. Appoint a project manager. This key person must have the ability, drive and experience to manage the diverse, complex interpersonal and political issues that will arise. The project manager must be able to master the issue of electricity supply to meet business needs as well as counselling, coaching key senior staff on the merits of the area and housing into which the company is moving. You need a high-quality individual to co-ordinate all the different functions and departments that will be required to relocate. This appointment is possibly the single most vital decision after the decision to relocate itself has been taken.

2. Appoint a steering committee. The steering committee will support the project manager and have overall accountability for the success of the venture. It will include representatives from the lines of business affected, as well as functional specialists such as architects, facilities management, legal, personnel and finance. Sub-committees under this steering committee can take specific responsibility for detailed logistics and planning activities.

# Creating the right environment

3. Appoint a relocation office. The office will consist of trained counsellors and administrative staff dedicated to supporting the relocation effort.

Having established this project organisation, and assuming new premises have been identified, the project manager will need to address a variety of key issues, including:

- Identifying the optimum use of space and provision of services in the new building. Specifically, the IT demands of the business need to be carefully considered.
- Considering the numbers, levels and requirements of staff and managers to be accommodated in the new premises.
- Defining the timing of departmental moves to the new premises, both to protect business as usual and to allow services to accommodate the staff in the new building.
- Considering individual needs and aspirations. For large relocation exercises a questionnaire to all staff seeking views on their intentions will be necessary, assuming all staff are being offered a job. Where only certain selected staff are being relocated, their individual views will need to be identified.
- Defining HR policy on the terms and conditions of those relocating. Where there are no jobs left in the original location, the terms of redundancy/early retirement will need to be defined. In a unionised environment, negotiations with the affected union(s) must be planned.
- Managing communications to all employees affected. From the viewpoint of managing key skills this is a most important aspect of any relocation. The full range of communications and consultative techniques should be deployed to encourage as many key staff as possible to relocate with the organisation. The techniques include:
  - Videos and information pack on the reason for relocation and the advantages of the new premises.
  - Letters to all staff explaining the background and process of the exercise.
  - Regular monthly written communication to all affected staff, keeping them up to date with the relocation timetable, and continuing to emphasise the attraction of the new premises.
  - Individual counselling sessions on education and housing issues.
  - One-day rail and road trips to the new location for groups of staff.
  - Briefings from internal and external sources on the new area. Local development corporation resources can be invaluable here.
  - Distributing copies of union-negotiated statements on terms, with full managerial briefings.

## Relocation terms

HR Managers interested in the detail of relocation terms should check the publications available.[15] They cover the terms available to groups or to individuals required to move from one area to another. The basic components of any relocation move are:

1. To encourage key staff to relocate, some form of assistance is necessary. This can include:

- A fixed monetary upper limit for expenses actually incurred, subject to receipts being provided. This allowance is normally tax-free.
- An agreed 'disturbance allowance' which is paid on relocation irrespective of actual expenditure. It may be defined as a percentage of basic salary (say 10 per cent) or as a monetary amount. Where a percentage is applied there is usually a monetary offer to assist lower-paid staff. This payment is normally taxable.

Both payments can, of course, be made. 'Claw-back' clauses in the event of the member of staff leaving within a defined period can be included.

2. With the housing market in a depressed state, moving key staff may also require a 'chain-breaking' clause. This means the company will buy the employee's house either directly or via a property agency such as Black Horse. The 'chain-breaking' price is generally fixed as the mid-point of two independent valuations. Whilst such a benefit obviously adds considerably to the cost of relocation, it may be the most important factor in persuading a key employee to remain with the organisation and relocate to the new premises. The same policy may also apply to the recruitment of key staff.

3. Other costs which can be reimbursed include:

- Legal costs of sale and house purchase.
- Estate agent's fees (sometimes with an upper limit defined to encourage shopping around).
- Building society fees and private survey fees (again with a fixed sum defined in advance).
- Stamp duty and land registry fees.
- Bridging loans – say up to six months.
- Removal expenses.
- Cost of storage of possessions if necessary.
- Allowance for travel and overnight expenses whilst house hunting.
- Costs of maintaining unsold property.

In those circumstances where an organisation is relocating all the operation, care needs to be taken to ensure that the relocation terms are not inferior to the redundancy/early retirement package. Those who cannot relocate still need the protection of a reasonable package. This is a difficult balance to achieve. Alongside redundancy/early retirement terms, counselling and other forms of assistance will be necessary for those staff not relocating. The steps taken by Pearl Assurance in this area are shown below:

1. We will help identify through individual counselling, the skills and experience of each individual who wishes to find alternative employment outside of the Pearl.

2. We will help identify individual's preferred career direction and target particular sectors of the labour market. Interviews with other companies will be arranged where possible.

3. We will provide information on specific jobs available in the relevant areas. Such information will be provided to us by the Department of Employment.

4. We will provide information on part-time and full-time training courses available.

5. We will provide skills training in writing CVs and in handling job interviews where these needs are identified.

6. We will provide reasonable paid time off for individuals to attend job interviews.

7. We will continue with counselling (if necessary) until the date of termination of employment with Pearl.

8. We will provide advice and guidance to individuals on taxation, DHSS and other Government benefits which are available.

9. Management have agreed that those members of staff who, although available for employment, remain unemployed at the expiration of the 12-month period (during which the current terms provide for the 4 per cent concessionary mortgage interest to continue), will have that concession extended for the period for which they remain employed.

You will appreciate that at this stage our efforts will be directed to persuading individuals to relocate with us to Peterborough. However, in the latter part of 1988, once the counselling processes on relocation are completed, we can then turn our attention to the above initiatives to assist staff who wish to seek alternative employment.

## Relocation issues

If relocation can make a significant impact on managing key skills by improving retention of staff and facilitating easier recruitment, it can create major problems too:

- Protecting the flow of business during the move.
- Maintaining the morale of staff who have decided not to relocate.
- Managing the recruitment and retraining exercise necessary in the new premises.
- Handling the complex logistics problems, especially if there are delays in completing the new premises.
- Controlling the cost of the exercise.

Experience suggests that organisations can expect 20–25 per cent of their staff at lower levels to relocate, 60–75 per cent at the technical and managerial levels. Since it may anyway be cheaper to recruit new lower-level staff in the local labour market than relocate, HR Managers may not object to this. It all depends, of course, on who leaves the company. If all the more experienced staff who are more easily marketable leave, the consequences for 'business as usual' could be serious. Similarly, while more managers can be expected to stay with the organisation (pension being a key retention device here) even losing 25 per cent can be very damaging. This reinforces the earlier stated view that massive efforts need to be devoted to individual counselling and communications to key staff.

With possibly 75 per cent of clerical or semi-skilled staff leaving the organisation, retaining them in the old location until the new staff are fully operational is yet another difficulty. Redundancy and early retirement terms should be payable only if the individual leaves at the date set by management., For longer-service staff whose severance terms will be higher this is a powerful device. It is less persuasive to junior staff. Organisations have added other 'loyalty bonuses' to end-pay to assist with this problem.

With staff waiting to go, and new staff being recruited and trained, the 'old staff' can assist in retraining in the new location, and can be temporarily accommodated in the new premises. However, with both groups in employment there is 'double manning' for a time. This is expensive and tends to be an underestimated cost of relocation.

In summary, relocation can give an organisation more cost-effective space, premises designed for its needs, and staff with lower turnover and higher morale. It will take vision, courage and problem-solving skills of the highest order to realise these advantages in full.

## THE WORKING ENVIRONMENT

Relocation provides the opportunity to create a new working environment. Without this opportunity it is still possible to refurbish existing premises. This is a costly option but organisations are increasingly having to redesign their premises as a result of growth in information technology and organisational changes.

> What's new is that organisations are setting up IT networks between and within buildings; they are installing up to one or more computer terminals per desk; new technologies like compact disc data storage and videos are coming in, while other seemingly modern technologies become obsolete and are phased out. What's also new is the rate of organisational change. Thus organisations can have what is called a churn rate – the number of people moving location within the building per year – approaching or even exceeding 100 per cent. This is not just

## Creating the right environment

A taking B's seat. It is a continual reorganising of people on a project basis and this requires continual reorganising of space.[16]

The logistics issues are enormous – moving partitions, reorganising power supplies and lighting to handle IT networks, reconnecting telephone lines and so on. Many older buildings cannot be repartitioned in this way, or at least not without high costs. No wonder Facilities Management is a function rapidly gaining credibility!

Much work is currently being undertaken on modelling buildings, to match buildings better to both organisational requirements and the needs of the staff themselves.[17] Again IT requirements are likely to be at the fore from a business viewpoint. From an HR perspective, building design provides the opportunity to provide for staff interaction informally. The design of the new British Airways Terminal at Heathrow has been reported as showing BA's desire to use architectural resources to achieve corporate goals, including supporting an open management style.[18] In this, American experience has pointed the way. Steelcare Stafor's Corporate Development Centre in Michigan was designed:

> To encourage people to stop and talk to each other, and to wander away from their desk to go and see what someone else is doing. The concept starts in the foyer, which has been christened 'the Town Square' because everybody has to pass through it to both enter and leave the building. Each floor has balconies overlooking it which encourages the feeling of being part of a community.[19]

There are 'productive coffee areas', areas for 'management clusters' and other spaces for interaction. The object is to provide an environment enabling 'creative thought and design'. Interestingly, this building has been designed to accommodate a matrix form of organisation in that functional 'neighbourhoods' overlap in open-plan areas. Each interdisciplinary group also has a separate project room near its open-plan area.

Open-plan offices have their critics, not least because of difficulties in concentration and the need, certainly of first-line management, for privacy when conducting appraisal or disciplinary interviews. In an open-plan office, private rooms must therefore continue to be available, and partitioning can reduce disruption from other areas of the office.

If design can support business goals, it can also support retention through the provision of desirable facilities. These facilities can include the following:

*Shops on site.* These can sell convenience foods as well as standard confectionery. There are examples of travel agents, florists, video hire shops and hairdressers being provided on site. On-site shops will be of greater importance in buildings remote from a shopping centre. In business parks such shops can be shared between various companies. It is usual to subcontract the management of these company shops.

*Banks.* Banks will be willing to provide a limited on-site presence if the number of potential customers justifies the capital and running costs. On-site cash dispensers are, however, increasingly the option preferred by the banks. Philips Business Systems are reported as having installed sixty 'staff cash' points in three years. Installation costs are £20,000, running costs approximately £2,000 per annum.[20] Careful consideration needs to be given to the location of these facilities.

*Sports facilities.* On-site sports facilities are popular with staff and increasingly seen by organisations as relevant to enhancing staff productivity, and reducing absenteeism by encouraging staff fitness. Even without a swimming pool they can be costly investments, but the investment can be extremely worthwhile. The advantages do not just arise from a healthy workforce, vital though that is. Staff are more likely to interact cross-functionally and at all hierarchical levels in a sporting context. The support and team spirit arising can be vital to the maintenance of a quality workforce. Arrangements for sports do not have to rely on purpose-built centres. Local schools or sports clubs can be persuaded to share their facilities in the early evening, and lunchtime jogging routes can be easily established.

*Health.* The provision of on-site medical and dental facilities is also increasing. Preventive medicine seminars can be held and screening arrangements introduced. They can cover subjects such as breast cancer and cervical smear testing. This is another area that will be a focus of greater attention in the 1990s.

*Library and archive.* Important for encouraging self-development and in the archive presenting the history of the organisation. Library facilities can support the company communications programmes.

*Staff restaurants.* A key benefit. Extra attention is being given to the effective design of such restaurants to provide a relaxing but efficient environment. Single-status restaurant facilities have been largely accepted as the preferred approach to dining for the 1990s.

Not all staff have a place of work which can include such facilities. Home working has increased, and developments in 'lap top' computers will lead to even greater flexibility. This reinforces the need for organisations to respond creatively to building design, especially if the building may not be needed in future!

## SUMMARY

Creating the right environment is more than an important staff benefit: it provides opportunities for increasing productivity and customer responsiveness. It is also a vital component in the HR vision. Working time flexibility, including part-time working and annual hours arrangements, can enable overtime and other costs to be reduced whilst better matching working time to customer demand. At the same time, employees value the increased blocks of free time which can arise in these innovative arrangements. Part-time working allows women returners in particular to manage the resumption of their career and child care needs better. These working time arrangements can also improve individuals' quality of life, a subjective concept admittedly, but one which embraces travelling time and location of work. Relocation from city centres can have similar advantages whilst providing the organisation with improved space and savings on rents, rates and location allowances. New premises can be designed to support corporate objectives, including improved communications. A working environment which includes a fitness centre, medical facilities, library and other components can be incorporated. Organisations lacking the scale to support such benefits can still take steps to improve the working environment of their staff, with pay-offs in lower absenteeism levels, and higher morale and productivity generally.

## REFERENCES

1 See, for example, PHILIP LYNCH, 'The abuse of overtime', *Industrial Society*, December 1985, p. 22.

2 PHILIP LYNCH, 'Annual hours – an idea whose time has come', *Personnel Management*, November 1988, p. 46. See also STEPHEN CONNOCK, 'Workforce flexibility – juggling time and task', *Personnel Management*, October 1985, pp. 36–8.

3 The point is elaborated by PHILIP LYNCH, 'Making time for productivity', *Personnel Management*, March 1991, pp. 30–5. See also CHRIS CURSON (ed.) *Flexible Patterns of Work*, IPM, London 1986, pp. 50–8.

4 The evidence is reviewed in PAUL BLYTON, *Changes in Working Time – an International Review*, Croom Helm, Beckenham, 1985, pp. 125–36.

5 See ACAS, *Labour Flexibility in Britain*, Occasional Paper No. 41, ACAS, London, 1987.

6 See the survey in IRS *Employment Trends* 453, 5 December 1989, pp. 5–9.

7 IDS, *Part-time Workers*, Study No. 459, June 1990, p. 8.

8 LEI DELSON, 'European trade unions and the flexible workforce', *Industrial Relations Journal*, Vol. 21, No. 4, winter 1990, p. 269.

9 C. BREWSTER and S. L. CONNOCK, *Industrial Relations: Cost-effective Strategies*, Hutchinson, London, 1985, p. 117.

10 *Job Sharing*, IDS Study, No. 440, August 1989, p. 2.

11 Jones Lang Wootton prediction quoted in *Office Environment*, March 1990, p. 22.

12 As reported in *Group Relocation*, IDS Study No. 448, December 1989, p. 17.

13 Quoted in David Lucas, 'Assured move', *Personnel Today*, 22 January 1991, p. 33.

14 Wendy Smith, 'Home truths about moving away', *Office Environment*, March 1990, p. 23.

15 See for example, IRS *Employment Trends*, No. 432, 'Relocation Survey 1: Background and trends', 24 January 1989; No. 433, 'Relocation Survey 2: High-cost moves', 7 February 1989; No. 436, 'Relocation Survey 3: Controlling costs, administration and eligibility', 21 March 1989; No. 437, 'Relocation Survey 4: Scheme basics, bridging loans and disturbance allowances', 4 April 1989.

16 Barrie Evans, 'Smarter than the average building', *Management Today*, December 1990, p. 39.

17 See, for example, John Rawson, 'Modelling buildings and users', *Architects' Journal*, 22, 29 August 1990, pp. 40–3.

18 Frank Duffy, 'Masters of change', *Architects' Journal*, 13 June 1990, p. 31.

19 Elizabeth Daly, 'A living experiment', *Premises Management*, January 1990, p. 15.

20 Sue Bloodworth, 'Workers' playtime', *Office Environment*, July 1990, p. 18.

CHAPTER 9

# Conclusions: implementing HR strategies

It is a common failure in organisations that fine plans are produced but almost nothing changes. Why is this? There are many reasons. Staff can become cynical if there are a succession of new initiatives, each announced with much aplomb but little follow-through. If senior management appear more interested in presentation than in substance, why should anyone else bother? In addition, and more fundamentally, there will be concern over personal security and individual power arising from new visions and strategies. Igor Ansoff[1] has summarised well the circumstances in which managers will resist change, which include:

- when managers are uncertain about the impact and implications of the change;
- when they are called upon to take risks which are uncongenial to them;
- when managers feel that the change may make them redundant;
- when they feel incompetent to perform in the new role defined by the change;
- when they feel they will lose 'face' with their peers; and
- when they are incapable and/or unwilling to learn new skills and behaviour.

There may be some individuals who lack the necessary skills, adaptability and openmindedness to embrace the changes signalled in the HR vision. If they have skills which can be utilised, all well and good, although this would presumably not be in a 'change-agent' capacity. Otherwise the HR Manager may need to develop a training plan or, alternatively, if the difficulties are more fundamental, an out-placement strategy. Enhanced early retirement schemes can be the most effective and acceptable mechanism for managing individuals who cannot adjust to the new organisational requirements.

So what other steps can senior managers take to ensure that real change takes place consistent with the HR vision? Philip Sadler[2] discussed this question by suggesting the following options:

- Discussion, debate and modification of the mission until it meets with general agreement.
- Develop simple statements of core values – the simpler the better.

- Provide details of the standards of performance and behaviour required.
- Intensive communication, using all possible channels.
- Integrate the desired changes into training and induction programmes.
- The behaviour of top management must exemplify the new culture.
- Decisions on recruitment, transfers and promotion must reflect the norms of the new culture.
- Use symbols, logos and other devices to reinforce change.

The importance of effective communication is clearly underlined in these options.

The chairman of General Electric has been quoted as saying, 'Without question, communicating the vision, and the atmosphere around the vision, has been, and is continuing to be, by far the toughest job we face.'[3] This chapter on implementing the HR vision and strategies therefore begins with a review of effective communication.

## COMMUNICATIONS

Most HR Managers will recognise the central importance of effective communication to the management of change. Most will wish to emphasise the importance of involvement, as well as communication, to building commitment to the vision and strategies at all levels of the organisation. Many techniques can be adopted for this purpose, including:

*Use of multi-disciplinary project teams.* These can add value by testing out in detail the dimensions of the vision, and developing associated strategies. They can be crucial to the success of the change project and can develop among the participants a sense of shared purpose, a commitment to change, a trust and an enthusiasm for the direction of change which can be harnessed to the benefit of the organisation overall. As Gerry Johnson and Kevan Scholes put it, 'individuals are likely to become not only identified with and party to the changes but also involved in the partial implementation of those changes; it may be that they go back into their functional operations as disciples of change'.[4]

*'Disciples of change', 'change agents', 'ambassadors', 'exemplars'.* The identification and deployment of such 'change heroes' can be a further vital component in implementing the HR vision and strategies. Hopefully, these people will be known to the HR Manager through the management development process. They will be persuasive advocates of change, and will be influential among their peers. Utilising their skills and commitment may require separate briefing mechanisms.

*Staff briefings.* These provide management visibility, and enable staff to hear direct from the top the key components of the vision. Opportunities for discussion and debate will add to the sense of identification with the change process. Communication meetings in which the participants passively receive information may be useful in communication terms but may be less success-

## Conclusions

ful in building commitment and enthusiasm. Further processes enabling the participants to internalise the components of change, and 'own' them, will be necessary for successful implementation. As the experience of Shell use has shown:

> The effective implementation and communication of the philosophy throughout the Company can be achieved only if its mode of implementation manifests the spirit of the philosophy. Verbal or written communication alone will not suffice; it is essential that all employees be enabled to relate the philosophy to themselves by participating in the implementation of the philosophy in their particular parts of the Company.[5]

*Written communication.* Accepting that emotional commitment may not follow reading the company newsletter or HR vision statement, written communication continues to perform a vital role in providing relevant, up-to-date information to staff. Documents can be professionally presented, with imaginative use of illustrations, for ease of future reference. Extracts from the HR vision can be reproduced on the back of visiting cards, in poster form or in other simple ways which reinforce the key message.

*Videos.* A rapidly growing component of communications programmes, these can enable senior management to be seen by all staff in a way impossible in large organisations. There remains the danger that videos may be passively received, but it can be reduced through using the video as the basis of subsequent discussion.

*Training and induction.* These provide an excellent opportunity for the HR vision and strategies to be communicated to staff – especially important for new recruits, who need to know the values and behaviour expected within their new organisation. If the HR vision is changing the role of first-line and/or middle management, then supervisory and management training programmes will be an ideal opportunity for aspect of the new role to be discussed. British Airways introduced a number of training events in their culture change programmes, including 12,000 customer contact staff, through a 'Putting People First' programme, and 1,400 managers through a 'Managing People First' course. Each day of the management programme has been described as follows:

> Day One was Urgency, which we were told 'should come from the leader, not from events'. Day Two looked at Vision – 'having the image of the cathedral as we mix the cement' – creating a mental picture of what is required and what is possible. Day Three concerned Motivation, 'management by expectation – expect the best, and catch them doing it right'. Trust was considered on Day Four, 'giving confidence to the individual to act alone and spirit to the group to act together', with Responsibility – 'believing that I am in charge of my own behaviour' – filling the final day.[6]

*Trade union briefings.* For many organisations with established collective bargaining arrangements and high trade union membership, the knowledge and understanding of the union officials of the HR vision will also be vital. Without it, when the officials are asked for advice or guidance by the members, they may at best give a passive response, or at worst show hostility. Such hostility can be a major barrier to the effective management of change, and can often be avoided by early and genuine consultations. Problems may remain, and the implementation of new HR strategies may be opposed by the unions, despite detailed consultation. In these circumstances 'trade-offs' can be sought, time scales can be varied or an appeal made to the employees direct. Most HR Managers and trade union officials will not want confrontation – the willingness to negotiate will generally secure acceptable compromises. Early consultation can certainly reduce the risks of industrial relations problems.

*Setting individual objectives.* The process of performance management was described in chapter 7. In this context the focus is on the translation of HR strategies into specific team and/or individual objectives and communicating them to job holders. Priorities should be assigned, and processes of measurement defined. Performance standards can seek to define the requirements at each level. This process needs to be applied with rigour, even though there will be flexibility in how the objectives are to be achieved.

In practice, organisations will use most, or all, of these approaches. As John P. Kotter put it:

> Communicating the direction as often as possible (repetition is important) to all those people (subordinates, subordinates of subordinates, bosses, suppliers, etc.) whose help or co-operation is needed; doing so, wherever possible, with simple images or symbols or metaphors that communicate powerfully without clogging already overused communication channels and without requiring a lot of scarce management time; making the message credible by using communicators with good track records and working relationships, by stating the message in as sensible a way as possible, by making sure the words and deeds of the communication are consistent, and generally by demonstrating an unswerving dedication to the vision and strategies (so-called 'leadership by example').[7]

## THE HR MANAGER AS 'CHANGE AGENT'

The HR Manager has a central role in many of those processes which drive change in an organisation. They include:

- The recruitment of quality staff against new criteria.
- Training and development strategies.
- Performance management, including processes for setting objectives, and recognising and rewarding achievement.

## Conclusions

- Communication.
- Organisation development.

Such a handle on many of the key forces for change provides a vital role for the HR Manager. The HR Manager is more likely to have a grasp of subjects such as organisation values, style, power and culture.

If the HR Manager is to act as a 'change agent', what personal characteristics are required? Rosabeth Moss Kanter identified certain qualities in the manager as innovator which are highly relevant to the HR Manager:

- Comfortable with change – such managers are confident that uncertainties will be clarified.
- Clarity of direction – they select projects carefully and have long-term horizons.
- Thoroughness – they prepare well and are professional in presentation. They have insight into organisational politics.
- Participative management style – they encourage others to be part of the team.
- Persuasiveness, persistence and discretion – there is a realistic grasp of what is possible.[8]

The skilled HR Manager will also take note of the steps described by Rosabeth Moss Kanter in building commitment to change:

- Allow room for participation in the planning of the change.
- Leave choices within the overall decision to change.
- Provide a clear picture of the change, a 'vision' with details about the new state.
- Share information about change plans to the fullest extent possible.
- Divide a big change into more manageable and familiar steps; let people take a small step first.
- Minimize surprises; give people advance warning about new requirements.
- Allow for digestion of change requests – a chance to become accustomed to the idea of change before making a commitment.
- Repeatedly demonstrate your own commitment to the change.
- Make standards and requirements clear – tell exactly what is expected of people in the change.
- Offer positive reinforcement for competence; let people know they can do it.
- Look for and reward pioneers, innovators, and early successes to serve as models.
- Help people find or feel compensated for the extra time and energy change requires.
- Avoid creating obvious 'losers' from the change. (But if there are some, be honest with them – early on.)
- Allow expressions of nostalgia and grief for the past – then create excitement about the future.[9]

Aligning themselves with the 'architect' model[10], the HR Managers' contribution occurs at board level, and the corporate plan is prepared with human resources issues in mind. A creative role is expected from HR, but within a business-centred approach. Core competences for the HR Manager will therefore not just embrace the 'change agent' skills identified above but will include a significant business orientation. The HR Manager contributes to business strategies and implementation, and in turn recognises and manages the business implications of decisions taken by HR. In particular, the cost implications are evaluated and the benefits in measurable terms are analysed. In undertaking such an analysis of costs and benefits for the business the effective HR Manager is proficient in the financial language of his line colleagues. Initiatives are clearly costed and HR ratios are continually deployed to measure the effectiveness of HR strategies. The effective HR Manager is aware of the fundamental importance of customer service and continually evaluates his actions in relation to the end customer – be the customers internal or external. It is to this subject of measuring HR effectiveness that we now turn.

## MEASURING HR EFFECTIVENESS

Measuring HR effectiveness is becoming more sophisticated. Basic indicators for assessing HR effectiveness often include:

- HR staffing as a proportion of total staffing.
- Staff costs/total costs.
- Staff costs/income.
- Staff costs *per capita*.
- Work load *per capita*.
- Staff costs per unit of work load.
- Staff turnover rates.
- Sickness absence rates.
- Costs of benefits.
- Costs of recruitment *per capita*.
- Training costs/total costs or *per capita*.

Effective HR measurement systems will:

- Focus on results directly related to the HR vision and HR strategies.
- Not rely on one measure but develop multiple measures to gauge effectiveness.
- Keep things simple – choose up to ten basic indices.
- Be widely communicated to employees.
- Track progress over time, derived from baseline data.
- Be used! Measurement for its own sake is unnecessary. Measures should be evaluated, and strategies adjusted if necessary.

In 1989 Jack Phillips and Anson Seers identified twelve ways to evaluate HR management, including:

# Conclusions

- Cost–benefit analysis: comparing the costs of HR programmes and services to the benefits derived from them.
- Goals and objectives: specific targets and objectives are defined and performance evaluated against these targets.
- Progress-oriented approach: evaluating the efficiency of the internal functioning of the HR function, using, say, length of time to fill vacancies.
- Human resource auditing: a detailed analysis over an extended period of HR activities against defined baseline data.
- Attitude survey approach: measuring overall satisfaction, commitment and other variables through questionnaires assessing the attitudes of employees.
- Tracking HR costs: HR costs in comparison with internal and external factors such as total costs, work load or sales income.
- HR accounting: extension of accounting principles to HR, including accounting for human capabilities.
- Reputational approach: feedback from users, judged against defined benchmarks.
- Performance measures: linking key HR measures to organisational performance, including productivity and quality.
- Index of effectiveness: a single composite index of effectiveness for the HR function.[11]

All the relevant approaches are captured in these options.

There are certain common threads which need to be considered in developing HR measures:

- Decide what you are doing it for. What is the object of the measurement? Is it to improve quality, reduce costs, improve cycle time, improve responsiveness to changing customer needs? Decide which aspect of the HR vision and strategies are most important to track progress.
- Decide on appropriate performance measures. What factors are most relevant to your organisation?
- Establish where you are now on those factors. This provides the HR Manager with baseline data on current levels of performance.
- Establish long-range objectives linked to the time frame of the HR vision. Where do you want to be in five years time on:

  Staff turnover?
  Benefit costs?
  HR costs *per capita*?
  Training costs?
  Sickness absence?
  Time to fill vacancies?
  Income per employee?

  Identify where you don't want to go. What measures would suggest a worsening?
- Establish intermediate performance standards against these factors to use

as milestones to judge progress towards the achievement of targets.
- Prioritise the factors – not all will be equally important.
- Generate data in intangible areas. For example, to assess the effectiveness of internal communication it will be necessary to undertake an attitude survey of employees to establish a satisfaction index. From these base data, targets for improving the satisfaction level can be set.
- Regularly review the performance data on HR effectiveness and take action if necessary by adjusting HR strategies and implementation. Encourage regular debate on the indices, and their meaning.

HR Managers are likely in future to be subject to close scrutiny of their effectiveness. It may be preferable to take the initiative. Having developed the HR vision and HR strategies, as this book suggests, these associated HR operating ratios and performance measures should be developed alongside vision and strategies.

## FINAL THOUGHTS

Developing the HR vision is about articulating the long-term HR goals, core values, key behaviour and underlying philosophy which derive from, support and complement the business mission and strategies. It will be realistic yet visionary; specific enough to be meaningful yet general enough to be applicable in different parts of the business. It will appeal to staff at all levels by demonstrating a clear direction which captures the emotions. From the HR vision will come HR strategies, objectives, milestones, performance measures. All will be integrated and cohesive, deriving from the business mission and ultimately judged on the success of the business in fulfilling that mission.

And what substantive richness is here for the HR Manager! New competences to be developed. New reward strategies, reflecting new priorities. New working time initiatives. New sources of labour. New forms of organisation, including project management. New channels of communication. Underlying all these are the continuing business pressures charted in chapter 2. Recession sharpens the focus on competitiveness, a focus already clear from the processes of deregulation, privatisation, liberalisation, growth in overseas competition, and so on, which has characterised the 1980s and early 1990s.

What a challenge, too, for the HR Manager! There is increasing recognition that HR must be an integral component of the strategic planning process, and that effectiveness in HR will be to the organisation's competitive advantage. A challenge, too, to the business understanding and conceptual strengths of the HR Manager. This book has explored the components of the HR vision, but deliberately with feet firmly on the ground. As information technology develops, the potential for changed employment relationships is enormous. This will in turn impact upon HR processes in ways as yet unforeseen. In the chapters of this book HR vision and strategies have been considered which are future-oriented, pro-active, professional and practical. To have been too speculative would have reduced the applied nature of the book. Future HR Managers will have to grapple with these as yet still speculative developments. Hopefully, the core values and HR goals articulated in the HR vision will be rigorous enough to provide continuing guidance through the increasingly rapid changes which will characterise the last decade of the twentieth century.

## REFERENCES

1 IGOR ANSOFF, *Corporate Strategy*, Penguin, London, 1987, p. 241.

2 PHILIP SADLER, *Designing Organisations*, Mercury, London, 1991, p. 144.

3 JACK WELCH, quoted in JOHN P. KOTTER, *A Force for Change: How Leadership Differs from Management*', Collier-Macmillan, London, 1990, p. 51.

4 GERRY JOHNSON and KEVIN SCHOLES, *Exploring corporate strategy*', Prentice Hall, Englewood Cliffs, N.J., 1988, p. 314.

5 ANDREW CAMPBELL, MARION DEVINE and DAVID YOUNG, *A Sense of Mission*, Economist Books, London, 1990, p. 210.

6 *Ibid.*, p. 123.

7 KOTTER, *op. cit.*, p. 60.

8 ROSABETH MOSS KANTER, 'The middle manager as innovator', *Harvard Business Review*, July–August 1982, p. 96.

9 ROSABETH MOSS KANTER, 'Managing the human side of change', *Management Review*, April 1985, p. 55.

10 SHAUN TYSON and ALAN FELL, *Evaluating the Personnel Function*, Hutchinson, London, 1986, p. 23.

11 JACK J. PHILLIPS and ANSON SEERS, 'Twelve ways to evaluate HR management', *Personnel Administrator*, April 1989, pp. 54–7.

# Index

Abbey National 139
Acquisitions 17–18
'Adopt-a-school' schemes 85
Advertising, recruitment 63–6
Age distribution of staff, measuring 48–9
Age profile of the work force, changing 38–9
Annual hours contracts 145–50
Ansoff, Igor, 165
Appraisal schemes 130–32
Armstrong, Michael 95
Assessment, 360° 127
Assessment centres 73–4, 125–7

BAT Industries 115–16
Bennison, Malcolm 53
Birmingham and Midshires Building Society 131
Boeing Corporation 138–9
Bonus payment schemes 104–5
Boot's the Chemist 140
Bramham, John 4–5
Brewster, Chris 4, 95–6
Brighton Borough Council 78
British Airways 32–3, 161, 167
British Petroleum 126–9
Bus cards, as a recruitment tool 67
Building design, and corporate goals 161–2
Business portfolios, reshaping of 16–17
Business strategies, current 15–18
Business strategies, influences on 8, 9–15

Cadetship schemes for students 85–6
'Cafeteria' remuneration 105–7
Campbell, Andrew 24
Career break schemes 79–83
Career conventions 87
Career management 132–6
Cars, company 107–8

Cash rewards, for help in recruiting 69
Cassels, Sir John 111
Casson, Jonathan 53
'Change agent' role of HR Managers 165, 166, 168–70
*Changing Culture: New Organizational Approaches* (Williams *et al.*) 28–9
Channel Four 65
Child care options 77–9
Communicating the HR vision 166–8
Competences 113–22, 128–9
Competitive pressures on organisations 10–12
*Competitive Strategies* (Porter) 8–9
Computer-assisted job evaluation 94
Conditions of employment 107–9
Connock, Stephen 4, 95–6
Constable, John 113, 138
Core skills, sought in graduate recruits 70–71
Corporate culture 28–9
Cost pressures on British business 13–14
Cost reduction strategies 27
*Creating the Environment for Total Quality Management* (Kearney) 19
Crèches, workplace 78
Crosslee (tumble drier manufacturer) 146–7
Curnow, Barry 59
Customer service, new focus on 19–20
Customer service competences 121, 123

Decentralised organisations 17, 34
Demand-side trends in the labour market 43–5, 46
Demographic changes 37–47
Deregulation of British business 12–13
*Designing Organisation – the Foundation for Excellence* (Sadler) 30

# Index

Developing countries, increasing role in world trade 10
Development opportunities 136–7
Development strategies 4, 111–43
Devolution of authority 17, 34–5, 90
Disinvestment 16
Distribution of staff by age, sex etc., measuring 47–50
Dixon's Group 76
Dulewicz, Victor 115–16

Early development opportunities, the need for 135–6
Educational trends 39–43, 46, 47
Equal opportunities monitoring 48, 52
Esso 82
'Excellent marketeers' 19, 20
Expatriate managers 116
*Exploring Corporate Strategies* (Johnson and Scholes) 28
External labour market trends 37–47

Flatter organisations, as part of HR vision 35–6
Flexible manufacturing systems 21
Flexi-time schemes 150–51
Functional distribution of staff, measuring 48–50

General Electric 166
Grade distribution of staff, measuring 48–9
Graduate output of universities 42–3
Graduate recruitment 70–72
Grampian Health Board 30–32

Handscomb, Richard S. 111
Harmonisation of terms and conditions 107
HAY job evaluation schemes 97
Health care facilities, on-site 162
Hendry, C. 1
Henley Management College 118–20
Herriot, Peter 59–60
Higher education, numbers entering 40, 42
Hoechst UK 121–2
Housing assistance schemes 108
HR architecture 26, 27
HR effectiveness, measuring 170–72
HR Managers, the role of 4–6, 168–70

HR strategies 3–4, 165–73
HR vision, components of 29–33
HR vision, defined 2–4, 27–9
*Human Resource Planning* (Bramham) 4–5
Human resourcing, and personnel management 5
Humble, John 1

IBM (UK) Ltd 139–40
Incentive payment schemes 104–5
Induction programmes 167
*Industrial Relations: Cost-effective strategies* (Brewster and Connock) 4, 95–6
Innovation strategies 26
Institute of Manpower Studies 40–42, 76, 83
Insurance industry, competences required in 121, 123
Interest rates 13–14
Internal labour market, and manpower audits 47–55
International managers, and the competencies they require 116

Japan, increasing role in world trade 10–11
Job evaluation 91–5, 97
Job profiles 69–71
Job sharing 154–5
Johnson, Gerry 28, 166
Joint ventures 17–18

Kanter, Rosabeth Moss 169
Kearney, A. T. 19
Kotter, John P. 168

Labour force, size and age profile of 39–40
Labour market trends 37–55
Lateral movements within organisations 133, 135
'Leadership through quality' programme (Rank Xerox) 32
Leaflets, as a recruitment tool 67
Legge, Karen 5
Leicester City Council 81
Length-of-service distribution of staff, measuring 49–50
Liberalisation of British business 12–13

Local authorities, and performance-related pay 100, 103
Locational distribution of staff, measuring 48–50
Lynch, Philip 145–6

McBeath, Gordon 2, 115
McCormick, Roger 113, 138
MacKay, L. 130
*Making of British Managers* report 113, 138
*Making of Managers* report 11–12, 113, 138
Management training, international comparisons 112
Managerial competences 117–21
Manpower audits 47–55
Manpower context 37–47
*Manpower Planning Handbook* (Bennison and Casson) 53
Manpower plans 45–7
Manufacturing, current trends in 19, 21–2
Marketing, new focus on 18–19
Market rate job evaluation 95
Market-related salary scales 97–8
Market research, in recruitment 60–62
Market scarcity supplements to pay 102, 104
Mergers 17–18
Merit pay 99–101
Missions, corporate 24
Mortgage subsidy schemes 108
Mumford, Alan 136
Murlis, Helen 94

National Council for Vocational Qualifications 113, 121
National Health Service 91
National Provident Institution 156
National Westminster Bank 100–101, 118–21
Nevens, Michael 19
Norman, Philip A. 111

Older workers, new roles for 63, 76
Open days, as a recruitment tool 66–7
Organisational implications of HR vision 33–5
Organisational manpower plans 45–7

Paddison, Lorraine 64

Part-time working 152–4
Pay bargaining, levels of 90–91
Pearl Assurance 67–8, 85–6, 158–9
Pensions 109
Performance management 130–32
Performance-related pay 99–102, 104, 130
Personnel management, development of 4–5
Peterborough Regional College 85–6
Peters, Tom 2, 30, 34
Pettigrew, A. 1
Phillips, Jack 170–71
Porter, Michael 8–9
Posters, as a recruitment tool 67–8
Potential appraisal 124–5
Potential assessment 122–4
*Practical Manpower Development* (McBeath) 2
Pritchard, Derek 94
Private medical schemes 108
Privatisation, government programme of 13
Project teams 35, 134–5, 166
Psychological profiling 127
Productivity, measurement of 55–7
Profit-sharing pay schemes 105
Promotion statistics 52
Purcell, John 4

Quality, and quality programmes 6, 19, 26–7, 32

Radio advertising, as a recruitment tool 69
Rajan, Amin 43
Rank Xerox 32, 65–6
Recruitment 59–72
  audits 74–6
  advertising 63–4
  agencies 69
  brochures 71–2
  statistics 50–51
*Recruitment in the 90s* (Herriot) 59–60
Redesign of premises 160–61
Regional variation in numbers of school leavers 40–42
Relocation 144, 155–60
Resourcing strategies 3, 59–88
Restaurants, on-site 162
Reversion to lower-grade jobs 133, 135

# Index

Reward strategies 3, 89–109

Sadler, Philip 30, 165–6
Sainsbury's 76
Salary maxima and minima 99
Salary structures 95–9
Samuel, P. J. 54–5
Scarce supply, categories of staff in 44
Scholes, Kevin 28, 166
School leavers, numbers in the workforce 38–42, 84–5
School leavers, recruiting 76
Schools liaison 85–6
Schroder, Professor Harry 118–21
Seers, Anson 170–71
Segmentation of market, in recruitment 62–3
Selection, and selection tests 73–4
Senior managerial competences 115–17
*Sense of Mission, A* (Campbell et al.) 24
Sex distribution of staff, measuring 47–50
Share option schemes 105
Shell International 116–17, 167
Shift working, different forms of 152–3
'Single status' terms and conditions 107, 162
Skills profiles 69–71
Sponsorship schemes, for students etc. 85–6
Sports facilities, on-site 162
Staff briefing 166–7
Staff distribution by age, sex etc., measuring 47–50
Staff-level competences 121–2
Steelcare Stafor 161
*Strategic Leadership – the Missing Links* (Handscomb and Norman) 111
Strategic review of corporate HR 24–7
Sub-contracting 18
Succession planning 133–6
Supervisory competences 117–21
Supply-side demographic trends 37–9, 45–6
SWOT analysis of corporate HR 25–6

Targeting, in recruitment 63–6
Technological change 14–15
Tesco Stores 63–4, 76
Thorn-EMI 16
*Thriving on Chaos* (Peters) 30
Torrington, Derek 1, 130
'Total quality' programmes 6, 19, 26–7, 32
Trade unions 34–5, 56, 168
Training 136–40, 167
Training Commission 113, 117–18
TSB Trust 156
Turnover statistics and costs 53–5

Undergraduates, and what they want from a job 71–2
Unemployment statistics 37–8
Untapped recruitment resources 76–87
Unisys 29

Vacancies, analysis of 51

Wheeler, David 63–4
W H Smith 70–71
Women
    increasing presence in the labour market 38, 152
    monitoring their distribution in the workforce 50–51
    'returners' 39, 47, 48, 63, 76–83, 144, 152
    targeted recruitment of 65–6, 152
    'women only' management development schemes 83
Working environment, modification of 4, 144, 160–62
Working time flexibility 145–55
Workplace nurseries/crèches 78

Yarrow, George 13
Young people
    in the labour market 38
    recruitment of 84–7
    what they want from a job 84